The Journal of
MAARTEN HARPERTSZOON TROMP
Anno 1639

T0384566

J. Luvens. ad viv. del.
J. de Frey f aquâforti 1801

Marten Harpertz Tromp.

J. de Frey excudit amstelodami

"Bestevaer"

(from the etching in the possession of the author)

Emery Walker Ltd. ph.sc.

The Journal of
MAARTEN
HARPERTSZOON TROMP

Anno 1639

Translated and Edited
by
C. R. BOXER

CAMBRIDGE
AT THE UNIVERSITY PRESS
1930

CAMBRIDGE
UNIVERSITY PRESS

University Printing House, Cambridge CB2 8BS, United Kingdom

Cambridge University Press is part of the University of Cambridge.

It furthers the University's mission by disseminating knowledge in the pursuit of education, learning and research at the highest international levels of excellence.

www.cambridge.org
Information on this title: www.cambridge.org/9781107536838

© Cambridge University Press 1930

First published 1930
First paperback edition 2015

A catalogue record for this publication is available from the British Library

ISBN 978-1-107-53683-8 Paperback

To

THE MEMORY OF
MY MOTHER

Horas non numero nisi serenas

CONTENTS

ILLUSTRATIONS

CHARTS

*This map is available for download from www.cambridge.org/9781107536838

PREFACE

At this present time when the history of the seventeenth century is being re-written, much has been done by English writers to reveal the true story of our Navy under the Stuarts, and to restore to their rightful place the names of several forgotten naval worthies of that period. But there is still room for a work dealing with our re-doubtable opponents and neighbours on the other side of the North Sea. It must surely interest students of British naval history to know what manner of men they were who once burnt our ships in the Medway—to say nothing of waging against us the three most stubbornly contested maritime wars which this world has ever seen.

This Journal, which is now printed for the first time, affords us a remarkable insight into the life at sea of "Jan Maat" who was our Jack Tar's "opposite number". Not only this, but we also get from it an interesting portrait of the great Admiral Maarten Tromp, one of the noblest and most sympathetic figures in the richly-crowded canvas of Holland's Golden Century. Finally, together with the little-known Portuguese and English sources which are used in the text, the Journal gives us a vivid picture of one of the most fateful episodes of that romantic age.

C. R. B.

THE SOURCES

FOR

THE STUDY OF THE CAMPAIGN
OF 1639

The increasing interest shown by English historians in naval
matters would seem to afford a valid reason for the publication
of the journal kept by Tromp on board his flagship during the
fateful months of 1639 culminating in the destruction of a
Spanish Armada in the Downs.

It is true that the story of the ill-fated Armada of 1639 has
already been ably told by Dr M. G. De Boer in his work—
De Armada van 1639 (Groningen 1911), but although he
made use of nearly all that had appeared in print on the affair—
whether in Holland, Spain, France or England—up to the
time that he wrote, yet there were some obscure but important
contemporary sources which escaped his vigilant eye, whilst
naturally a good deal of water has flowed under the historical
bridge since then. Hence I trust that the present work will
serve to show not only that it amplifies Dr De Boer's study, but
also that it amends and corrects it in some important particulars, albeit I do not differ from the general conclusions
reached by my predecessor in this same field. The materials
which I have drawn upon, will be found summarised in the
Bibliography at the end of the book, but it will be convenient
here briefly to discuss the importance of the various works
consulted and the method I have adopted.

In the first place, the materials on the Dutch side are
naturally of most weight. The *Journal* itself (on which a detailed
descriptive note is printed *infra*) was already used not only by
Dr De Boer, but by the great naval historian De Jonge[1] and
other writers. But although its existence was well known to
students in Holland, nothing has appeared on it in English,
and Dutch writers have confined themselves to extracts dealing
with the outstanding events of the campaign, such as the battle
of October 21st, and have rather slurred over the prosaic but

---

1 *Het Nederlandsche Zeewezen*, Tweede druk, I, pp. 268–372, Haarlem
1858.

fundamentally important daily routine and dispositions of the fleet as described therein. Besides Tromp's *Journal*, we have the *Life* of his Vice-Admiral Witte de With, recently published for the first time by Captain S. P. L'Honoré Naber, R.N.N. (retd.),[1] which was written by De With's son-in-law as early as 1662. The journal of one of Tromp's captains, Zybrandt Barentsz Waterdrincker, was used by Aitzema[2] and is a valuable contemporary source, but the same cannot be said of the numerous pamphlets on the campaign, which possess in full measure that spiteful gossip in which that class of literature abounded.[3] I have myself been unable to see the majority of these pamphlets, but as they were known to De Jonge and Dr De Boer, I presume that these two gentlemen have abstracted what there is of worth in them.

The Resolutions—both Secret and Open—of the States-General[4] for the months of April-October are of course all-important, and have been used by De Jonge, De Boer and others. I was myself unable to see them, owing to lack of time, but Captain Naber kindly made a "Sommiere Inspectie" of the most important entries for September and October 1639, and all of those that he noted were already used by Arend in his *Geschiedenis des Vaderlands*.[5] This little known but extremely valuable Dutch History is almost entirely composed from the Resolutions of the States-General and those of the States of Holland. As an instance of the author's thoroughness, it may be mentioned that the Resolutions of the States-General for every single day in September and October are cited in his book, as well as many of those of the States of Holland. In view of this it is obviously quite unnecessary for anyone to wade through these voluminous entries again, since Arend has worked this rich mine of information so thoroughly. The

1 *'T Leven en Bedrijf van Vice-Admirael de With, Zaliger*, MSS. Rijks-archief, Admiraliteitscolleges, XL, 1 and 9, printed in 1926 in the *Transactions of the Historical Society of Utrecht*.

2 *Saken van Staet en Oorlogh*, IIe Deel, pp. 613–16, The Hague 1669.

3 Pamphletten Knutte. Nos. 4617–4632.

4 Manuscript in the Rijksarchief at The Hague.

5 Published at Amsterdam in 1874. I am indebted to Commander Warnsinck, R.N.N., for directing my attention to this invaluable work, and to Messrs Nijhoff at The Hague for the loan of a copy of the volume required, IIIe Deel, ve stuk.

popular Dutch works of the period such as Van den Bos' *Leven der doorluchtighste Zeehelden* are only of value in so far as they have drawn upon the sources already quoted, and should be used with discrimination.

Finally, of Dutch works published since De Boer wrote his study, I have used Elias' *Schetsen uit de Geschiedenis van ons Zeewezen*,[1] various articles in the *Jaarverslagen* of the Netherlands Historical Shipping Museum[2] and Professor Blok's *Frederik Hendrik*,[3] besides numerous other books for passing references which are quoted in the text. To those desirous of going somewhat deeper into the articles of Fruin,[4] Ising[4] and other Netherland historians on certain aspects of this campaign, I commend the work of De Boer. We now come to the Spanish side. Here I have confined myself to the invaluable Duro,[5] whom De Boer has already utilised to the full. My chief contributions however are the Portuguese sources which I have drawn upon extensively. The narrative of Admiral da Costa Quintella[6] was used by Duro and thence (second-hand) by De Boer, but both of these writers failed to realise that Quintella's narrative was merely a very concise—and not always quite accurate—précis of a much earlier Portuguese version written by a man who had been a participant in the events he describes. I refer to the *Epanaphoras de varia historia Portugueza* by Dom Francisco Manuel de Mello.[7] The author, who flourished in the first half of the seventeenth century, was one of the most celebrated Portuguese of his time. An expert soldier who served with distinction in Flanders and elsewhere, a gifted statesman, a writer of no mean ability, and a seaman

1 Published by M. Nijhoff, 1916–29. Five parts have already appeared. This compilation is especially valuable for the economic and administrative side of Dutch naval history.

2 At Amsterdam, 1919–29. Articles by J. F. L. Balbian Verster.

3 Vol. xiii of the *Nederlandsche Historische Bibliotheek*, Amsterdam 1924.

4 *Verspreide Geschriften*, ix, and Nijhoff's *Bijdragen*, Nieuwe Reeks, iv, p. 99.

5 *Armada Española desde la Union de los Reynos de Castilla y de Aragón*, iv, Madrid 1898.

6 *Annaes da Marinha Portugueza*, ii, Lisboa 1840.

7 I have to thank Professor Edgar Prestage, the leading authority on Dom Francisco Manuel, for the loan of an example of the second edition of 1676. This work is exceedingly scarce. The portion concerned is called *Epanaphora Belica* iv, *Conflito do Canal de Inglaterra*, Anno 1639, pp. 445–571.

of considerable—if painful—experience,[1] he has left us the
longest account of the whole expedition whether in manuscript
or in print, and the very existence of this narrative was unknown
to all others who have written on the campaign. Dom Francisco
Manuel was in command of one of the regiments raised for
service in Flanders; he was present at the assembly in La
Coruña, and graphically describes the situation there when the
French appeared on the scene. When the Armada finally sailed,
he embarked in one of the ships of the Dunkirk squadron
(which contingent he carefully describes), and participated in
the actions of September 16th and 18th, of which he gives us
a long account; and he was on board one of the ships which
escaped to Dunkirk on September 21st. Although he may not
have been present at the final drama on October 21st, he describes the battle, as well as the previous tortuous negotiations
with England, at great length from trustworthy eyewitnesses.
His impartiality is vouched for not only by his natural honesty
and fairmindedness, but also by the circumstances under which
he wrote; for although he had served in the Spanish Armada,
yet at the time his work appeared in its final form,[2] his country
was at war with Spain, so he had no cause to be unduly partial
to her. But his account is valuable for another reason, and this
is his meeting with Tromp at Falmouth in 1641. On this
occasion De Mello took the opportunity to ask Tromp many
questions on the battles of two years before, and we therefore
have several observations on his actions from Tromp himself,
and these are especially welcome in filling up the very meagre
details in Tromp's own laconic journal. Incidentally they also
provide a complete and convincing refutation of the scandalous
aspersions cast on Tromp in the *Life* of Witte de With—
refutations which it has not been hitherto possible to produce

1 He was in one of the ships lost in the disastrous shipwreck of the Portuguese
Armada on the French coast in 1627 (the greatest blow Portugal received after
the death of King Sebastião in Morocco in 1578) and took part in the even more
catastrophic expedition of 1639. His account of the shipwreck of 1627 forms
pp. 150–269 of his *Epanaphora Tragica*.

2 He drew up his first Relation immediately after the events, by order of the
Cardinal-Infant in 1639. This, together with a subsequent one of *circa* 1640, was
seized by the Spaniards on the outbreak of war with Portugal in 1640. The
dedication of the final Relation (to Francisco de Mello e Torres, the Ambassador
in England) is dated at Espinhel, Sept. 30th, 1659.

from the Dutch side. I have made copious extracts from the *Epanaphora* throughout this work, and those desirous of consulting the original for further details will shortly be able to do so in the forthcoming annotated edition of Dom Francisco Manuel's works which the great Lusitanian scholar Professor Prestage is bringing out at Coimbra.

With regard to the English side. The *Calendar of State Papers*[1] and that of the *Clarendon Papers*[2] have already been extensively drawn on by De Boer, but I think I may claim to have embodied some new material from the former. Almost at the same time as De Boer published his work in Holland, those of T. W. Fulton[3] and the Rev. G. Edmundson[4] appeared in England, and I have availed myself of these books, which De Boer was unable to do. In later years, the *Life of Sir Henry Mainwaring* edited by G. E. Manwaring and W. G. Perrin for the Navy Records Society has proved invaluable to me, whilst the *Travels of Peter Munday*[5] edited by Sir Richard Temple for the Hakluyt Society have also been laid under contribution. The most important English source, however, in my opinion, is the tract[6] published by Peter White, who was Master of the English admiral's flagship, and saw and spoke with Tromp daily for a month. This source was quite unknown to Dr De Boer and to all Dutch historians.

Besides the French works already used by De Boer,[7] I have made use of two very valuable books which have appeared since he wrote, namely Henri Malo's *Les Corsaires Dunkerquois et Jean Bart*, Paris 1912, and Charles de la Roncière's *Histoire de la Marine Française*, Paris 1920, both of which afford a good deal of new material.

The only German work I have used is the *Militärische Seetransporte von Spanien nach Flandern* of Dr Friedrich Graefe

1 *Cal. S.P. Dom.* 1639 and 1639–1640.
2 *Clar. S.P.* I and II.
3 *The Sovereignty of the Sea*, London 1911.
4 *Anglo-Dutch Rivalry*, 1600–53, Oxford 1911.
5 Vol. IV, *Europe*, in Hakluyt Society, 2nd series, vol. LV.
6 *A great sea-fight...Narrative of the principal passages transacted in the Downs*, Anno 1639.
7 (*a*) *Lettres du Cardinal de Richelieu*; (*b*) *Correspondance de Henri d'Escoubleau de Sourdis*; (*c*) *Lettres, Mémoires et Négotiations du Comte d'Estrades*.

in the German naval periodical *Marine-Rundschau* for January-March 1927, but as the author has studied all previous German works very thoroughly, for me to examine these again would only be redundant. To sum up, I may say that exclusive of what has been published since De Boer wrote his study in 1911, my chief sources have been Manuel de Mello on the Iberian side, Peter White on the English, and the *Journal* of Tromp itself on the Dutch side—all three extensive, contemporary and fair-minded.

INTRODUCTION

I. THE PREPARATION OF THE ARMADA

(a) The Concentration in La Coruña

As a result of the great victory of Nördlingen (September 6th, 1634), the young Cardinal-Infant Ferdinand, brother of Philip IV of Spain, made a triumphal entry into the Spanish Netherlands with the troops he had brought from Italy. But the effect of this success was not so favourable to the Imperialist cause as might have been expected, for the increased danger from the victorious arms of Spain and Austria tended to draw their rivals of Sweden, Holland and France closer together—a tendency which was confirmed in the Congress held at Hamburg in 1638.

In the meantime the Cardinal-Infant had more than held his own in Belgium against the attacks of France and Holland on two fronts. Breda, it is true, was lost to the Prince of Orange, Frederik Hendrik, in October 1637 after a determined resistance; but after this success, the Stadtholder, racked by gout and hampered by the intestine quarrels and provincial jealousies of the various States of Holland, relapsed into inactivity. Ferdinand on the contrary, after carrying the war almost to the very gates of Paris in 1636, avenged the loss of Breda by taking the offensive against the Dutch, and captured Roermond and Venlo. Nor was this all. In 1638 the Prince of Orange attempted to carry out the design on which his heart was secretly set, namely the capture of Antwerp,[1] but his plans were completely upset by the severe defeat inflicted upon a detached portion of his army under Count Willem van Nassau, by the Spaniards at the Dike of Calloo in June 1638. Nevertheless,

---

1 The fear of Amsterdam that Frederik Hendrik had ulterior designs on the assumption of the Crown, frequently led that city to oppose and obstruct his plans. He himself said to D'Estrades in this connection, "je n'ai pas de plus grands ennemis que la ville d'Amsterdam, mais si j'ai une fois Anvers, je les mettray si bas, qu'ils ne s'en relèvront jamais".

even these victories cost the Spaniards dear. Their losses at Calloo amounted to 1300 killed in half-an-hour's fighting, so that as one of their writers states, "they lost as much in men as they gained in reputation".

In view of this, it is therefore not surprising that the Cardinal-Infant addressed numerous and urgent appeals for reinforcements of men and money to the Court at Madrid. Nor did these appeals fall on deaf ears. Many members of the Council of State in Madrid had themselves served in the wars in Flanders, and thus were able fully to appreciate and to sympathise with the predicament of the Cardinal-Infant at Brussels. But although it was agreed that a determined effort should be made to send large and powerful reinforcements to Belgium, these could not be despatched overland like the force which Ferdinand had conducted in 1634. The reason for this was that Cardinal Richelieu had subsidised Bernhard von Weimar to enable him to take the field against the Imperialists in the Upper Rhine in 1638. Equipped with these supplies, Bernhard avenged his reverse of Nördlingen four years before by inflicting a crushing defeat upon the Imperialists at Rheinfelden, and before the year was out he had taken the strong fortress of Breisach, together with Breisgau and Freiburg. These successes not only opened the way of the French troops into Germany, but completely cut off the path of the Spanish reinforcements up the Rhine valley from Italy to Flanders. The only way left open for the despatch of men and money was therefore by sea. This of course was not a new way. On many previous occasions during the Thirty Years' War, troops had been sent to Dunkirk from Northern Spain and the undertaking had successfully been carried out in the two previous years.[1]

In September 1637 Don Lope de Hoces had set sail from La Coruña with a strong fleet carrying men and money which he successfully landed at Dunkirk; on his return voyage, he had the good fortune to fall in with some French and Dutch convoys, with the result that he entered La Coruña with

[1] For the transport of troops by sea between Flanders and Spain during the Thirty Years' War, see *Militärische Seetransporte von Spanien nach Flandern* (1631–9), by Dr F. Graefe in the *Marine-Rundschau*, 1927, Heft 1, 2, 3.

12 prizes, having destroyed as many ships by fire. In December of the same year he left on a second similar mission which was likewise successfully accomplished. Evading the fleet of Tromp and Witte de With which was cruising on the look-out for him between Portland Bill and Alderney, De Hoces sailed close along the English coast, in company with a Dunkirk squadron which had been sent to meet him; and having slipped past the Dutch fleet in the darkness and mist on December 12th, he came safely to Dunkirk with 38 sail carrying 5000 soldiers and a large store of bullion. His return voyage to Spain in March 1638 was even more profitable, for he entered La Coruña with about 20 Dutch and French prizes.[1]

The success of these expeditions led the Council of State at Madrid to determine upon an even more ambitious programme for 1639. They knew that although the Spaniards had twice evaded the watching fleet of the Hollanders, they could scarcely hope to do so a third time, whilst the powerful French fleet threatening their coasts had also to be reckoned with.[2] They therefore determined to assemble such an Armada, that its safety would not depend on its evading the enemy fleets, but that it would be of sufficient strength to force its way through to Dunkirk, if necessary, in the teeth of the combined Franco-Dutch squadrons.

With this object in view orders were given by the Court of Madrid to concentrate all available troops and ships which could be assembled by any means whatsoever, in the two maritime centres of La Coruña on the Atlantic Ocean, and Cartagena in the Mediterranean. The Italian contingents and that of Ragusa were to be assembled at Naples under the command of Don Antonio de Oquendo, and were to proceed thence to Cartagena and Cadiz to collect other troops and ships,

1 C. Fernandez Duro, *Armada Española*, IV, pp. 170–1. Tromp's *Journal* for 1637–8.

2 In 1638 the French invaded Northern Spain, captured and burnt the ports of Lezo, Renteria, and Pasajes in Guipuzcoa, together with some 16 galleons, built or building therein, and laid siege to Fuenterrabia. Don Lope de Hoces, trying to relieve this last place, was caught in the haven of Guetaria by the French fleet under De Sourdis, and the whole of the Spanish fleet was destroyed by a fireship attack with the loss of 4000 men, De Hoces himself escaping only in his shirt. (*Vide* C. de la Roncière, *Histoire de la Marine Française*, v, pp. 38–47, Paris 1920.)

after which this squadron was to unite with that of Don Lope de Hoces in La Coruña. The concentration in this last port soon included some 35 ships, comprising the squadrons of Vizcaya, Galicia, Portugal and Dunkirk. The Dunkirk squadron had originally put to sea on February 18th with 22 sail carrying some 2000 Walloon soldiers destined for Spain,[1] but the blockading squadron of Tromp had forced them to put back into the harbour with the loss of three of their ships, two of which were carried as prizes into Holland. The Dutch themselves had received such damage that they were temporarily compelled to give up the blockade, and on the day before Tromp left Holland to resume his post off the port, the Dunkirkers made their escape with 18 sail which duly arrived in La Coruña with 12 prizes that they had picked up on the way.

Amongst the troops raised to serve in this expedition, there were four *terços* or regiments which were formed in Portugal. One of these was commanded by Dom Francisco Manuel de Mello, who has left us a long account of the whole expedition,[2] and originally mustered 500 Portuguese and 600 Spanish soldiers, though the number of the latter was subsequently increased. The five Spanish regiments were commanded by the Mestres de Campo (or Colonels) D. Jerónimo de Aragón, D. Martin Alfonso de Sarria, D. Antonio de Ulhôa (whose regiment was composed of raw Neapolitan recruits), D. Gaspar de Carvalhal and D. Francisco Palominas.

In order to raise the necessary levies for this expedition the Conde-Duque of Olivarez, who was the prime mover of the whole affair, arranged with some private contractors to supply recruits at 21 ducats a head. In pursuance of this arrangement the contractors were empowered to seize—and actually did

---

1 It may seem odd that at the same time that the Spaniards were so desirous of sending men *to* Flanders, they should draw men away *from* that Province, but they were sorely in need of practised troops to withstand the French invasion. The idea was to send thousands of raw Iberian recruits to Flanders where they would be "licked into shape" in that school of warfare, whilst the Walloons would be repatriated in due course. In 1638 Olivarez wrote to the Cardinal-Infant, "The safety of Spain depends entirely on the coming of the Walloons"; and again, "...to rest assured, we require some 5000 Walloons".

2 In *Epanaphora* iv on pp. 445–571 of his *Epanaphoras de varia historia Portugueza*, 2nd edition, Lisboa 1676.

seize—more than 10,000 men from amongst all classes throughout the whole of Spain without regard to their age, occupation or walk of life. So thoroughly did the crimps do their work, that when some grandees tried to raise from their estates the men which they were bound to supply for the royal service, they could not find a single man to serve, although they offered 16 *reals* per diem as pay. Dom Manuel relates numerous instances of the abuses created by this press, and states that parts of Spain were almost entirely depopulated as a result of it.

The Armada of De Hoces[1] was made up of ships from the following squadrons. Some galleons of Vizcaya which had escaped the disasters of the previous year; they appear to have been under the personal command of De Hoces. The squadron of Galicia commanded by Don Andrés de Castro with Don Francisco Feijó as Almirante or Vice-Admiral. This latter individual was a brave and capable but unfortunate officer, and Dom Manuel observes that he was the author of an important treatise on naval warfare and tactics entitled *El Sargento Embarcado*. Portugal was represented by three vessels, the *Santa Anna, Santiago*, and the *capitana* or flagship *Santa Tereza*, which mounted 60 great guns of bronze, and carried 600 musketeers. This 1200 ton monster was the largest and most powerful ship in the fleet, and as Dom Manuel remarks, was worth an entire squadron in herself. This galleon had been built in Lisbon by Bento Francisco, the greatest Portuguese shipwright of the century.[2] There were also some vessels from Naples under the Almirante Don Pedro Veles de Medrano, whilst the squadron of San José, commanded by Francisco Sanches Guadalupe, was included in this La Coruña concentra-

1 Don Lope de Hoces y Cordova was a noble *caballero* of the city of his second name, and a brave and experienced seaman. He commanded fleets to and from the Indies from 1619 till 1636 on numerous occasions, and always with success. His expeditions to Dunkirk in 1637–8 were also successful, as we have seen, but Fortune subsequently deserted him until his death in this present expedition.

2 Over whom see Sousa Viterbo, *Trabalhos Nauticos dos Portuguezes*, II, pp. 57–9, Lisboa 1900. Peter Munday, who visited her in the Downs, calls her "the Fairest and biggest shippe off them all. Shee was built For an East India Carracke, & afterwards appointed for this Expedition." Some Portuguese writers say that she was expressly built as flagship for the European fleet, but Munday's statement that she was intended for a *Nāo da Carreira da India* is probably correct.

tion; but the best ships in it were those of the famous Dunkirk squadron under the command of the celebrated Miguel de Orna,[1] of which squadron Dom Manuel gives a curious account which it is interesting to compare with that in Henri Malo's work.[2] The vice-admiral of this squadron was Mathieu Rombout, who had been captured by the Hollanders under Piet Pietersz Heyn in 1629, whilst other celebrated captains included Josse Pieters, Salvador Rodriguez and Francisco Ferreira. Both these last-named individuals were Portuguese; Rodriguez, who was born at Almada near Lisbon, had risen from grumet in a Portuguese Indiaman to the post of Vice-Admiral of Dunkirk in the space of 39 years. Whilst still a lad, he had been captured by the English in an engagement with Downton's fleet in Swalley Hole, January 1615. Francisco Ferreira was a native of Angra do Heroismo in the Azores.

As it was well known to the Spaniards that the French fleet was likely to put in an appearance off the coast of Galicia to interfere with the concentration of this Armada, the Court at Madrid ordered the Governor of the Province, the Marquis of Valparaiso, to superintend the arrangements for its defence. Accordingly Valparaiso began to assemble the hordes of pressed and ill-found recruits within La Coruña, dividing them up into *terços* as they came in.[3] Not content with this, the Governor called out all the local militia, gentry and nobility, and by this means he collected 18,000 men within a narrow, impoverished town which could not properly support half of their number. The natural result of this foolish proceeding was that many of the men sickened and died, whilst famine and disease ranged unchecked throughout the fleet and army. In addition to this, there were not nearly enough arms or munitions to go round amongst this ill-assorted rabble, so that in the event of the threatened French invasion materialising, there was not much hope of an effective resistance being offered. The sailors, who also mistrusted the efficiency of their fellow soldiers, determined to secure their ships by constructing a large boom

1 Or De Horna. Born at Pamplona in Navarra Province of N. Spain. Under the name of Michiel Doorn he was well known to the Hollanders as one of their doughtiest opponents.

2 *Les Corsaires Dunkerquois et Jean Bart*, 1, Paris 1911.

3 Five of these regiments were formed.

across the harbour, from Fort San Antonio on the one side to that of Santa Luzia on the other; this boom was anchored by 50 strong sheet-anchors, and had a gap cut in the middle to permit of the entrance or exit of one ship at a time; the structure was further defended by ten well-manned shallops armed with swivel guns which patrolled around it day and night, and by batteries thrown up at vantage points on the shore. Dom Manuel assures us, however, that the real force of the boom by no means corresponded to the impression of prodigious strength which it produced in friends and foes alike. These preparations were still far from complete when the long-awaited French fleet appeared in sight.

(b) The French Expedition to La Coruña

Despite the annihilation of the relieving squadron of Lope de Hoces by De Sourdis in Guetaria (August 22nd, 1638), Fuenterrabia had gallantly held out until September 8th, when a relieving army under the Admiral of Castile and the Marquis of Valparaiso utterly defeated the besiegers under Condé and La Valette, and drove the French back over the border in headlong rout.

Richelieu was cut to the quick by the shame of this disaster and determined to strain every nerve to avenge it in the following year. Hence the appearance on June 9th, 1639, of a great French Armada of 73 sail carrying 25 companies of foot soldiers, off Cape Prior, some six leagues N.N.E. of La Coruña.[1]

The Governor—although, as we have seen, he was fully aware of an impending attack—had not yet allocated the various regiments to their posts, and consequently when the alarm was given, all was confusion worse confounded. Dom Manuel de Mello gives us a very graphic picture of the panic and despair which reigned in the town. He shrewdly observes that whilst the Spaniards individually are the most active and determined people in Europe, in matters affecting the common weal they are the laziest and most irresolute, and this (he says) was the reason for much of the ill-success of their

[1] De Sourdis' fleet comprised 40 ships of war, 21 fireships and 12 transports.

arms. Dom Manuel's own regiment[1] garrisoned the trenches defending the boom, and the fort of San Antonio which was the key to the position.

The cavalry, who were few in numbers and ill-armed, patrolled the beaches and the surrounding country, whilst various other units were stationed along the walls.

Shortly before the appearance of the French Armada, an English ship laden with cloth for the uniforms of the garrison arrived in La Coruña. The master of this vessel handed to the Spanish Governor a letter from the French commander stating "that he had captured that ship, and being informed of the needs of the Spanish soldiers, he sent it on as a present, and as a token that His Most Christian Majesty of France did not desire to make war upon his enemies with the aid of the elements, but only by force of arms and the justice of his cause".

Four days after this chivalrous message had been delivered, De Sourdis and his captains drew up a plan of attack at a nocturnal Council of War on June 10th.[2] One division was to mask the fort of San Antonio, another that of Santa Luzia, whilst the pinnaces of the fleet supported by 12 lightships were to try to hack a way through the boom; when a gap had been made, 12 fireships were to enter the harbour protected by another detachment of heavier ships, whilst the largest ships of the fleet were to cruise in the offing, ready either to meet any attack from the rear or to prevent the sallying-out of the blockaded Spanish ships. On the 11th, however, a further Council was held, and the majority of the French captains declared that the attempt would be foredoomed to failure owing to the converging fire from the forts and to the (imagined) strength of the boom. Despite the protests of a few bold spirits led by Abraham Du Quesne (later Admiral of France), the views of the majority prevailed, and De Sourdis cancelled the plan of attack. But he still did not give up hope of inducing the Spaniards to venture out, and dispatched a cartel to De Hoces, challenging him to come out and fight either ship for ship or squadron for squadron.[3] De Hoces prudently declined

1 Which consisted of 570 Portuguese and 600 Castilians—1170 men in all.

2 Details from C. de la Roncière, *op. cit.* pp. 50–4.

3 Henri d'Escoubleau de Sourdis, Archbishop of Bordeaux at the age of 34, was a sailor by inclination though not by profession. He served at the defence of

the offer and contented himself with sending out each day eight or ten Dunkirk frigates which sailed up and down outside the boom, but under the protection of the forts and galleons, exchanging occasional broadsides at long range with the French vessels, which on their side showed no disposition to close. Dom Manuel assures us that had the French been bold enough to attack within a few days of their first appearance they would undoubtedly have taken the place and burnt or sunk the galleons. He states that not only was there a general panic amongst the raw recruits of whom the garrison was composed, but that the supply of powder and shot was so scanty that express orders were issued that it was only to be used as a last recourse. To make matters worse, the Iberian captains quarrelled fiercely between themselves, whilst the place was hourly alarmed by the rumours and forebodings which spread amongst the soldiery and populace.

The blockade was not without an element of comic relief. De Sourdis had commenced a desultory long range bombardment of the city soon after his arrival, and one of the shots fell in the courthouse of the magistrates who had assembled to discuss the preparations for defence. Dom Manuel describes with evident gusto the terror caused by this incident amongst the lawyers, and he adds that after this occasion they invariably met in a subterranean cellar which served as a storehouse for provisions. The bombardment ceased with the sortie of the Dunkirk frigates, as the French were too occupied with them to continue their first efforts.

The appearance of an archbishop as the head of a fighting force caused great scandal to the whole of Spain,[1] and what

Ré against the English, at the siege of La Rochelle, and was appointed to the chief command in the Mediterranean in 1636, in fact if not in name. He retook the Lérins isles from the Spaniards in 1637, and in 1638 destroyed the fleet of De Hoces in Guetaria. He was the chief exponent of fireships, which arm of the service he brought to a high pitch of perfection, and used against the Spaniards with great skill. He was disgraced (on very inadequate grounds) for failing to prevent the Spaniards from relieving Tarragona in 1641 and died in exile.

1 Duro, referring to the refusal of the Pope to grant a dispensation to De Sourdis enabling him to bear arms, says that His Holiness thought that it ill became a Prelate to prefer the smoke of gunpowder to that of incense! But the Spaniards might have saved their breath to cool their own porridge, for in the person of the Cardinal-Infant, Governor of Flanders, they possessed one of the

irritated the Spaniards still more was the sight of the French ships riding off the bar "as if they had already completed the victory rather than only begun the battle". Dom Manuel mentions in particular the vast size and imposing dimensions of the vice-admiral ship called *La Reine*, which was named in honour of the Queen Mother, Anne of Austria, although he adds that she was a very clumsy and unsatisfactory vessel from the sea-going point of view.[1]

On June 23rd De Sourdis landed some 2500 men in the neighbourhood of Ferrol with orders to occupy that port. The Spaniards were on their guard, and Don Juan Fardo de Figueroa, the commander of the garrison, with the assistance of 2000 men hurriedly sent him by Valparaiso from La Coruña, forced the French to retire to their landing place after some four hours' skirmishing. De Sourdis intended to land more men on the next day to renew the attempt, but a storm sprang up and it was only with great difficulty that the crews already landed were disengaged and re-embarked. The weather grew steadily worse and mounted to a strong tempest from the S.S.E. On the advice of his captains, De Sourdis resolved to give up the blockade of La Coruña and seek the shelter of his home ports, whither the French set sail on the 24th. Before the rendezvous of Belle-Isle was reached, the fleet was scattered by a storm, and many of the ships had to put in to La Rochelle, Brest, Nantes and other ports, whilst the remainder, "all tottered and torn", struggled into Belle-Isle.

Sourdis, however, "ne cède ni au mal, ni à la fortune". He was resolved, he said, to finish by fire what the wind and water had denied him, and he still cherished hopes of repeating else-where his exploit at Guetaria. He proposed to Richelieu that he should attack either Fuenterrabia, Guetaria, Santander or La Coruña. Richelieu's reply was brief and to the point. Fuenterrabia would be a wasted effort, as Condé was in no condition to support the attack by land; Guetaria was not worth

doughtiest pillars of the Church Militant, whose "Apostolic blows and knocks" fell with equal force upon Catholic Frenchmen and Heretic Hollanders alike.

1 Although Dom Manuel calls this vessel *Reyna*, I suspect she was really *La Couronne* launched shortly before, as this ship was of 2000 tons burthen and famous for her size. Also, it was *La Couronne* which was serving as Vice-Admiral to this fleet, in which *La Reine* (1000 tons) was Rear-Admiral.

troubling about; Santander was too strong. As for La Coruña, if the boom could be broken by fireships, bombs, or a vessel laden with masonry, then De Sourdis could launch the fireship attack on which his heart was set; if not, he could at least resume the blockade of De Hoces. But (and this is noteworthy in view of what followed) on no account was he to risk the fleet without the practical certainty of a good success. France could not build another such within ten years.[1]

Scale: 1:5,000,000

(c) The Junction of De Oquendo and De Hoces

Early in the preceding spring, the Court at Madrid had issued orders for Don Antonio de Oquendo, the "Almirante General del Mar Oceano", and Commander-in-Chief of the naval forces of Spain, to proceed from the Mediterranean (where he then was) with the Italian and Levant squadrons to join De Hoces in La Coruña, picking up the Cadiz contingent on his way.[2]

1 Answer of Richelieu to the proposals advanced by the Sieur de Menillet on behalf of the Archbishop de Sourdis, Abbeville, July 7th, 1639 (vide De la Roncière, v, p. 53).

2 It was then the custom in Spain to divide the navy into squadrons, each of which took its name from the kingdom or province which was responsible for its upkeep and armament. Each squadron had its own General (= Admiral), Almirante (= Vice-Admiral), and Vice-Almirante (= Rear-Admiral). In 1616 the precedence of these various squadrons was regulated, the first three in order of seniority being those of Castile, Portugal and Aragon. The whole force was subordinated to the orders of the "Captain General of the Ocean Sea", who roughly corresponded to our Lord High Admiral.

Accordingly De Oquendo, after leaving Naples, sailed round
to Cadiz, where he arrived at the end of June, and thence he
beat up the coast of Portugal; he experienced great difficulty
in rounding Cape Finisterre, and for a time it seemed that he
was going to suffer the misfortune he had experienced in 1627;
for in that year he had vainly tried to weather the Cape for
37 days in succession, whereby he had been unable to reach
La Coruña, whither he was bound in order to join the expedition
of Don Fradrique de Toledo in aid of the Duke of Guise at the
siege of La Rochelle. On this occasion he was more fortunate,
and in the beginning of August he arrived at La Coruña with
his fleet of 22 sail.

With the junction of De Oquendo and De Hoces the Spanish
Armada now totalled some 70 sail, of which number 50 were
warships, whilst the remainder were transports, amongst these
latter being eight or ten English vessels freighted to carry
1800 Spanish soldiers.[1] De Oquendo himself flew the royal
standard in the *Santiago*, the Admiral ship of Spain, "burthen
about 1000 tonne, with 800 men, 60 peeces of Ordnance,
5 lanthornes & 2 galleries". She had been constructed in
Pasajes but completed and rigged in the dockyard at Lisbon.
As flagship of the Naples contingent there was the celebrated
San Agustin, "in whom strength and beauty were joined
together as rarely happens. She appeared to be a jewel made
of massy gold & bronze, rich and rare, so ornamented and so
strong was she".[2] She was later made Vice-Admiral to the
whole Armada and her place as flagship of the Naples squadron
was taken by the *Orfeo*. This contingent was commanded by
Don Pedro Velez de Medrano with Esteban de Oliste, a native
of Ragusa, as Almirante or Vice-Admiral. The great galleon
Santo Cristo de Burgos was the flagship of the so-called San
Josef squadron (all 12 ships of which had been bought or fitted
out by a Portuguese contractor named Afonso Cardoso), and
was under the command of Sanches Guadalupe.

1 The numbers given in contemporary literature vary between 50 and 80, but
from a comparison of the states in *Cal. S.P. Dom.* 1639 with the most reliable
Iberian sources, the above figures would appear to be correct, and they are
corroborated by the actual number of the Armada when it reached the Downs on
Sept. 18th, 1639—less one vessel taken by the Dutch and the nine English
transports, which made a separate voyage. See *infra*, Appendix IV.

2 Dom Manuel de Mello, *Epanaphora* IV, p. 482.

Of the remaining squadrons, we have already mentioned those of Galicia, Vizcaya, Portugal and Dunkirk, in the concentration of De Hoces, and the two others brought by De Oquendo were those of Don Martin Ladrón de Guevara and Jerónimo Masibradi. This last squadron bore the name of the General who had fitted it out on contract for the Crown, and was composed of nine ships from Ragusa on the Adriatic, of which place Masibradi was the native-born Governor. He himself was not present at this expedition, and his place was taken by the Almirante Matteo Esfrondati who was likewise a Ragusan. This contingent was also known as the "Escuadra de Bartelosa".

On board the 22 ships of De Oquendo's division were two regiments of infantry under the command of Don Gaspar de Carvajal and Don Antonio de Ulhôa, a Neapolitan; who had respectively Don Juan Acensio and Don Onufrio Ricio as sergeant-majors (or majors, as we should say nowadays).

Such was the quantity of the fleet; as to its quality, the relations differ a good deal amongst themselves. The Conde-Duque Olivarez, imprudently invoking the memory of 1588, called the Armada the finest which had been seen since then[1] and terms the men who manned it "muy buena gente". Dom Manuel, on the other hand, states that the majority of the troops were pressed men and raw recruits, although he says that there were many capable officers and quite a number of veteran soldiers amongst them. Don Francisco Feijó de Sotomayor, the Admiral of Galicia, wrote that not only were the men utterly useless, but that the supply of arms was totally inadequate, for in some ships there were no sidearms other than those of the officers. The testimony of this last individual is somewhat prejudiced, since he wrote from his prison in the Hague after the destruction of the Armada in the Downs, and naturally tried to explain away the disaster by painting all the previous circumstances as dark as possible.[2]

[1] "...y creo yo que en calidad, desde la jornada de Inglaterra acá, no se han visto iguales navios á los que VS. lleva". Olivarez to Oquendo, July 27th, 1639. (Duro, *op. cit.* p. 203.)

[2] His statement that in some ships there was only one gunner to every four guns, and those unskilful, is probably accurate, however, as the Spaniards inflicted astonishingly little damage on the Hollanders' ships when the fleets joined battle. His letter is printed in Duro, *op. cit.* pp. 227–35.

From the statements of the English captains who commanded the eight transports freighted to carry the Spanish troops to Dunkirk, we find that whilst the Armada itself consisted of 70 sail, "all warlike ships and well provided", the crews and soldiers on board were of indifferent quality. In fact the weak points of the Armada seem to have been more numerous than the strong.

No sooner had De Oquendo arrived at La Coruña than difficulties began to arise. His orders were couched in such vague and general terms that it was not clear whether the supreme command of the Armada should be given to him as "Almirante Real del Mar Oceano", or should devolve upon Don Lope de Hoces, who had command over a greater number of ships. To solve this vexed question, the Marquis de Valparaiso in his capacity of Viceroy of Galicia summoned a Council of the leading naval and military officers, at which the Duque de Villahermosa, Don Fernando de Borja, was also present, together with his brother Don Juan de Borja.

Valparaiso submitted two problems for the decision of the Council. Firstly, how to form the two divisions of De Hoces and De Oquendo into a single Armada with a single head. Secondly, how best to realise the two conflicting purposes for which the King had destined the Armada. These two objectives were as follows: To seek out and destroy the French fleet wheresoever it might be; and in the event of its having gone to unite with the Dutch fleet (as was thought probable), to attack and destroy it at all costs, even within an English harbour if necessary, without taking heed of England being a neutral and friendly Power; reasons of State demanded this, as it would be easier to satisfy the subsequent complaints of that monarchy, than to organise another such Armada as the Spaniards had now assembled against the enemy.[1] This objective conflicted with the other one of transporting the 10,000 odd soldiers as quickly and expeditiously as possible to Dunkirk.

With regard to the first proposition, the Council unani-

---

1 De Mello, *Epanaphora* iv, p. 484. "What is sauce for the goose is sauce for the gander!" In view of this categorical order to destroy the enemy in English harbours, the complaints of the Spaniards when they were caught in the trap they had meant for their enemies seem hollow. Unfortunately at that time the English had no idea that the Spaniards had any such order.

mously resolved to offer the command to Don Lope de Hoces, who had many friends owing to his generosity and charm of manner, whilst De Oquendo on the contrary was of a choleric and churlish disposition.[1] But De Hoces, for personal reasons, firmly rejected this proposal and announced his determination to serve under De Oquendo as a simple captain, without any flag-rank or command over a squadron, in the Portuguese galleon *Santa Tereza*, justly reputed to be the finest vessel in the fleet. Seeing that he was not to be moved from his resolve, the Council consented to this typically Iberian gesture, and then proceeded to elect Don Andrés de Castro, a member of the Council of War, and General of the Armada of Galicia, as Almirante or Vice-Admiral of the whole Armada under Antonio de Oquendo. This was a distinctly unfortunate choice, as this *hidalgo* had been educated and trained as a priest, having been Canon of Toledo Cathedral for many years, before leaving the service of the Cross for that of Arms. Events were to show, as Dom Manuel remarks, that the life of a man is not a theatre wherein he can play to perfection such totally dissimilar parts.

After the appointment of De Oquendo and De Castro, the Council proceeded with the discussion of the main problem of how to reconcile two diverse objectives. Many hours were spent in anxious discussion before the members came to a unanimous opinion, which was: That if the Armada could leave before September 15th it would scour the coast of Biscay in search of the French fleet; but if after that date, then it would steer straight through the Narrows to Dunkirk: "since there was every likelihood of encountering the French and Dutch fleets in the Channel at that time (either separately or together), with every chance of victory as the whole maritime strength of Spain was concentrated in that fleet".[2] This resolution was

---

[1] Don Antonio de Oquendo, born in the Province of Guipuzcoa at San Sebastian, began his naval service in the galleys of Naples at the age of 16. In 1609 he was General of the fleet of Cantabria and in 1611 of the flota of Mexico. In 1621 he commanded an expedition to Pernambuco, and in 1623 was General of Guipuzcoa. For refusing the presidency of Panama he was imprisoned for a time but soon released. In 1631 he had made his celebrated voyage to Brazil, when he fought his homeric duel with Adrian Pater's flagship. In 1637–8 he served in the Mediterranean.

[2] *Epanaphora* IV, p. 488.

forwarded to King Philip IV at Madrid for his approval, but to everyone's surprise it was cancelled by the Council of State, which ordered instead "that the voyage should be made direct to Flanders, but that if on the way the Armada fell in with any enemy fleet, it was to venture the whole of its ships and treasure in the attempt to destroy this at any cost".[1]

On the receipt of these categorical instructions, preparations were rapidly pushed forward to enable the Armada to sail. The state of affairs on shore left much to be desired. The military officers quarrelled amongst themselves on questions of seniority, whilst their miserable men, ill-paid, half-starved and unarmed, died or deserted by hundreds. In order to make up the required numbers, the Marquis de Valparaiso carried out a press in the surrounding country with such severity and thoroughness that no man of any degree, high or low, escaped. Dom Manuel says that it was the most sorrowful and unhappy day seen in Spain for many a long year, and that not even the hardest heart could watch unmoved the miserable prisoners, all chained together, being driven into the city, followed by crowds of wailing women and children deprived of the only bread-earners in their families. All the chief officers of the Armada retired within their houses in order to avoid any appearance of having approved of this brutal measure. But Valparaiso was not to be denied and ordered the 2000 hapless wretches who had been forcibly collected to be embarked on the same night. This gave rise to still more harrowing scenes, which are vividly described by Dom Manuel, who was the chief embarkation officer, and he assures us that his health was broken for three years by the strain he underwent at that time. Nevertheless he managed to ship some 10,000 soldiers (of sorts) on board of the Armada within two days. The charitable Cardinal Spinola (son of the great Ambrosio de Spinola) who was then occupying the See of Santiago de Compostella, somewhat eased the intolerable situation of the crews and troops by distributing amongst them

---

1 *Epanaphora* IV, p. 489. This downright statement should suffice to dispose of any lingering doubt that there may still be in the minds of some historians as to whether the Spanish Armada really had orders to fight the Dutch, or merely to slip through to Dunkirk without engaging them if possible. It is clear from this, that the destruction of the enemy's fleet was regarded as of more importance than the introduction of the reinforcements into Flanders.

a vast amount of money, clothes and food, whilst he also gave generous alms to the sick in the hospitals. Nevertheless, the condition of the men was still pitiable when the Armada was ready to sail.

Whilst these scenes were being enacted in La Coruña, De Sourdis, whom we left refitting his fleet at Belle-Isle at the end of June, was once more in a position to put to sea. Just about the same time as De Oquendo effected his junction with De Hoces in La Coruña, the French Armada set sail.[1] Having received advice that there were two galleons on the stocks at Santoña near Laredo, De Sourdis, who evidently had no mind to try conclusions with the united Spanish Armada, resolved to proceed thither and destroy them. This he was enabled to do on August 16th, having first captured Laredo on the 14th. After this petty success he cruised off Santander for some time and then returned home.[2]

On August 27th, 1639, the Spanish Armada set sail from La Coruña on its ill-fated voyage. The order of battle is printed in Appendix IV of this work, but as the formation of the fleet laid down therein differed from the order in which it set sail, the latter is here reproduced from Manuel de Mello's account. First of all came the royal flagship with the Admiral-General Antonio de Oquendo, who had taken Miguel de Orna, the Admiral of Dunkirk, to act as flag-captain and general adviser on board the *Santiago*. Astern of the *Santiago* came the *San Salvador*, the Dunkirk flagship, commanded by Don Jerónimo de Aragón. Next came the Vice-Admiral Matthieu Rombaut on board the *Nuestra Señora de Monteagudo*, followed by the galleon *San Francisco* of the same squadron; this vessel was commanded by the Portuguese Salvador Rodriguez, who had his countryman Dom Manuel de Mello on board. Next astern was the *San Vicente Ferrer* commanded by another Portuguese, Gaspar Ferreira, and this vessel was followed by the remainder of the Dunkirk squadron. This contingent was followed by the

1 Comprising 33 ships, 10 pinnaces, 16 fireships, 18 frigates and 9 flyboats carrying 1630 men of the Regiment de la Couronne (De la Roncière, *op. cit.* p. 53, note 3).

2 The pillaging of Santoña and Laredo was described by the Spaniards as "más robo que empresa, más de corsario que de capitán, más de ladrón que de Conquistador".

San Josef squadron of 12 ships led by their flagship *Santo Cristo de Burgos*, commanded by Vice-Admiral Francisco Sanches Guadalupe. Next in line came the Ragusa (or Bartelosa) squadron under the orders of Vice-Admiral Mateo Esfrondati. The nine ships comprising this division[1] were followed by the Portuguese galleons with the great *Santa Tereza* bringing up the rear. Don Lope de Hoces, with the gallant Catalan Don Thomaz de Echaburu as his ship's-captain, was on board the *capitana* or flagship of Portugal, but she had no "flag, pendant, or other sign to distinguish her save only her great size". On board this vessel were 600 musketeers in addition to the crew. Astern of the *Santa Tereza* came the galleon *San Josef* carrying the sergeant-major of the whole Armada, Don Gaspar de Carvajal, followed by the galleon *San Juan*. They were followed by the squadron of Naples led by Dom Pedro Velez de Medrano in the superb *Orfeo*. Then followed the squadron of Guevara,[2] commanded by D. Antonio de Ulhôa in the *San Pedro el Grande*. The rearguard was brought up by Don Francisco Feijó de Sotomayor in the *Santiago*, flagship of Galicia, followed by the remainder of his squadron. Behind these came the nine English ships hired as transports, and last of all came the *San Agustin*, formerly the *capitana* of Naples, now Vice-Admiral to the whole Armada under the command of Don Andrés de Castro. Such was the Armada, in which, according to the books of the Fleet-Paymaster, 25,000 rations were distributed daily. It carried 97 infantry and 53 naval captains, three "generals", six colonels, six vice-admirals, four councillors of war, munitions in abundance, and money for the payment of the troops till the following summer to the tune of 800,000 ducats.[3]

On the same day that it set sail the Armada "bore into the Bay of Biscay",[4] but if this was in the hope of finding the French fleet, that hope was vain. Although De Sourdis had written to

1 Capitana, *San Carlos, San Blas, Santa Cruz, San Nicolas, San Jerónimo, San Pablo* and two others.

2 *San Pedro el Grande, El Gran Alejandro, San Esteban* and *Santiago.* [N.B. There were six *Santiagos* in the Armada.]

3 *Epanaphora* IV, pp. 495–7.

4 The eight or nine English transports being bound by their Charter Party to go directly for Dunkirk stood straight for England and safely arrived at Plymouth on Sept. 13th. See *Cal. S.P. Dom.* 1639, pp. 476–7.

express his willingness to encounter the Spaniards,[1] such was not the desire of his master. Richelieu, as he himself said, preferred to let others have the task of "tirer les marrons du feu". In what manner the Hollanders drew his chestnuts out of the fire for him we shall now see.

[1] "Tout venoit à nous; je lève l'ancre pour aller au devant, et si on se rencontre il y aura combat" (De Sourdis to Richelieu, Aug. 26th, 1639; De la Roncière, *op. cit.* v, p. 55).

RICHELIEU

II. TROMP'S CRUISE IN THE NARROW SEAS

(a) Battle of Dunkirk and the Summer Cruise in the Channel

In the year 1637 the Lieutenant-Admiral of the States of Holland, Philips Van Dorp, together with his Vice-Admiral Lieffhebber had been relieved of their commands for reasons into which it is not necessary to go here.[1] In their place were appointed respectively Maarten Harpertszoon Tromp and Witte Corneliszoon de With, both of whom were born in Den Briel and had served as flag-captains of Piet Heyn.[2] The appointment of the *pikbroek* Tromp instead of the *jonkeer* courtier Van Dorp gave rise to the hope that the state of the Dutch navy would be greatly improved, both in quality and quantity; for owing to Van Dorp's incompetence, to administrative difficulties, and above all to the parlous financial situation, the condition of the States' navy left a great deal to be desired.[3]

Within a few weeks of his appointment, Tromp was at sea on a cruise to intercept the Spanish fleet under De Hoces, which as we have seen (p. 3) was bound from La Coruña to Dunkirk with money and soldiers. Tromp and De With vainly cruised in the entrance of the Channel between Portland Bill and Alderney in their search for this fleet, which, as we saw, slipped past them in the thick and misty weather into Dunkirk

[1] They are detailed in Arend, *Geschiedenis des Vaderlands*, III Deel, v stuk, pp. 125–7; Edmundson, *Anglo-Dutch Rivalry* (1600–1653), pp. 111–12; and T. W. Fulton, *Sovereignty of the Sea*, p. 313. Briefly the reasons were dissatisfaction at Van Dorp's failure to prevent the English ship-money fleets from forcing the Dutch herring fishers to pay toll in 1636, and the ineffective way in which he conducted the blockade of Dunkirk.

[2] The German scholar Dr Friedrich Graefe is now engaged upon a detailed biography of Tromp which is to be completed in three vols. The first (down to 1637) is due to appear in 1929. I am therefore excused from the necessity of giving a biographical sketch of the Admiral. For Witte de With see the *Leven en Bedrijf* written by his son-in-law in 1662 and first published by S. P. L'Honoré Naber in 1926. Cf. Bibliography at end. M. H. Tromp was born April 23rd, 1598, of burgher parents, so he was not a "tarpaulin" in the strictest sense of the word.

[3] See Elias, *Schetsen uit de Geschiedenis van ons Zeewezen*, I, pp. 81–114, The Hague 1916.

in mid-December. Undaunted by their failure, Tromp and
De With were at sea again in the first months of 1638, to try
to intercept the Spaniards on their return voyage to Spain, but
once more De Hoces was too sharp—or too lucky—for them
and made his way home in safety. This time the Hollanders
had cruised in two divisions; one under Tromp himself between
the Lizard and Beachy Head, and the other under De With in
the "Vlacke Zee" or southern part of the North Sea. The escape
of De Hoces and a squadron of Dunkirkers induced Tromp
to carry out a more or less close blockade of Dunkirk itself, but
owing to the greater handiness of the famous frigates, and to the
Flemish seamen's intricate knowledge of the chaos of shoals
and banks off their ports, the undertaking was barren of useful
results. In August and October two strong squadrons made
their escape and in December the majority of the Dutch ships
returned to their home ports empty-handed.[1] But their time
had not been wholly wasted. The years 1637 and 1638 were
those in which the Hollanders learnt by bitter experience how
to conduct a cruise in the Channel in the most advantageous
way. 1639 showed how they had profited from those lessons.

In January of that year the States-General had received information of Olivarez's intention to bring over a squadron
from Dunkirk to join the concentration in La Coruña, and at
the same time to transport the 2000 Walloon soldiers of whom
he had such desperate need.[2] Tromp was hurriedly ordered to
put to sea to forestall the escape of the Dunkirkers, and after
a preliminary visit to Falmouth, he appeared off Dunkirk on
February 7th with 12 ships. The Marquis de Fuentes, the
Governor of Dunkirk, contemptuous of the small strength of
the Dutch squadron, gave categorical orders for the fleet
destined for La Coruña to sail without delay. Accordingly at
"creak of day" on February 18th, 1639, Miguel de Orna put
to sea with his force of 12 galleons, 3 pinnaces, and 5 transports
carrying the Walloon soldiery. Of the fierce and well-contested
action which followed, the Dutch and Spanish accounts are
well known,[3] but the version which follows is a contemporary

1 De With's *Leven*.
2 Cf. p. 4, note 1 of this present work, and Arend, *op. cit.* p. 177.
3 De Jonge, *op. cit.* 1, p. 269, and Malo, *op. cit.* pp. 348–51.

English one and as it has never been reprinted since the exceedingly scarce first and only edition of 1649, I reproduce it here as the testimony of an impartial witness:[1]

The 8th [o.s.] of *February* 1638. There came from under the fort at *Mardick* neare *Dunkirk*, 12 sayle of the King of *Spaynes* men of Warre, having in their Company sixe other ships called *floyes* [fluiten], full of Soldiers bound for the *Groyne* in *Biskay*, the wind was at E.S.E. when they set sayl out of the *Splinter*, which was about 8 in the morning, at the same time there was 16[11] sayle of *Hollanders* riding in *Dunkirk* Road, under the Command of *Heare Martyn hartezan van Tromp*. They likewise set sayle and run to the Westwards between the *Brakes* and *Splinter* before the *Dunkirkers*, and did attend their coming out between *Graveling* and *Mardick-hoock*, and as soon as they came within shot one of the other, the Fight began and continued for 4 houres a very sore fight, in so much that Admirall *Tromp* was forced twice to carreen and stop his leakes, the water being smooth and very little wind, and the tyde of ebbe being spent, about noone the wind shifting westerly the *Dunkirkers* bore roome again for succour under *Mardick*-fort, and the *Hollanders* after them, still in fight one with the other, the Vice Admirall of *Dunkirk* the Hollanders did take; for as report went she had lost the use of her steeridge, her rutherhead being shot. But as I conceive it was for want of good Pilotage, and being in that distraction shee ran aground upon the wester Tayle of the *Splinter*, and fearing that the *Hollanders* might come and take out her Provisions, they set her on fire, and so burnt her and all her provisions, not saving so much as her sails that were at the Yards.[2]

As a result of this "bloody fight" Miguel de Orna was compelled for the nonce to give up his attempt to escape, but Tromp on his side was forced to retire to his own ports to refit his ships which had been very roughly handled during the action.

Historians frequently—and as a rule quite justly—contrast the inefficiency and slowness of the over-centralised Iberian Government, with the freer and less hidebound methods of their Dutch and English opponents. But there are times when a strong autocratic administration—especially if spurred into activity—has considerable advantage over a decentralised body which has to consult its component parts before taking any

1 *A Memorable Sea fight...Narrative of all the Principal Passages...Transacted in the Downes*, 1639, by Peter White, 1649.

2 Tromp had also taken two galleons of 34 guns commanded by Captains Mény and Petit, and the Dunkirkers lost over 1600 men in killed, wounded and prisoners (Malo, *op. cit.*).

From the pen-and-ink drawing by Willem Van de Velde (de Oude) in the Nederlandsch Historisch Scheepvaart Museum at Amsterdam

BATTLE OFF DUNKIRK (FEBRUARY 18TH, 1639)

drastic action. Such an occasion in fact now occurred.[1] Although Fuentes, mortified by the defeat of the Dunkirkers in sight of himself and other noblemen who had driven along the shore "to see the fun", threw De Orna and his Vice-Admiral Rombout into prison after the action, he soon came to his senses and restored them to their posts. By dint of forcible pressing and seizures, and by straining every nerve in the dock-yards, the defeated squadron was repaired, re-manned, re-equipped, and put to sea again within a month. On March 12th De Orna sailed out of the now unblockaded harbour and reached La Coruña safely with some prizes.

Meanwhile what of Tromp? The Lieutenant-Admiral of Holland had put into Hellevoetsluis on February 21st with his two prizes and 250 prisoners. Gold chains and medals, and fair words, were showered on him and on his captains for their gallantry, but his urgent appeals for reinforcements were shelved. Thanks to the complex and cumbersome system of Dutch naval administration, with its five Admiralty Boards,[2] its Directories, hired ships and other conflicting and parochial interests, even with the best will in the world it was not an easy or an expeditious matter to fit out or to repair a fleet. When, as in the present case, some provinces showed a disposition to shirk their fair share of the burden, the ensuing confusion and delays would have tried the patience of Job. Eventually after heroic efforts on his part, Tromp put to sea on March 15th—with four ships! Luckily for Tromp—as he himself said—De Orna had already sailed three days earlier with his powerful squadron, otherwise it would have fared ill with the gallant Dutchman had he met his greatly superior force off Dunkirk.

For all the material benefit that had ensued, the action of February 18th might just as well never have been fought and

---

1 Another such occasion was that of the recapture of Bahia in 1624. See Quintella, *op. cit.* pp. 217–21.

2 *I.e.* those of the Maas (or Rotterdam), Amsterdam, Zeeland, Friesland and the North-Quarter. For the constitution, powers and procedure of these Admiralty Boards, and for a survey of the whole system of naval administration in Holland at that time, see De Jonge, *op. cit.* 1, pp. 194–201, 255–8, 322–33, 374, and J. E. Elias, *op. cit.* 1, pp. 89–112. As already noted this latter work is of particular importance for the economic history of the Dutch navy, and corrects the too rosy picture painted by De Jonge.

won. De Horna had escaped to La Coruña with his 2000 sorely-needed Walloons and with the practised Flemish seamen to reinforce the gathering Armada. Spain—strategically if not tactically—had won the first round.

The news that the Spaniards had gone served, however, to bring the wrangling politicians back to some sense of reality. Tromp had returned again when he found his bird had flown, and at the end of March some 15 warships were lying in Hellevoetsluis—which Prince Frederik Hendrik had appointed as the chief base of the fleet in 1632[1]—without anything having been done to help them put to sea again. But things now took a turn for the better. The wrangling parties in the States-General, who had been bitterly disputing amongst themselves and with the Prince of Orange on the latter's proposals for the reorganisation of the fleet on a unified basis,[2] came to a compromise on their differences and made some efforts to fit out a fleet capable of meeting the threatened danger. Tromp himself, who had several times appeared in person before the States-General, took his leave of that august body on April 23rd and journeyed via Den Briel to his flagship at Hellevoet. Although he found the *Amelia* "ongereddert als oyt gezien is", thanks to his energy and zeal he was able to put to sea on the 29th. On May 2nd whilst in the Narrows he was joined by Vice-Admiral Jan Evertsen of Zeeland with six ships of that province, and various other odd ships, bringing his fleet up to 20 sail in all. He now resolved to proceed to his old cruising ground off Portland Bill, whither he sailed after setting ashore his pilot (of all people!) at Dover, with orders to send on any ships which came that way to join the flag off Portland. A week later he reached this rendezvous, and the next few weeks were spent by the fleet in "plying to and again" between Portland Bill and the Race of Alderney. Frequently the fleet spread out over a distance of four or five sea miles, and every ship that passed through was searched irrespective of her nationality. One thing

1 "Generale haven ende plaets van ververschinge der kust-schepen", Aitzema, *Saken van Staet en Oorlogh*, ii, p. 589.

2 These are exhaustively dealt with by Arend, *op. cit.* pp. 149–61, and Elias, *op. cit.* i, 128–9, and 133–7. See also pp. 122–5 of the same author on the vexed question of the abortive "Compagnie van Assurantie". Original documents thereon in Aitzema, *op. cit.* ii, pp. 593–600.

that will probably strike any reader of the *Journal* very forcibly is the frequency with which Tromp had his ships careened. There was scarcely a day when one or more of his ships were not absent on the careen, either in Falmouth, Guernsey or in some other suitable place, or even at sea. This desire to keep the ships so clean was probably due to the numerous demands made upon them for scouting and chasing work, and also to enable them to cope with the swift-sailing Dunkirkers if some of these should chance to fall upon the rear of the fleet, as was feared.

It is interesting to compare the dispositions adopted by Tromp whilst waiting for the expected Spanish fleet, with those adopted by Robert Blake in somewhat similar circumstances in February 1653 when he was cruising in the Channel in expectation of Tromp's arrival with the Bordeaux convoy from the Isle de Ré.[1] It must be admitted that the comparison is in Tromp's favour. His arrangements left nothing to chance. By his daily plying to and again with his fleet between Portland and Cape la Hague he covered the narrowest stretch of this part of the Channel very effectively. To make still more sure that the Spanish fleet could not slip past by hugging the English (or French) coast as De Hoces had done in December 1637, Tromp stationed pairs of *spions* or scouts off Start Point and the Casquets on May 16th.

On the next day a letter was received from Prince Frederik Hendrik containing three points which were debated in Council on the following day. They were: (1) the rigorous searching of all ships for possible Spanish men or money; (2) the possibility of hiring an English ship to sail to La Coruña to "spy out" the Armada's strength; and (3) to send some ships to the mouth of the Channel in order to get advanced warning of the coming of the Spaniards. The first proposal was already in operation, but the Prince's orders provided a welcome pretext for enforcing a stricter visiting of neutral ships—albeit "in the most civil manner". With regard to the second point, Tromp had

---

1 S. R. Gardiner, *History of the Commonwealth and Protectorate*, II, pp. 156–7. His strictures on Blake however are somewhat too severe. For a juster estimate see *Letters and Papers relating to the first Dutch War*, 1652–4, vol. IV, *Introductory*, pp. 5 ff., and J. Elias, *op. cit.* IV, pp. 76–81. Nevertheless a comparison of the two situations is in my opinion to the advantage of Tromp. Cf. *infra*.

already (on the 12th) sent Captain Hollaer to La Coruña for news of the Armada, but it was now resolved to send another two captains, instead of any Englishman, on whom no reliance could be placed. Their orders were to watch what way the Armada took, and so soon as they saw whether it was round Ireland or up Channel, they were to come sailing up the Channel firing off their guns at frequent intervals to alarm Tromp's fleet. So far as the third point was concerned, it was resolved that some captains should be sent to cruise off Portland and Guernsey whilst Tromp with the *gros* cruised midway between them. As there were already *spions* off Start Point and the Casquets—all these scouts were of course relieved from time to time—it is obvious that Tromp's net was cast fairly wide and that little or nothing was left to chance.

That this was so, is proved by the large number of ships which were boarded and searched by Tromp or by his scouts. Almost every day one or more vessels were visited in this manner, and a good deal of news was thus obtained, some of it reliable, some of it much the reverse. The concentrations in La Coruña and Cadiz, the movements of the French fleet under De Sourdis, and the progress of affairs in Brazil, were all reported from time to time. As the daily doings of the fleet are fully recorded and annotated in the *Journal*, there is no need here to go into anything save a broad outline of the chief events.

On June 11th Tromp heard from the master of an English vessel from San Lucar, that five of his compatriots' ships had been freighted to carry soldiers from Cadiz to Dunkirk, which tidings were confirmed by various other ships subsequently. On June 16th a letter was received from the States which mentioned, amongst other things, that the Dunkirkers were causing havoc in the North Sea, but left it entirely to the discretion of Tromp whether he would send a squadron to protect the traders and fishers there or not. At a council of war it was decided to dispatch Commander Banckert with five ships to cruise in the North Sea for a month.

On the 27th one of the *spions* returned from La Coruña with the news that the Armada had sailed, but an examination of the captain's logbook convinced Tromp—quite rightly—that the information was false. The same day a Danziger was stopped, who said that the five above-mentioned English ships would be up with the fleet within 24 hours, and so it proved.

These vessels were the *Experience, Providence, Industry, Rainbow* (Admiral) and *Swan*, carrying about 2000 Spanish soldiers raised in Andalusia under the command of Dom Simão Mascarenhas, son of Dom Jorge Mascarenhas, a great Portuguese minister. This officer—or so it is alleged—out of jealousy to his comrades, persuaded the Spanish Government to let him sail with his regiment on board these five English ships (which being neutrals it was thought would be passed by the Dutch) to Flanders in advance of the remainder of the expedition; his hope being that if he could reach Dunkirk before the Armada, he would be given rank and precedence over all the other colonels.[1] On June 28th three of these ships were stopped by Tromp and on their refusal to strike,

he showed them *Amelia's* teeth, which caused such fear amongst them that they immediately fell into a state of weakness and faintheartedness. The Admiral on seeing this, visited their illness like a good Doctor, and found that they had their belly full of Spaniards, which they had intended to be brought to bed of in Dunkirk. But the aforesaid fright has caused a miscarriage, and thus they brought into the world at sea 1070 Spaniards, whom the Hollander Mid-Wives and Dry-Nurses have forthwith wrapped in swaddling clothes, so that they shall as speedily as possible taste of Rotterdam's beer or water,—being hourly expected here.[2]

Of the other two ships, one escaped into Cornwall and the other to the Isle of Wight. A large consignment of money which the English had on board was not touched by Tromp, on the assurance that it was for English merchants at Dover and not the King of Spain's.

On July 4th, news was received from Holland that the Dunkirkers, taking advantage of the absence of the blockading squadron, and of the weakness of the regular convoys, had

---

1 Dom Francisco Manuel de Mello in his *Epanaphora* iv, p. 464.

2 From a very rare contemporary Rotterdam News-Letter. Commander J. C. M. Warnsinck, R.N.N., has in preparation an article on this amusing episode. For Tromp's own account see under June 28th and 29th in the *Journal, infra.* Other accounts are in *Cal. S.P. Dom.* 1639, pp. 275, 290–2, 306, 328. The account of De With in his *Leven en Bedrijf* (p. 111) is mere personal butter. De Boer, *Armada van* 1639, is wrong as regards Jan Evertsen's alleged part, but shows up that infernal liar, Dom Simão Mascarenhas, in his true colours.

greatly increased their depredations, and were "grazing right lustily" amongst the fat pastures of merchantmen in the North Sea. As the Armada showed no signs of undue haste, and since the French fleet was known to be prepared to cope with it (or with some of it), the Council of War resolved that Tromp with the main body of the fleet should do a "turn" of 10 or 12 days in the North Sea, taking as cruising ground a square formed by the River Maas, Orfordness, Dunkirk and the North Foreland. Two scouts were to be left off the Isle of Wight, on the look-out for the Armada (should it come after all) and to keep an eye on the English transport which had put into Cowes road with her Spanish soldiers.[1]

Whilst Tromp was cruising in the Channel on the watch for the Armada, his policy of searching all vessels for Spanish contraband aroused the ire of the English, always extremely sensitive on such matters.[2] But as luck would have it, the time was a favourable one for the Hollanders, as Charles I's ship-money fleet, which in previous years had worried the Dutch fishers in the North Sea and kept a jealous eye on English "rights", was now busily employed elsewhere. The outbreak of the troubles with Scotland consequent on Charles' ecclesiastical policy in that kingdom, had called not only the army but also the fleet to the north. Thus rumours of the approach of the French fleet and of the Hollanders, to say nothing of that of the Spaniards, caused no little perplexity to the English authorities. At first they were more afraid of De Sourdis than of Tromp. On June 2nd, 1639, Thomas Smith, the secretary of the Lord High Admiral, wrote to Sir John Pennington, Admiral of the Fleet in the Firth of Forth: "'Tis said they (the French) intend to come this way and are for Dunkirk, to prevent which the Spaniards have as good a fleet at the Groyne and another at Cadiz coming this way, so that our little *Wren* must piss in the sea for fear.... Twenty-two sail of the Hollanders attend about Portland the coming of the French fleet to join therewith".[3] At the end of May several English vessels were

1 These were landed at Portsmouth on July 23rd and marched overland to London, *Cal. S.P. Dom.* 1639, p. 391.

2 For complaints of these "insolencies" see *Cal. S.P. Dom.* 1639, pp. 274, 290, 292, 306, 382–3, 397.

3 *Cal. S.P. Dom.* 1639, pp. 214–15.

assembled in the Downs, and whilst a small squadron "plyed two and again between Dover and the Ness and so back to the Downes" each week,[1] the other vessels were employed on the Dover-Dunkirk convoys. The complaints of the "insolencies" of the Hollanders however grew in volume to such an extent, that the King ordered Pennington to return to the Downs from Scotland, whence he sailed about the same time as Tromp left his cruising ground in the Channel for the North Sea.

(b) The Cruise in the North Sea and Blockade of Dunkirk

On July 5th Tromp was off Cape Grisnez with 20 sail, and that same day 11 enemy frigates were sighted, which, although he held after them all that day and the next, escaped by the use of sweeps. A Council of War on the 6th confirmed the resolution of cruising until July 15th-16th in the North Sea for the protection of the fishery and accordingly the fleet proceeded to the appointed cruising ground "between the Maas, Orfordness, Dunkirk and the N. Foreland".[2] Each of the captains was given a station to cruise on, and two rendezvous—Hythe and the North Foreland—were selected for the ships to assemble at on the expiration of the time limit. On the 10th the Spanish officers and priests taken on June 28th were landed at Rotterdam. This cruise was totally unproductive of any results, and the only noteworthy event which occurred was an outbreak of sickness amongst the crews, which the cargo of a captured enemy ship laden with fruit did a good deal to assuage.

On July 17th Brederode rejoined with the squadron with which he had been cruising between Wight and the Narrows, and as news was received that the departure of the Armada from La Coruña was likely to be postponed until October, it was resolved that the main body—gros—of the fleet should

1 *I.e.* well clear of the Hollands Fleet which was "plying to and again off Portland" (*ibid.* p. 275). Not until the end of his cruise did Tromp go east of the Wight, and the English obviously avoided meeting his fleet lest they should be compelled to undertake a task beyond their powers in trying to stop him searching ships for Spaniards.

2 Commander Brederode with five sail had been detached to cruise between the Wight and the Narrows.

return to the old cruising ground between Portland and the Casquets, and accordingly they proceeded down Channel. On the 19th news was received of the taking of the Rouen convoy by Dunkirkers,[1] whereon Tromp resolved to detach Vice-Admiral Jan Evertsen with a *vliegant Esquadre* or flying squadron of seven ships to range the seas between Texel and Portland for the audacious Dunkirkers. On the 27th Tromp resolved to go to Falmouth to careen some of his foulest ships, and detached Vice-Admiral De With to take up a station off Portland. Contrary winds however prevented Tromp from reaching Falmouth, so that he put into Guernsey instead at the end of the month in order to careen the ships and refresh the crews.

On the same day that Tromp abandoned his fruitless cruise in the North Sea (July 17th), Admiral Sir John Pennington arrived in the Downs from the Firth of Forth with the *Antelope*. Here he found a squadron of eight sail[2] awaiting him, but owing to lack of provisions and inadequate supplies he could not put to sea to chastise the "insolencies" of the Hollanders as the merchants of Dover so ardently desired. The Secretary of State Windebank informed him that he would in due course receive orders to

go with some of the fleet to the Westward, to prevent sundry like insolencies to those which have been lately committed upon the King's subjects, to the great interruption of trade, and not without some reflection upon his Majesty in point of Honour. The English merchants' complaints go very high; and it concerns His Majesty not a little, both in reason of State, in honour, and benefit, to be sensible of them, and to put some timely redress to those disorders, especially in his own seas, or else his sovereignty will run hazard to be lost.[3]

Pennington in his reply took a much more reasonable view of the alleged "insolencies" of the Dutch. He pointed out that Tromp could scarcely be expected tamely to permit the English to transport Spanish troops to Flanders, and stated that he had done nothing beyond his plain duty and "otherwise

1 See *Journal* under that date, and *Cal. S.P. Dom.* 1639, p. 392, where the loss is estimated at £100,000.

2 *Vanguard, Victory, James, Unicorn, Leopard, Providence, Henrietta Maria* and the City of London's ship *Unicorn.*

3 *Cal. S.P. Dom.* 1639, p. 383.

used the English with all civility and courtesy, not offering to meddle with any of their goods or moneys, which lay upon the decks in chests, with the King of Spain's arms upon them.... In truth I think the English masters have committed the greater insolency and deserve to be punished, in undertaking a business of that nature without special warrant, for their presumption herein has produced no good effect".[1] He pointed out that in any case the strength and quality of his fleet was too small to enable him to use force against the Hollanders—and all the more so since the French fleet was expected to join with them before long.

The King and the Lord High Admiral Northumberland did not share Pennington's eminently reasonable view, and on July 25th, Windebank wrote informing him that he was to go "westward" with his fleet to "keep the trade free and open as well to his Majesty's subjects as to others in league and amity with his Majesty". Captain Carteret was to be left in charge of the convoys to Dunkirk. These orders were repeated on the following day, and Pennington wrote in reply on July 27th that he would be ready to leave in a day's time albeit only four of his ships were fit to sail.[2] Contrary winds, however, held him up until July 30th, when he put to sea on hearing that a Hamburger ship named the *Fortune* had been taken by two Dutch vessels from out of Dover Road. Although he could not catch the culprits, he brought five other Dutch ships which he found into the Downs, and did not release them until they had made humble apology.[3]

In the middle of August, as all the news received of the Armada tended to show that it could not sail before October, and since the depredations of the Dunkirkers were continually increasing, Tromp resolved to resume the blockade of Dunkirk. He arrived off the place on August 15th and held it blockaded with the *gros* of his fleet until September 5th. This operation,

1 *Cal. S.P. Dom.*, p. 390.
2 *Ibid.* p. 399. A "state of the fleet consisting of 19 sail and how they are dispersed this 17/27 July 1639", is calendared on the same page.
3 A full account of the incident in *ibid.* p. 411. The five Dutch ships seized were *Utrecht* (28) Captain Brederode, *De Prins Willem* (32) Captain Pietersz, *Deventer* (28) Captain Post, the *Overijssel* (26) Captain Farant, and the *Tertholen* (18) Captain Hollaer. Cf. Tromp's *Journal* under Aug. 8th, 11th and 15th.

like the cruise in the North Sea, was barren of any useful result and that for three reasons. In the first place, a large number of frigates had already escaped; secondly, the wooden fort or *Houten Wambuis* of Mardijck prevented the Hollanders from making full use of the *Scheurtje*, or inner road, and kept them at a respectable distance; lastly, the uncanny knowledge of the Flemings of the chaos of banks off their port stood them in such good stead that on every dark and windy night one or more frigates slipped out.[1]

Tromp's difficulties were further increased by the numerous English traders, which under convoy of royal vessels sailed in and out of the blockaded harbour as they liked. In these circumstances there was little hope of effecting anything useful.

Acting on instructions from the Lord High Admiral, Pennington wrote to Tromp, categorically prohibiting the examination of English ships in the Channel, to which he returned a firm reply maintaining his right to search merchantmen for Spanish soldiers.[2]

The "dog-in-the-manger" attitude of the English brought its own revenge on them on one occasion, when one of the convoyers grounded on a shoal outside Dunkirk and a couple of French privateers came up and carried off a merchantman under the very nose of the stranded warship, whose captain vainly appealed to Tromp to interfere.[3]

This deliberate flaunting of the blockade by the English brought no advantage to any of their countrymen save the Dover merchants, and opposition against the huge ship-money fleets which were being used for such doubtful purposes steadily hardened through the land.[4]

---

1 De Boer, *op. cit.* p. 29, and Tromp's *Journal*, Aug. 15th–Sept. 5th, 1639.

2 For these letters see *Cal. S.P. Dom.* 1639, pp. 444 and 457, where they are reproduced in full. See also Tromp's *Journal* under Sept. 3rd.

3 See *Journal* under Aug. 28th.

4 That the ship-money fleets were, potentially at any rate, of great value has been proved by G. E. Manwaring in *Life and Works of Sir Henry Mainwaring*, pp. 226–94 (N.R.S. publ. 1920).

(c) Tromp's final Dispositions

With the continued delay in the appearance of the expected Spanish fleet, both the States-General on shore and the admirals at sea were forced to reconsider the measures which they had adopted. It was difficult to decide whether it was best for the fleet to await the Spaniards off Dunkirk itself—where at least they would certainly be met—or to return to its old cruising ground off Portland. The situation was further complicated by the presence of Pennington's strong squadron in the Downs, and by the alarm caused by the Dunkirkers in the North Sea where (it was said) 30 or 40 of them were ranging. Finally, it was still uncertain whether the Spanish Armada would come "North about" or up Channel, or if indeed it was coming at all this year. The city fathers may well be excused for scratching their heads over this problem, but as events showed they took the wisest course. For when at the beginning of September, sure news arrived from Antwerp of the imminent approach of the Armada, they resolved that "the business would perforce have to be left in the hands of God and to the energy and courage of the Lieutenant-Admiral".[1]

Tromp himself had made up his mind on September 5th that a change of plan was necessary. In view of the comparative futility of blockading Dunkirk, he resolved on that day to sail with 13 ships to cruise between Beachy Head and the Narrows. Witte de With was to be left with ten sail before Dunkirk in order to hinder, if he could not prevent, the exit and ingress of the Dunkirkers; whilst Banckert, who was absent on guard of the fishery in the North Sea, was to take over the command from De With on his return to Dunkirk, when De With would rejoin Tromp in the Channel with some of his ships.[2]

Tromp with his detachment weighed anchor the next day and stood over to the English coast. The following day he paid a visit to Calais, and shortly afterwards steered westwards again. When about half seas over he sighted seven "tall ships",

1 *Resolutions of the States of Holland,* Sept. 6th, 1639 (Arend, *op. cit.* p. 189).
2 For the situation in the first fortnight of September see *Journal,* Sept. 5th-15th; Aitzema, *op. cit.* II, p. 609; and the *Leven en Bedrijf* of De With, p. 112.

which proved to be English royal vessels.[1] As soon as he discovered what they were, he tacked about and sailed away from them; he was evidently anxious to avoid any unnecessary meeting which might have led to serious difficulties in view of the strained situation then prevailing. The English on their side were equally anxious to avoid him, as several warships which were sighted in the next few days made away from the Hollanders as soon as they saw who they were. Tromp continued to stop and search all merchantmen he met, however, and several English ships were visited in this way.

Whilst Tromp was thus cruising between Beachy and the Narrows with his 13 sail, Commander Banckert had relieved De With off Dunkirk on September 13th. On the next day the Vice-Admiral left with five ships to join Tromp, who was then off the Sussex coast. How timely his departure was the sequel will show.

[1] Apparently Vice-Admiral Sir Henry Mainwaring, who had been detached by Pennington to cruise in the same part of the Channel as Tromp. Pennington himself was still in the Downs.

JOACHIMI

III. THE FIGHTS IN THE CHANNEL

(a) *The Action of September 16th*

The Spanish Armada, which had left La Coruña at the end of August, continued on its voyage without any incident worth the telling until September 15th. That morning the Spaniards fell in with an English ship which had been spoken by Tromp on the previous day. The master of this vessel informed De Oquendo that Tromp with his 13 sail was cruising between Calais Cliff and Beachy. This news caused the greatest joy amongst the Spaniards, who had thought it certain that De Sourdis and his fleet had united with the Hollanders, and that they would have their work cut out for them. But now they learnt that the Dutch were not only alone, but in such small strength, "there was no one in the Armada who did not regard them as already defeated, and the victory as Spain's".[1]

Least of all De Oquendo. Some of the more prudent of his captains thought that in view of the approaching conflict, they ought to be issued with clearer and more detailed instructions than those which they already possessed. Accordingly, seven or eight of the senior naval and military officers proceeded on board De Oquendo's flagship, and assembled in his cabin. The Spanish commander however was so contemptuous of his opponents that he thought it totally unnecessary to fall in with his captains' views. Dom Manuel de Mello, who was one of those present in the cabin, gives us a graphic account of what took place. De Oquendo, rough and impatient as ever, closed the brief discussion with a sentence which (says Dom Manuel) he could never forget: "Ea señores! El enemigo es poca ropa, cada uno haga su mejor, que yo lindo caballo tengo; la Real darâ buenos exemplos!"[2] "Such", observes the Portuguese

1 *Epanaphora* IV, p. 500.
2 *Ibid.* p. 501. These words, "See, Gentlemen! The enemy is but small fry; let each one do his best, for we have an easy task; the Flagship will set a good example", were spoken by De Oquendo on a similar occasion some eight years before, prior to his encounter with Adrian Pater's fleet off Pernambuco in 1631. On that occasion the Dutch admiral had lost his ship and life after a homeric duel with De Oquendo's flagship; no doubt it was the hope of repeating his memorable success in the former action, which caused De Oquendo to act in the same way eight years later.

soldier, "was his confidence, greater without a doubt than his prudence". By this time the Spaniards were off Selsea Bill and in sight of the Hollanders to the S.W. of Beachy Head.

So soon as Tromp discovered the 67 sail of the Armada, he hoisted the white flag as signal for a council. It was at once unanimously resolved to send off Captain Tjaert de Groot post haste, to sail eastwards shooting off his guns four times in every half hour, to give the alarm to De With off the Sussex coast and to Banckert off Dunkirk. His orders were to send all ships he met with to join the flag forthwith, in order to attack the enemy with some prospect of success.

At sunset the Spaniards lay hove to "with their heads to the south", whilst Tromp, who was about three miles S.-E. from them, lay by the lee to wait for them, the wind being at W. by S.

At day-break on September 16th the Spanish Armada got under weigh. Their ships were scattered about "in incredible disorder" and were in no formation of any sort or kind. The wind was between W. and N.W. (or thereabouts), and Tromp did his best to beat up towards the Armada. The Spaniards were so astonished at seeing Tromp making towards them, instead of flying from them, that they seriously thought for a time that his squadron was probably an English one and not Hollanders at all! But they were soon undeceived. Captain Tjaert had met De With with five sail off Dungeness on the night of the 15th-16th and these five sail were now to leeward of Tromp's squadron, trying their best to come up with him. Tromp, seeing that he could not get the weather-gauge of the Armada, bore away before the wind and soon united with De With's squadron.[1] Of what followed this meeting we have sharply divergent accounts.

If we can trust the contemporary *Leven en Bedrijf* of De With, written in 1662 by his son-in-law Walter Bremen van der Hagen,[2] the real hero of the subsequent action was not "Bestevaer" but De With himself. According to this account, Tromp behaved—both before, during, and after the fight—like

[1] The foregoing from De Mello's *Epanaphora* IV, Tromp's *Journal*, and De With's *Leven*.

[2] MSS. in the Rijksarchief at The Hague, published by S. P. L'Honoré Naber in 1926, *vide* Bibliography.

an abject poltroon. At the Council of War on the 15th he is said to have left his captains to decide what action to take, and to have washed his hands of any responsibility. On the 16th it is averred that he had no wish to give battle, but was overruled by De With, who was basely abandoned by him in the fight. Numerous other similar instances of alleged cowardice on Tromp's part are also recorded.[1]

Now all this, I am firmly convinced, is the sheerest nonsense. De With was the bravest of men and undaunted by any danger, as the whole course of his life showed. But he had the defects of his qualities. Throughout a long and active career at sea, he seldom got on well with either his superiors or his subordinates. Often disliked by those equal to or above him, hated and feared by those below him, his jealousy, ill-temper and vindictiveness roused the enmity of nearly all those with whom he came into contact.[2] Dr De Boer has clearly shown that the whole of his *Leven en Bedrijf* is permeated by a spiteful hate of Tromp, and confutes his version of the events of that memorable September day by a comparison of other Dutch contemporary sources.[3]

But these sources, being Dutch, might be considered too partial by some ultra-strict writers. I think, however, that I can quote other references which should settle the matter once for all. From the account of Dom Manuel de Mello—translated and printed in Appendix I—and from that of Peter White (which follows), we see that the honour of this action belongs to Tromp and to Tromp alone. These two witnesses for the defence (so to speak) are beyond suspicion, for one was an enemy and the other an unbiassed neutral. Both state that it was Tromp alone who addressed the Council of War, and announced his intention of giving battle without asking its opinion. Both agree that he deliberately formed his squadron into line, and maintained it in that formation for some length of time—at that period a novel though not unique practice.

1 *Leven en Bedrijf*, pp. 112–16, etc.

2 On one occasion in the English war of 1652–4, when Tromp had been replaced in the supreme command by De With, the crew of the *Brederode*—Tromp's flagship—refused to allow De With on board and hounded him away!! When a senior officer is treated by his men in this manner, there must be something radically wrong with his character. And this was not an isolated incident.

3 In his *De Armada van* 1639, pp. 29–31. But his note 2 on p. 34 is rubbish.

Both give De With his due as a brave and valiant officer, but in neither of their narratives can there be found the slightest trace of any want of conduct or courage on the part of Tromp. Their versions, moreover, are to a large extent corroborated by other trustworthy contemporaries, such as one of De With's own subordinates—Captain Waterdrincker—in his *Journal*.[1] But having dealt with this vexed question to boring point, it is time to return to the scene of action.

Tromp and De With effected their junction "thwart off Beachy" at about 8 a.m., and the decision to fight was confirmed by their drinking a glass of wine together in the Admiral's cabin. Tromp now formed his 17 sail into line and drove southwards "under small sail" to await the onset of the 67 ships of the Spanish Armada which bore down upon them with all sail set. Of the memorable action which follows, the two best accounts of the rival fleets—those of Tromp and De Mello—are printed in this book, and it is interesting to compare them with that of Peter White, whose version—so far as I know—has hitherto been overlooked.[2] There are a few mistakes in it, but on the other hand he gives some details which are wanting in both the Dutch and Iberian accounts.

Presently after daylight, this present day aforesaid, the wind being at N.N.W. this Fleet [*i.e.* the Spanish] being to the Eastward of *Wight*, thwart of *Arundell*, The Hollander discryed them being right to Leeward off them,[3] upon which Admirall Trump called a short Councell, and incouraged all his Fleet now to behave themselves like Men, and then with Gods assistance he doubted not, but they should doe their Country good service and gain themselves honour, the which all resolved with heart and hand to performe, and having the Starboard tacks aboard, held it up close upon a wind, and as they came neare unto them, they

1 From which we see that Tromp beat up towards the Spanish Armada *before* he bore away to join De With, a statement also confirmed by De Mello. From De With's account one would imagine that he was running away from the Spaniards until De With met and stopped him. For Waterdrincker's journal see Aitzema, II, pp. 613 ff. Dr De Boer, whose account of this action and that of the 18th is the weakest part of his otherwise excellent study, gives a wrong reference to this. He also says the Hollanders kept out of musket-shot, which is untrue. Cf. De Mello's version in Appendix I.

2 *Memorable Sea-fight*, pp. 4–5. But Cf. *Dom Manuel de Mello—Esboço Biographico* by Professor Edgar Prestage, p. 114, *n.* (3), Coimbra 1914.

3 *I.e.* the Hollanders were right to leeward of the Spaniards.

From the portrait of 1649 by Jan Lievens in the Kweekschool voor de Zeevaart at Amsterdam

LIEUTENANT-ADMIRAL MAARTEN HARPERTSZOON TROMP (1598–1653)

payed a little roome to get from amongst them, and likewise to try how
their Ships did sayle by the *Spanyards*, and perceiving that they went
better than the most part of their Enemies, they laskt it away with a
fathom of the Sheat to the Eastward, and the *Spanish* Admirall and some
other that were the best saylers gave them chase and the rest of the Fleet
followed; the *Hollanders* perceiving that they had got the Admirall and
a part of the Fleet from the rest, shortened sayles, and about 9 of the
clock in the morning the Fight began; the *Hollanders* still as it were
flying from them, but Birtht [berthed] themselves so, having a faire gale
of wind, that in following each other they were but two Ships length a
sunder,[1] and when they looft [luffed] up to give their broad sides, one
was cleere of the other. But the first broad side that one of the foremost
ships of the *Hollanders* gave, by what accident no man knoweth, the Ship
blew up all to pieces, but some of their men were taken up by the *Span-*
yards; which accident was much lamented by the *Hollanders* for the losse
of the Ship and Men, and likewise for the want of her force, being a good
Ship of 36 Pieces of Ordnance.[2]

Likewise after this another mischance hapned aboard their Vice-
admirall *de White*, he having a barrell of Powder in his Round-house to
fill Cartridges, which by negligence was fired and blew up the Round
house whereon the Drummer was beating his Drum, who was likewise
taken up by the *Spanyards*;[3] the fire was presently quenched and not much
disheartening to the *hollander*, but a mighty encouragement unto the
Spanyards, who did still pursue their Fight; and the Hollanders in a
seeming flight behaved themselves so well, that at 3 a clock afternoon the
spanyards began to grow weary, having his Masts and yards shot, strook
[struck] his Topsayles and lay by the Lee, and staid for the rest of his
Fleet, and when they came up they all lay by the Lee together, to repaire
their Masts, and rigging, upon which the *Hollander* run to Leewards off
them out of shot, and likewise clapt his Ship by the Lee...etc.

A comparison of Peter White's account with those of Tromp
(*vide Journal*) and Manuel de Mello (*vide* Appendix I) shows
that there is general agreement as to the way in which the action
started, and the course of the fight. But there is one important
difference between the Portuguese account and the other two.
This concerns the reasons for which De Oquendo broke off

1 De Mello says they were even closer, less than one ship's length apart.
Cf. Appendix I.

2 *De Groote Christoffel.* That the Spaniards picked up many of her men is
confirmed by Tromp's *Journal, q.v.* De Boer's statement on p. 32 of his *Armada*
is erroneous.

3 This confirms De With's own account of the incident on p. 114 of his
Leven en Bedrijf. Dr De Boer who places it in the action of the 18th (*Armada,*
p. 34) does less than justice to De With in this respect.

the action. Peter White, as will be seen, agrees with Tromp that the Spanish admiral was *afgevochten*, *i.e.* that he had received his belly full. Dom Manuel de Mello admits that the Spanish Admiral *himself* was *afgevochten* but would have us believe that with the majority of the Armada it was far otherwise. He tells us that at the very moment when the distressed condition of the royal flagship compelled De Oquendo to retire from the fight, the Hollanders themselves were in a desperate position; not, as he admits, by reason of the losses they had suffered, but because of their situation. Tromp's squadron, he says, was now penned in by the 67 sail of the Armada extended in crescent formation, somewhere between the mouth of the Somme and the coast south (or north) of it.[1] This is not unlikely if we consider that during the whole time which the action lasted, both fleets had been driving before the wind in a S.E. or S.S.E. direction. Since the wind was at N.N.W. Tromp obviously could not escape from being driven on to the lee shore formed by the French coast unless he forced his way through the midst of the Armada. In fact he was caught like a rat in a trap, and if we follow De Mello the situation of the two fleets at about 3 p.m. was somewhat as follows:

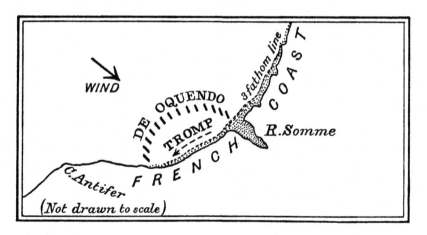

(Not drawn to scale)

1 *Epanaphora* iv, p. 510: "...os tinha reduzidos a hum breve sitio, entre a terra, e o Rio".

Now, when success seemed within his grasp, De Oquendo broke off the action. Why? De Mello gives two answers. One suggestion, which was widely current in the Spanish fleet, was that De Oquendo being himself *afgevochten* and unable to continue the action, was so jealous of his subordinates achieving a victory without his help that he deliberately recalled them. The other reason—which was advanced by De Oquendo himself as the ostensible cause of his determination—was that he feared lest his great galleons should follow the Hollanders too close inshore, and be wrecked on the dangerous banks. This excuse is the one invariably alleged by English and Spanish writers whenever their countrymen had the worst of any action with the Dutch off the Flemish or French coasts, and it will not bear a moment's examination.[1] These writers always say (as does Dom Manuel on this occasion) that the Dutch knew these dangerous coasts like the backs of their own hands, and that their opponents were wholly ignorant of them. This is absurd on the face of it, as amongst all the huge English fleets which fought the battles of the three Dutch wars, there must have been not one but numerous pilots who were acquainted with those coasts, almost if not quite as well as the Hollanders themselves. In the case of De Oquendo there was even less excuse. For amongst his Armada were 13 sail of Dunkirkers, and these renowned corsairs knew the shoals and banks of these coasts every bit as well as Tromp himself. If De Oquendo really thought his galleons in danger, why did he not send in the 13 Dunkirkers and some other light vessels to tackle the Dutch? Or if not this, he had only to stay where he was *vis-a-vis* the Hollanders and they would then be still at his mercy. But he did none of these things, and in my opinion there can only be one rational explanation. Be that as it may, he himself, as all accounts agree, was compelled to "lie by the lee" in order to repair his shattered ship, as were many of his consorts, and the remainder of the Armada followed suit about two hours afterwards.[2]

1 This excuse was trotted out as the reason for not following up the Dutch after Lowestoft (1665), Schooneveld (1673), St James' fight (1666), and after every other victorious or indecisive battle fought off the Dutch coast, in all of the wars from 1652 onwards.

2 It is interesting to compare this situation on the evening of Sept. 16th, 1639,

Tromp, whether or not he was actually in a difficult situation, similarly hove-to to leeward of the Armada until nightfall, when he drove northwards with the S.W. wind which had sprung up, having been joined by two more ships.

He could be well contented with what he had done. With 16 ships—all of which, save two, were of the same strength as English fourth rates—he had beaten off the onslaught of 67 sail of the proudest ships of Spain, led by one of her greatest admirals. Not only this, but he had handled them so roughly that the Spaniards were now definitely on the defensive. This much is admitted by all their writers. When De Oquendo had cast about to the northward at 3 in the afternoon, the initiative had passed from his hands into those of Tromp.

The action of September 18th was the necessary complement to the earlier battle, and that of October 21st formed the pendant to the whole campaign. But the issue had really been decided on September 16th, and by nightfall on that date Tromp was master of the situation.

(b) *The Action of September* 18th

By sunset on the 16th Tromp was five miles E.S.E. of Fairlight, whilst the Spaniards lay to windward and two miles W.S.W. of him. At midnight the Admiral missed the enemy's lights, and lay over to the E.N.E. under small sail till daylight on the 17th, when Cape Grisnez bore four miles E.N.E. of him. At nine o'clock the Spaniards were sighted to the N.W., between Dungeness and Hastings.[1]

Owing to the calm and lack of wind Tromp was unable to get up with them, but the Spaniards were not left undisturbed. Vice-Admiral Sir Henry Mainwaring with six sail fell in with the Armada during the afternoon, and found the Spaniards in

with that of Tromp on the last day's action of the three days' fight, Feb. 28th–Mar. 2nd, 1653. On this last occasion, Blake's fleet had cornered Tromp and his convoy to the south of Cape Grisnez at nightfall on Mar. 2nd. The English pilots swore that Tromp would never weather the headland, but during the night he did so, and gave the English the slip. See Gardiner, *op. cit.* pp. 160–3; Elias, *op. cit.* III, pp. 90–1; and *Letters and Papers*, IV, p. 12.

1 Tromp's *Journal*; Peter White's *Sea-fight*; and Aitzema's journal of Waterdrincker.

distress, "having been shrewdly torn and beaten by only seventeen of the Holland ships in their first encounter (a shameful thing, considering the number of the Spanish ships and their ostentation before to chastise both the French and the Hollanders)".[1] Nevertheless De Oquendo refused to strike his flag until Mainwaring made a "faire shot" at him.[2]

When the English had left the Spaniards in peace the Armada slowly made its way with the S.S.E. wind as far as Folkestone, where De Oquendo "anchored to stop the Ebbe, and the *Hollanders* did the like, being some 4 or 5 miles from them, right in the wind of them; the *Spanyards* bearing from them N. by W.". It was now sunset and Tromp hoisted the white flag as a signal for council. He proposed to attack the enemy soon after midnight, at which time the moon would be up and the ebb tide spent. After some discussion this was agreed to, and it was resolved that in order to minimise the risk of mistaking friends for foes, the following distinguishing marks would be displayed. The *Amelia* was to carry two lights in the poop and one in the maintop, whilst the remainder were to carry one light in the poop. In addition to this, all ships were to display a bonnet on the poop; and finally, they were to keep as close together as possible.[3] At 11 o'clock Tromp weighed anchor, and followed by his 18 sail stood after the Spanish fleet which was still 67 sail strong. During the whole night the Hollanders continued to fire four guns in every half hour as a signal to Banckert who was feeling his way towards them from Dunkirk.

By 2 a.m. on the morning of September 18th the Hollanders having the weather-gauge of the enemy, and "the tyde of Ebbe being spent" they "bore up all together upon the Spanish fleet and steer'd with them N. by W.".[4] First of all the Hollanders bore upon De Oquendo's flagship, "and gave him every one their broadside, and tore him exceedingly, and then to work pell-mell with all the Fleet, and continued the fight, the

1 *Clarendon State Papers*, II, p. 71.
2 A full account of this incident in Peter White's *Sea-fight*; and another in Mainwaring, *op. cit.*
3 Waterdrincker's journal, Aitzema, *op. cit.* II, p. 614. This provides a valuable confutation of the balderdash in De With's *Leven en Bedrijf*, p. 115.
4 Peter White, *op. cit.* p. 7. N. by W. should probably read E.N.E.

Ordnance going off so fast, that it was a wonder to those that heard and saw them".[1]

In the early hours of the 18th, Tromp was joined by Banckert with nine sail, which provided a welcome reinforcement for the Hollanders. At daybreak the two fleets were off Dover and Banckert came aboard the *Amelia* to ask for orders. If we are to believe Dom Manuel de Mello, who gives us by far the longest and most interesting—if not always the most reliable—account, Tromp now changed his plan of attack.

The Portuguese writer informs us that the Dutch admiral formed his 30 sail into two equal divisions, one led by himself and the other by De With, with which he simultaneously assaulted the van and rear of the Spaniards. The Armada was ranged in a parallelogram-shaped formation, so that only the ships on the flanks were able to use their guns to some purpose, the fire of those in the centre and to leeward doing more harm to their own consorts than to their opponents.[2] It is quite possible that something of the sort actually did take place. Tromp in his *Journal* does not mention this formation, but his own account—and that of Waterdrincker—is so brief that it only amounts to four or five lines in all. Peter White, who was an eyewitness and gives us an excellent and graphic picture of the battle, is also silent on the subject; but it does not conflict with anything in his own version.[3] On the other hand the *Leven* of Witte de With actually confirms the Portuguese account to a large extent, although it implies that the idea was the Vice-Admiral's own.[4] Be this as it may, there is no foundation for what many modern writers claim as the first instance of "the breaking of the line". The origin of the notion that Tromp employed this (later) classic manœuvre on this occasion for the first time, is due to a misreading of De Mello by his countryman Quintella,[5] which having been copied by Duro[6] has since passed into accepted currency. It is probably true that—for a time at all events—Tromp's fleet fought in two detachments, but (and

1 Peter White, *op. cit.* Cf. Manuel de Mello's graphic account in Appendix I.
2 *Epanaphora* iv, p. 517. Cf. my translation in Appendix I.
3 *Op. cit.* pp. 6–8.   4 *Leven en Bedrijf*, p. 116.
5 In his *Annaes da Marinha Portugueza*, ii, p. 346, Lisboa 1840.
6 *Armada Española*, iv, p. 210.

this is the crux) the Spaniards were *not* in line. They were formed, as De Mello specifically says, in a vast square or parallelogram four or five ranks deep, and therefore there can be no question of the "breaking of the line" when there was no line to break.[1]

But "revenons à nos moutons". When the fleets were off Dover:

> The Wind being then at S. and by W. the *Spanish* fleet hal'd over for the French coast, and the *Hollanders* to windward off them, still continuing their fight upon the *Spanish* and *Portugall* squadrons,[2] the *Dunkirkers* keeping still on the lee-boughs off them without shot, and all the *Lubeckers* and other ships that had the Soldiers in them, were a good berth ahead of them all, some of them being as we did conceive that lookt upon them out of the *Downes* with prospective Glasses were past *Callice* [Calais].[3] About 9 a clock we could perceive one of the great *Spanyards* which proved the Admirall of *Sivill*,[4] lie with her head to the westward, with her mayn-yard shot downe, and her mayn-top-sayle stroke.

This great galleon together with a hired Danish ship was taken by five sail detached by Tromp for the purpose.[5]

Meanwhile the Hollanders hammered the Armada so stoutly, "especially the Vice Admirall of the *Holland* fleet, (as the *English*men which were amongst the *Spanyards* did relate unto us) that the *spanyards* laid downe their Armes and would not fight; so that they shot not one Piece of Ordnance in almost halfe an houre, the which wee could very well perceive out of the *Downes*". At this critical moment the Dunkirkers and De Oquendo tacked about upon the two captured vessels to

1 Tromp himself, of course, as we have seen, adopted the line ahead formation on the 16th and also (apparently) in the first attack on the morning of the 18th.

2 The Portuguese squadron bore the brunt of this action; the flagship *Santa Tereza* having fired over 1520 great shot from her starboard battery alone! Cf. Appendix I.

3 Sir John Manwood writing from Dover Castle at the same hour, stated that the fleets were then "in sight not half seas over between Dover and the high white cliffs opposite", *Cal. S.P. Dom.* 1639, p. 491. It is evident that Peter White overestimated the distance that the Spanish van had gone, as the fight ended almost exactly in mid-channel.

4 Seville—yet another name for the *capitana* of Masibradi, Esfrondati, Bartelosa or Ragusa as the Iberian accounts indifferently term it!

5 And not by Peter White's personal friend "Captain Forrant a valiant Frenchman" alone, as he would have us believe (*op. cit.* p. 8).

rescue them and were successful in one instance. Tromp seeing this, and "the Powder in his Fleet being almost spent, about 10 aclocke hee made sayle and stood away to the westwards from them, having taken one of the Spanish fleet...and then hee stood for Calice to supply himself with powder".

Modern Dutch writers are fond of affirming that the Spaniards broke off the action first, but that this was not the case is proved by the accounts of Peter White and De Mello. Both of these writers are equally emphatic in stating that the Spaniards had been very roughly handled during the fight, and had suffered much heavier losses than the Hollanders. Tromp himself told De Mello two years later that the lack of powder was his sole reason for breaking off the action, and this is further corroborated by his *Journal*. But even now that Tromp was compelled to retire to Calais to replenish his exhausted ammunition, the Spaniards were unable to take advantage of the fact. In the first place, the majority of their ships were so torn and shattered that it was doubtful if their masts and rigging would stand much further strain. Secondly (and not one modern writer has noted this point), "the tyde of Ebbe being spent...the wind being at South and S. by W. and the flood being come they could not fetch over unto the *French* coast, but was forced to beare towards the *Downes* and anchored with all his fleet, between the South Foreland and Walmer Castle...where they rode with their Flags aloft there being 65 Sayle of them".[1]

From a careful comparison of the accounts of Peter White and De Mello (the Dutch contemporary versions are unfortunately too brief to be of real use at this point), we come to the following conclusions:

If Tromp had been plentifully supplied with powder, he would in all probability have taken or destroyed three-fourths of the Armada before the remnant could have reached Dunkirk.

As matters actually stood, if De Oquendo had not cast about to relieve his two captured ships,[2] but had continued on his course eastwards, he might have reached Dunkirk with the

---

[1] Peter White, *op. cit.* pp. 8–9.

[2] "...except they would have lost that ship, the which the Admirall [De Oquendo] would not give way unto, etc." (Peter White, *op. cit.* p. 9). This refers to the retaken Bartelosa flagship.

majority—if not all—of the Armada, since Tromp's ammunition was gone.

Owing to his delay, he had no other course than to steer for the Downs in view of the prevailing wind and tide, and of the battered condition of many of his ships. Once in the Downs, his last chance of victory, faint at best after the action of the 16th, was gone. For to reach Dunkirk with his great galleons he had to pass through—or just outside—Calais road, where Tromp lay replenishing his munitions. A study of the charts will show that there is, and was, no other way. Tromp at Calais held the key to the situation, and De Oquendo's fate was virtually sealed.[1]

[1] Most writers have overlooked this fact owing to their using seventeenth-century plans and maps, which are more decorative than accurate. For the proper study of the whole of Tromp's campaign in 1639 modern Admiralty Charts are essential. Captain S. P. L'Honoré Naber, R.N.N. (retd.) first indicated this point to me.

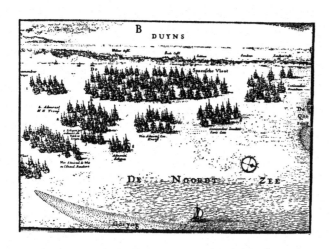

IV. THE DOWNS

(a) *The Blockade of De Oquendo's Fleet*

No sooner had Tromp dropped anchor in Calais road at 4 o'clock, than he sent an urgent request to the Governor of the town—the Comte de Charost—for ammunition. Even whilst the battle was still raging on the morning of the 18th, he had sent one of his smaller ships to that port for the same purpose, and hence the Governor was not unprepared. Within a few hours he had supplied his allies with over 28,000 lb. of gunpowder and a vast store of shot of all calibres. Early next day, Tromp called a council, as a result of which it was decided to send De With with the prize and his own damaged ship to Holland, with the news of the fight,[1] whilst Catz was to remain at Calais to take further supplies on board. Abram Crijnsz. was also detached on convoy duty, so that when Tromp weighed anchor and stood over to the English coast at 8 a.m. he had only 24 sail with him.

The Spaniards meanwhile had been lying off Dover endeavouring to refit, but no sooner did they sight the Dutch squadron than

like men scared out of their wits, albeit they had a windward tyde, and might have got up all their Anchors before the *Hollanders* could get halfe seas over, or come neare them by 4, or 5 leagues, the most of them like mad men cut their cables in the halss [hawse] and came into the Road and anchored to the Southwards off us, the Admirals saluted us with 7, and 5 pieces, the Vice-admirals with 5, and 3 Pieces. After which the Hollanders came all in, and saluted us every Ship and anchored to the Southwards off the *Spanyards*.[2]

Sir John Pennington now sent Peter White aboard the *Amelia* to warn Tromp that he was not to attack the Spaniards in the Downs, "the which he promised me faithfully to obey". In order, however, to prevent any chance of a conflict, Pennington gave the Spaniards his own berth—"the best of the

---

1 De With reached Goeree on the 21st and made his report to the States-General on the following day. One of the survivors from the *Groote Christoffel*, Wouter Pietersz., had already narrated the particulars of the fights to the States-General on the 21st. De With rejoined Tromp with four ships on Sept. 28th.

2 Peter White, *op. cit.* p. 11; De Mello also agrees that Tromp only had 24 sail.

Road"—and interposed his squadron between the rival fleets. During all the time that the three fleets lay in the Downs, the English would not permit either the Spaniards or the Hollanders to wear any colours, which caused them no little annoyance.

Two days later, on September 21st, De Oquendo, who had given up all hope of forcing his way through to Dunkirk, determined to send 13 of his best sailers—the majority Dunkirkers—away to Flanders under cover of night, by way of the Gull Stream, which was left unguarded by the Hollanders. The plan was successful, and by nine o'clock next morning the 13 ships carrying 3000 soldiers and a million of money were anchored safely under Mardyck fort.[1]

Here we come to what "Mr Punch" would term "another headache for the historian". Tromp in his *Journal* asserts that Pennington had passed his word that the Spaniards would not escape out by the north end of the Road, and that therefore he (Tromp) had not placed any ships there. Pennington, on the other hand, admits that he told the Dutch admiral he did not think it possible for the Spaniards to escape, but added that if Tromp liked he could detach some ships to watch the Gull Stream, which he did not do. The Dutch version will be found in the *Journal, infra,* so in fairness to both sides I give the English version as related by Pennington's skipper, Peter White:[2]

after noone Admirall *Tromp* sent his Vice-admirall, and Rereadmirall, and some other Captaines to desire leave from Sir Iohn, that some of their ships might ride to the Northwards of the *Spanyards,* fearing that some of the Spanyards might run away in the night, to the which *Sir Iohn* made answer, that the Channels were narrow and the nights darke; so that hee was verily perswaded they could not, nor would not put it to such a hazard as to goe that way, yet he sayd, that if so be that they did doubt of any such thing, they might if they pleased send some of their Ships to ride to the Northwards in the mouth of the Gulls, and likewise at the inner Channel, between the *Brakes* and *Quearns,* and at the North sands head; but to ride to the Northwards of them in the Road, hee would by no meanes condiscend unto it, with which answer they return'd, but did not send any Ships to the Northwards as aforesaid.... At daylight in the

1 De Mello, *Epanaphora* iv, pp. 533–6. Cf. De Boer, *op. cit.* p. 44, who says two millions of silver bullion.

2 Peter White, *op. cit.* pp. 13–17. Cf. Tromp's *Journal* under Sept. 22nd and 28th.

morning the wind continuing, wee did misse 13, or 14 sayle of the small
Spanish ships that rode to the Northward of us, the which did trouble Sir
Iohn Pennington exceedingly; afternoone...the Hollanders sent aboard
unto Sir *Iohn*, to desire leave that they might ride to the northwards of
the Spanyards, the which he presently granted with an expression of
sorrowfulnesse that the Spanyards had made such an escape.

Accordingly 14 Dutch ships took up their station in the Gull
Stream to prevent a repetition of such an incident.

Tromp complained about this escape to the Dutch ambassador, Joachimi, who told the Dutch version of the affair to
Charles I. The result was that Pennington was taken severely
to task about it, and dispatched Peter White to remonstrate
with the Dutch admiral. If Tromp's account is correct, Peter
White and Captain Slingsby admitted that in reality they were
responsible, as they had *ordered* Tromp in Pennington's name
(but not apparently with his knowledge) to stay berthed to
southwards.[1] On the other hand, Peter White in his account
says that he did nothing of the sort, and that the blame of
the whole thing was placed by Tromp upon the shoulders of
Commander Catz, who thus by common consent was made the
scapegoat.[2] I confess it seems to me a very difficult question to
decide who was really to blame, and my readers must judge the
affair for themselves.

In any event it was no use crying over spilt milk, and Tromp
now devoted all his energy to the task of tightening up the
blockade, and of preparing his fleet for battle. In this he was
loyally supported by his Government. The news of the actions
of September 16th and 18th, and De With's forceful ex-
position of the situation to the States-General on the 22nd, had
roused the whole of Holland to immediate and effective action.
The most energetic measures were taken by the States-General
to increase the strength of the fleet. Commissioners were dispatched to the five admiralties to hasten on the refitting of old
ships and the purchase of new ones, and to take up all ships
from convoy duties. The East and West India Companies—
especially the last—were called upon to supply their quotas,
and orders were given to buy up all suitable merchantmen for

1 See *Journal* under Sept. 28th.
2 Peter White, *op. cit.* pp. 15–16. It must be remembered in this connection
that Pennington was strongly pro-Dutch and a zealous "anti-papist".

conversion into men-of-war. The Prince of Orange was asked to supply musketeers from the army for service afloat, a request with which he readily complied, and troops were detached for this purpose from the garrisons of Breda, Den Bosch, Briel and elsewhere.[1] Within a very few days of the receipt of Tromp's first messages, reinforcements began to come in, and every single day for a month he was joined by some ships from Holland, with the result that on October 18th Tromp informed Peter White that he had 103 sail of men-of-war and 16 fireships under his command. Well might the wretched Spaniards have asked in their astonishment whether it rained ships in Holland!

Nor were the States-General behindhand in giving specific instructions to Tromp. On the very day that they received the first news (September 21st) they drew up a Resolution couched in the most uncompromising terms, ordering Tromp to attack and destroy the Armada wherever and whenever possible. This order was repeated on numerous subsequent occasions,[2] and the Prince of Orange, Frederik Hendrik, likewise repeatedly wrote to Tromp instructing him in the same sense and ordering him to ignore English protests, whether backed up by force or not.

In view of these facts, it is bootless for us to concern ourselves with the diplomacy adopted by Charles I and his advisers on this occasion, nor are the manoeuvres and intrigues of the Spanish and Dutch ambassadors at London, and of their supporters, of more importance. Furthermore the diplomatic reactions of the blockade in the Downs have been dealt with very ably by numerous other writers, and there is no need to go over the same ground here.[3] It is only necessary to observe that Charles I's shifting and devious policy was dictated by two main firm and undeviating considerations. Firstly, his resolve to use the opportunity to extort the money of which he

1 Details of the measures taken by the States-General in Aitzema, *op. cit.* II, pp. 610–13, 614. For their *Resolutions* during this time see Arend, *op. cit.* pp. 191–200. Letters from the Prince and the States are also frequently mentioned in Tromp's *Journal* at this period, *q.v.*

2 *Resol. Stat. Gen.* Oct. 9th, 1639; *Secr. Resol.* Oct. 14th, 1639, etc. *Vide* Arend, *op. cit.* pp. 196–8. The Prince daily conferred with the States over the affair in hand.

3 The best account is in De Boer, *op. cit.* pp. 43–64, but the works of Gardiner and Edmundson are also useful.

was so sadly in need from the Spaniards in their predicament. Secondly, to bring pressure to bear on the Spaniards to restore the Palatinate to his nephew Karl Ludwig—a design on which his heart was set—by holding Tromp's fleet over them as a sword of Damocles, with Pennington's squadron as the thread. If these facts are borne in mind, his apparent vagueness and indecision of purpose, "blowing now hot now cold" on one or other of the rival parties, becomes clear.[1]

But what neither he nor his courtiers realised, was that all these unsavoury negotiations to sell the neutrality of England to the highest bidder were wasted on Tromp, in view of his secret but categorical orders. Charles might talk of his resolve not to be affronted in "his own Chamber", Joachimi might deliver long-winded speeches and letters *ad nauseam*;[2] the once proud Spaniards might—and did—make pitiful and humiliating appeals for protection; but the Dutch were not to be deterred from their purpose; and every living soul in the English squadron, from Pennington down to the smallest cabin boy, was fully aware of this fact. All through the month in which Tromp was gathering his forces, and preparing his fireships, he was playing with De Oquendo as a cat plays with a mouse. Peter White, who was in daily—almost hourly—contact with Tromp, leaves us no illusions on that score, and it is clear from his account that Pennington had none either.

Leaving on one side, therefore, the negotiations which were continually proceeding at London, The Hague and Paris, and which were powerless to affect the issue by a hair's-breadth, we can briefly examine the chief events which took place in the Downs during the blockade.

Tromp showed his hand quite early. Already on September 24th he told Peter White "that if the weather should storme

---

1 This much is clearly shown by the Rev. G. Edmundson in his *Anglo-Dutch Rivalry*, 1600–50, pp. 105 ff. Cf. "It must be money that must carry the business", as Windebank wrote to Hopton the ambassador in Spain.

2 Arend, *op. cit.* pp. 192–4. A long version in Manuel de Mello, *Epanaphora* iv, pp. 544–56, wherein are also to be found details of the position adopted by Laud (who was evidently not so very anti-Dutch after all), Windebank, Endymion Porter, Northumberland and other influential nobles. Although Dom Manuel's account contains several inaccurate details (noticeably about Pennington), on the whole his information was surprisingly sound.

up as it doth usually at this time of the yeare, *Within short time the King of* England *would have all the* Spanyards *Guns; the Countrey people would have the Ships, and the Divell would have the men*". "Meaning"—observes Peter sapiently—"that they would all drive a shore if not worse." On another occasion— September 28th—after the worthy skipper had told him that the English were 25 sail strong, Tromp replied, "I would that your Fleet were away, and so many *Spanyards* in your place, mann'd with their own Nation, and then I would not fear to buckle with them all". Finally, on October 18th, a few days before he actually struck his blow, Tromp told Peter White outright that his orders were "...without limitation, for to fall upon his enemies whersoever he found them, not exempting any road or place"; though he added as a sop that he would not do so "before he gave our Admirall notice by a Letter".[1]

During all this time that Tromp was continually being rein-forced from Holland, Sir John Pennington was in a most unenviable position.[2] He was no friend to Spain—as his words frequently show—but he did his best to enforce respect for the neutrality of the Road on the Hollanders. The Spaniards com-plained bitterly of his unduly favouring the Dutch, but as the Hollanders likewise were not backward in accusing him of favouring their enemies, it is obvious that in reality he acted with the utmost fairness. He deputed Peter White to act as his intermediary with Tromp—who spoke English very well— whilst Captain Slingsby performed the same office with the Spaniards, "for he had their language very perfect".

On several separate occasions he invited the Dutch and Spanish admirals to dinner with him, but they both excused themselves from accepting, and a contemporary Englishman notes with approval "that Tromp would not be intreated to foole away his time in Feasting".

Three days after Tromp had anchored in the Downs, the eight English transports which had left La Coruña with the Armada, and put into Plymouth in mid-September, anchored

1 Peter White, *op. cit.* pp. 14 and 39.
2 On Sept. 18th Pennington's fleet consisted of *Unicorn* (admiral), *Henrietta-Maria* (vice-admiral), *Antelope, Bonaventure, Dreadnought, Providence, Second Whelp, Third Whelp, Roebuck,* and the *Unicorn* (City of London's ship) (Peter White, *op. cit.*).

in the Downs with 2000 soldiers on board.[1] This caused both Tromp and Pennington considerable annoyance, and, acting on orders from the Court, the latter placed them under embargo for some time, although most of the soldiers were surreptitiously shipped away to Dunkirk.

On the same day the Spaniards asked for the two tides law to be applied to them, but Pennington answered "that he could not doe the *Hollanders* that injustice, but did advice them to make all the speed that they could and get into Flanders before the wind came Easterley, otherwaies they would have more enemies out of *Holland* then they did expect".[2]

On the 25th Pennington detained ten merchantmen in the Downs to strengthen his squadron[3] and by the end of the month he had about 30 sail at his disposal. As the owners of the detained merchantmen made bitter complaints to the King, the majority of them were discharged before long and Pennington had only his own squadron to rely on. Some eight or ten ships were fitted out at London and Chatham to join the English fleet, but as they remained wind-bound in the Thames until after the battle was over, they had no effect on the result. From time to time friction arose between the English and Dutch over questions such as the searching of English vessels bound for Dunkirk, the seizure by a Dutch captain of two ketches full of Spaniards at Margate and so forth, but they were all settled satisfactorily (at any rate to the Hollanders) through the mediation of Peter White.[4]

A further source of anxiety to Pennington was the possibility of a French fleet coming to reinforce the Hollanders, but although this prospect greatly alarmed the English Government, in actual fact there was no danger of anything of the kind. The States-General had indeed written to Paris to ask

---

1 The *Exchange, Peregrine, Assurance* and five others (*ibid.*).

2 The two tides law (*i.e.* allowing a fugitive to have two tides start before his pursuer) was introduced by Sir William Monson in 1605, but it was only intended to be applied to single ships or at most to a few.

3 *William and Ralph* (18), *Hope* (16), *Anne Bonaventure* (24), *Speedwell* (25), *John and Thomas* (22), *Leopard* (20), *Dorset* (18), *Golden Eagle* (22), *Mary* (16), and the *Martha* (15) (Peter White, *op. cit.*).

4 See Tromp's *Journal*, and also Peter White, *op. cit.* pp. 15–16, 19, 21, 24, 25–30, 37.

that De Sourdis' fleet might be sent to join that of Tromp as speedily as possible, but both the King and Richelieu were away in the south of France. The cardinal, as we have already seen, was resolved that others "should pull his chestnuts out of the fire for him"; and this was not lost upon the Dutch ambassador in France, who wrote to the States-General to say that no reliance could be placed on any aid from the French fleet.[1] Tromp himself evidently knew this, as throughout the whole of his *Journal* he never once hints at the possibility of any active co-operation with De Sourdis. Probably this lack of French help was not unwelcome to him, as he, in common with many of his compatriots, must have desired to finish off the task he had begun so well without any outside aid. French assistance in practice was limited to the support of Joachimi's protests by the French ambassador in London—who gained over Queen Henrietta Maria—and to the help freely extended to Tromp's fleet by the Governor of Calais.

Whilst the situation of Tromp was improving from day to day, that of the Spaniards grew steadily worse. In answer to Charles' (indirect) demands for the payment of £100,000 in return for his guarantee to protect the Spanish fleet, Cardenas, the Spanish ambassador, replied that he might as well have asked for a million, as it would be equally impossible to secure either sum. The Cardinal-Infant was endeavouring to obtain £50,000 of the amount from Antwerp money-lenders, when the blow fell on October 21st and there ceased to be any longer a Spanish fleet to protect.[2] It must be admitted, however, that the Spaniards did singularly little to help themselves. They constantly and querulously complained of real or fancied Dutch

1 Manuel de Mello alleges that Richelieu went so far as to give secret orders to De Sourdis that, whilst making every appearance of haste, he was not to put to sea until the affair should be settled one way or another (*Epanaphora* IV, p. 541). This reminds one of Louis XIV's orders to his admirals for the campaign of 1672, which led to the controversy about the battle of Solebay. On the other hand, perhaps Richelieu was only giving the Dutch "tit for tat", as he had frequently had cause to complain of the lack of support afforded him in the field by the Prince of Orange on the Belgian frontier in 1638 and 1639, "Le Prince Henry est sans courage, il ne prend ville ni village".

2 Cf. Gardiner, *Fall of the Monarchy*, I, pp. 265–75, and Edmundson, *Anglo-Dutch Rivalry*, p. 128.

aggressions, and would take few or no steps in their own defence, throwing themselves entirely on the mercy of the English, who were soon tired of their unwelcome guests.[1] They complained—quite justly—that the English sold them powder at an exorbitant price, which, when it came, was of inferior quality and quantity to the amount contracted for. But when Tromp offered them 500 barrels free of charge if they would only come out and fight him, they shuffled out of accepting this chivalrous gift on puerile pretexts. Tromp on his part was only too anxious to enable them to put to sea, and even went so far as to fetch their spare topmasts from Dover for them. The Spaniards thanked him politely but still remained where they were.

During the time that the three fleets lay watching each other, numerous Englishmen of all classes came to visit them. Amongst them were the 80-year old Captain-General of the Army, the Earl of Arundel; Theophilus, Earl of Suffolk, "Lord Warden of the sinck [sic!] Portes"; the Pfalzgraf Karl Ludwig; Lord Conway, Lord Holland and many others. Some of them were a source of amusement to English and Dutch alike. Arundel and his sons visited Pennington's flagship on a day (October 9th) when Tromp had "heaved out his foretop Saile". Whereon, "The Lord *Marshall* hearing, that we doubted, the fight might presently begin, he would not stay to dinner with Sir *Iohn*, albeit he did most solemnly invite him. But went presently abord of Admirall *Tromp*, where he had an excellent good pickle *Herring* for his Break-fast, and from thence he went ashore". At other times, the aristocratic sightseers were a positive nuisance. Tromp told Peter White that Lord Conway and Colonel Goring had wished to serve in his ship, and Lord Conway had even had the effrontery to ask for Tromp's great cabin for himself "that he might set up a Bedstead in it"! Tromp pointed out that he had nowhere else to live or sleep, and that anyway the cabin was required for the daily Councils of War held aboard the *Amelia*. Conway was

1 The silly legend that the Armada was destined for England and not for Flanders, has already been thoroughly disposed of by Manuel de Mello (*Epanaphora* IV, pp. 525 ff.), Gardiner, *op. cit.* p. 273, and Edmundson, *op. cit.* p. 127, and it is therefore astonishing that it should be dished up again by G. E. Manwaring on p. 285 of his book.

not deterred, however, until Tromp told him "that he had neither Cooks nor Cook-rooms to dresse his meat in, for said he, for my part I can make a meal with a pickled Herring, and a Ham of Bacon".[1] But it was not until Sir Henry Mainwaring told Conway and Goring that they would make themselves a laughing-stock, if they persisted in their foolish resolve, that they finally gave up the idea.

More welcome no doubt was a visitor like Peter Munday.[2] This Cornish traveller has left us an interesting account of his visit to the three fleets and accurately defines the situation in each of them. With regard to the Spaniards he says: "They have aboundance of men in their Fleete, butt most part sickly, tattered, and questionlesse inexpert either for souldiers or saylers; all in generall perplexed in this extremity...to say the Truth the Spaniard is become as it were a prey unto them [i.e. the Dutch], for I have heard themselves say, some thatt it is even a Lost Fleete, others wishing their shippes uppe in our River or the Like". He found a great contrast aboard the *Amelia*, "where I found them lusty, healthy and Frolicke, encouraged by former good successes, and this present Fortunate oportunity which they will hardly let goe". Well might he define the situation as "a doubtfull State businesse, soe intricate thatt the like hath not hapned to England these Many yeares. How itt possibly May bee carried without the incurring ill will off one off the 3 Nationes, Spanish, French or Dutch. God turne all to the best".[3]

By the middle of October, Tromp was ready to strike. His fleet was more than double in number that of the Spaniards, and Pennington, having discharged the majority of the detained ships, could be held in check by a squadron detached for the purpose.[4] On October 7th Tromp had imparted his secret orders of September 21st to his flag-officers, and, after some further discussion on the 8th, it was finally unanimously resolved at a general Council of War on the 11th to attack the

1 Peter White, *op. cit.* p. 24.

2 His *Travels* have been edited for the Hakluyt Society in five scholarly volumes by Sir R. Temple.

3 *Travels of Peter Munday*, Hakl. Soc., Series II, vol. LV, pp. 39–41, 1925.

4 On Oct. 8th Tromp had 65 sail, De Oquendo 54, and Pennington 24, of which only 10 or 12 were of strength.

Armada at the first opportunity that wind and tide should afford. Rear-Admiral Catz had been detached four days before to cruise between Dover and Ostend with a squadron of ten ships on some frigates which were expected from Dunkirk, but as he had rejoined that day (11th), De With was now ordered to contain the English (if necessary) with an observation squadron of 34 sail including 4 fireships. On the 13th Tromp divided the remainder of the fleet as follows: he himself with 11 warships and 3 fireships was ranged opposite the Spanish admiral and his squadron; Vice-Admiral Evertsen with 14 sail including 1 fireship was berthed opposite Don Lope de Hoces in the great *Santa Tereza* and the Portuguese contingent; Rear-Admiral Catz with 9 sail including 2 fireships was opposed to the few Dunkirk ships left and some others. To complete the envelopment of the Spaniards, Commander Denijs was placed at the south end of the Downs, and Houtebeen against the northernmost ships of the Armada with eight and seven sail respectively, including fireships. The Council further unanimously resolved not to begin the action until the wind came from between N.W. by W. and W.S.W.[1] De With alleged subsequently that it was at this Council on the 13th that Vice-Admiral Jan Evertsen was detailed to command the observation squadron against the English, which he refused to do with "botte Zeeuse woorden", whereon (it is alleged) De With patriotically undertook this thankless task. This story gained considerable currency during the first English war,[2] and is still believed in Holland, but I firmly believe it is nothing more than another of De With's jealous libels. There are two reasons for this standpoint. Firstly, from Tromp's *Journal* it appears that the observation squadron was already detached on October 11th, that is, two days *before* Tromp called the Council of his own division. Secondly, Jan Evertsen's 14 sail was composed

1 See *Journal* under Oct. 13th. It is noticeable throughout the *Journal* what great importance Tromp attached to his fireships, of which he eventually had 16 or 18. Probably his zeal for this arm was largely founded on De Sourdis' exploit at Guetaria in 1638, when he had destroyed 18 Spanish warships with 4000 men at a cost to himself of under 100 casualties. From this list we see that Tromp had ± 86 sail in all, but he was still receiving reinforcements and continued to do so up till the 21st.

2 *I.e.* in *Rotterdams Zeepraatjen*, p. 25, 1653.

entirely of Zeeland ships and captains; and in view of the strong provincial jealousy which then existed in Holland, it is well-nigh impossible that a Hollander like De With would have been placed over a contingent entirely composed of Zeeland ships, when there were two or three flag-officers of that province in the fleet. There are plenty of other reasons, but I trust these will suffice to disabuse any Dutchman who still labours under the delusion that such a gallant compatriot behaved as a poltroon on this occasion.

Meanwhile things in the Armada had gone from bad to worse. It is true that on October 16th some 20 sloops had come from Dunkirk with much needed gunners and stores for the fleet, but there was little fight left in the majority of the Spaniards.[1] On the 14th they shot dead a man in one of the Dutch ships, which gave Tromp the excuse he had been waiting for. Although Mainwaring and two other English captains went aboard Tromp's flagship "to excuse it as a mis-chance done by some untuterd Rascall", yet "Admirall *Tromp* was exceedingly angry, and said that he would be with them tomorrow morning". This, coupled with Tromp's admission to Peter White on the 18th that his orders were "without limitation, for to fall upon his enemies wheresoever he found them, not exempting any road or place", induced Pennington to send up his nephew, Lieutenant Thomas Pennington, by express to London to ask for definite orders as to how he was to comport himself when the inevitable action began. Charles' response was the reverse of helpful, and may be summed up by one of its sentences which ran "...you must make as handsome a retreat as you can in so unlucky a business".[2] With this cold comfort Pennington had to be content.

At noon on the same day that this message was received (October 20th), a hoy came into the Downs with 500 barrels of powder for the Spaniards, which had been purchased (at a fantastic price) from the Earl of Newport, Master of the Ordnance. Owing to delays on the part of Newport's sub-

---

1 De Mello has it that De Oquendo was willing enough to come out and fight, but that the majority of his officers opposed him. The English sources (especially Peter White) imply that De Oquendo was loath to leave on any terms, and they are corroborated by Tromp's *Journal*.

2 *Cal. S.P. Dom.* 1639–40, no. 47.

ordinates, it was some hours before the hoy was made fast alongside De Oquendo's flagship and the unlading begun. However 100 barrels were delivered on board the *Santiago* when

the night came on, and the wind increased, wch made a litle popling Sea, so that the Spaniards put off the taking out of the rest untill the morning, which might have been all taken out and disposed of before night, had the Earl of *Newports* men attended as they should have done, upon so weighty a busines as that was, which did much discontent our Admirall. The Hollands Admirall had birtht himselfe to the N. East-wards of the Spaniards; and his Vice-Admirall, and Reare-Admirall with 30 of their best men of Warre, and 3 fireships, Birtht themselves to the N. Eastwards of us.[1]

Pennington knew well enough what these movements fore-shadowed, and in actual fact Tromp launched his attack next day.

(b) *The Destruction of the Armada*

The looker-on, it is said, sees most of the game. In the belief that this is so, we cannot give a better description of the action of October 21st than that of Peter White:[2]

In the morning at 4 of the clock the wind at N.N.W. Foggie weather, we did heare a piece of Ordnance to the N.N. Eastwards of us, the which we tooke to be a warning Piece from the Hollands Admirall, for all his Fleet to prepare themselves for the Fight, wch proved according to our expectation, for at daylight most of the Hollanders had their Top-sailes out, and their sheats hauled home, whereupon our Admirall called a Councell, and we with all our Fleet made preparation, and tore downe all our borded Cabbins betweene the Decks, and heav'd them over-bord. At the Councell we all agreed to turn up to the Northwards, to get the wind of them, the Hollands Admirall and all his fleet standing in under

Friday 11/21. The *Hollander's* set sayle to get the wether of the *Spanyards*.

1 Peter White, *op. cit.* pp. 41–2. This agrees fairly well with De Mello's version in *Epanaphora* IV, pp. 562–3.

2 For Tromp's own account see his *Journal* under Oct. 21st. Other Dutch versions in De With's *Leven*, p. 118, Aitzema, *op. cit.* II, p. 615, and De Boer, *op. cit.* pp. 65–70. The best Spanish account is that of the Vice-Admiral Francisco Feijó de Sotomayor, printed in Duro, *op. cit.* IV, pp. 232–5, and the next best that of Dom Manuel de Mello, *Epanaphora* IV, pp. 564–71. Pennington's own account is in Mainwaring, *op. cit.* I, pp. 283 ff. and *Cal. S.P. Dom.* 1639–40, pp. 26–7; but Peter White's, pp. 42–6, is the fullest of all, and agrees well with Tromp's.

the Flood to get the wind of the Spanyards,[1] but the wind was so little that they could hardly stem the flood. We set sayle and stood off to the Northwards with all our Fleet, being but 9 in number *viz.* The *Vnicorne* Admirall, The *Henrietta Maria* Vice-admirall, these two of the second ranke, the *Bonadventure*, the *Antelope*, the *Dreadnought* of the third ranke, the *Providence* of the 4th ranke, and the *Greyhound* Pinnasse of the 6th ranke, and two Merchant men *viz.* The *Unicorne* Capt. Popham, and the *Exchange* Capt. Browne; we all set sayle and stood off, and the Hollands Vice-admirall with the 30 Ships of warre, and the 3 Fireships without us did the like, who it seemes were ordered to attend upon us. By that tyme that we were under sayl, *Hollands* Admirall was very neare the *Spanish* Admirall, the weather being somewhat misty and thick; we heard a piece of Ordnance, and some of our men said that it went from the *Spanyards*, presently after that we heard another, after which whole broad sides without number, and instantly after this, came a Hollands Captaine abord to our Admirall, with a very large letter written in *Dutch*,[2] wch Capt. did protest that they brake not the Peace; for the *Spanyards* shot the first shot, Sir *Iohn* answered that might very well be so, but it was because they came so neare him with their Fireships, by which they brake the Peace, the Ordnance went off wonderfull fast, for the space of almost halfe an houre, in which time there came such thick Fog that they could not see one ship from another, neither could wee see any of them, whereupon the Fight ceased, for they could not tell when they shot, whether it would hurt their foes or their friends, wee being now by gesse [guess] (for we could neither see Ship nor Land) and far enough to the Northwards to wether them, wee cast about, and stood in towards the shore; & all the *Hollanders* that wayted upon us did the like, and kept close to windwards of vs, the wether not being so thick where wee were, as it was neerer the shore where the great Fleet was. We stood in thus halfe an houre in all which time we heard not one Piece of Ordnance, which caused our Admirall, to doubt that they might all chop to an Anchor, untill it cleered up, and demanded of mee what I thoght of it; I answerd, that I doubted that they were all come to an Anchor vntill they could see one another, and likewise I said to him, that if they were Anchored, the tyde of Ebb being come wee stood in, we should fall to Leewards of them, and bring our selues in danger of both their shot, and be unable to help either party; upon which he demanded of me, what course I thought best fitting to be taken; to the which I answered, that if he pleased, it being very little wind, we might let drop our Anchor for a very small time, and to have it ready to heave up againe vpon a sudaine and not to take in our sayles, onely to strike our Tapsayles upon the Caps,

The Fight began, it proved very thick and foggie.

1 Manuel de Mello says that De Oquendo's was the first ship of all, amongst friends or foes, to get well under sail.

2 This letter (translated) is printed in full in *Cal. S.P. Dom.* 1639–40, pp. 28–9, and dated "from the *Amelia* in the Downes, October 11/21".

and to hall up our fore sayle in the Brayles; and if so be the *Hollanders* that waited upon vs did the like, If he thought fitting he might either send to them by message, or begin to fight with them; this Councill being approved of by him, we brailed vp our fore-sayles, and the *Hollanders* did the like, then we stroke our topsayles, they likewise stroke theirs, then wee let drop our anchor, and all our fleet did the like, but the *Hollanders* did not let fall their anchors. Our Admirall sent presently to all our fleet to be very ready to wey, for hee did intend to wey as soone as the *Hollanders* should be falne a little to Leewards off us; within halfe an houre after we anchored, the *Hollanders* were falne a little to Leewards of us, we all weyed our anchors and stood in after them, upon the wether gage of them,[1] and presently after when it cleered up, we did see Admirall *Tromp* & his fleet all in a huddle together, right thwart of *Deal* Castle, and all the Strand full of ships, at which ships the *Hollanders* let fly their Ordnance as fast as they could; and we with our fleet, and also the Castle of *Deal* shot as fast at them, upon which they bore roome and made all the haste they could after the rest of the *Spanyards*, which were run away as far as the S. foreland, being in number 25 sayle of the better sort of their ships, and there was vpon the shore 25 sayl of Spanish fleet, one of them being the Vice-admirall of Spaine, *Don Andrewes de Castro* Comander,[2] who run a ground and 6 or 7 more all in a huddle together betweene *Wamer* Castle and the village of *Kingsdowne*, and a fire-ship amongst them, which burnt two of them and had fired the bowl-sprit and foremast of another, but they quenched it; also their was 2 *Hollanders* ashore between *Deal* and *Sandowne* Castle, the two Castles shot at them, but they shot again; (to begin where I left) the *Hollanders* bore away to the Southwards, shooting at them ashore as they past by, and some of them ashore shot at them, and we following them our fleet plyed our Ordnance upon them, as fast as we could charge and discharge, but they ne're shot one shot at any of us, so wee chased them out of the Road, but the more wee chased, the farther they were from us, and our Admirall perceiving some more *Hollanders* coming from the Northwards through the *Guls*, fearing that they might, if wee did run out of the Road, haull in and take these ships from the shore, for the better securing of them anchored against *Kings-downe*. The wind hartned on and was with the *Hollanders*

1 Thus Pennington had outmanœuvred De With who was now powerless to interfere with the English. He evidently realised this himself, as he made no effort to watch them any longer but joined Tromp and Evertsen in the attack on the *Santa Tereza*. *Vide Leven*, p. 118.

2 In the *San Agustin* (56), ex-flagship of Naples, the finest ship in the fleet after the *Santiago* and *Santa Tereza*. Spaniards, English and Hollanders all agree in their accounts on the cowardice of this officer who deliberately ran his ship on shore. This poltroon was subsequently appointed Vice-Admiral of a Fleet in 1640—an appointment which throws a lurid light on Spanish naval maladministration in the seventeenth century.

From the pen-and-ink drawing by Willem Van de Velde (de Oude) in the Nederlandsch Historisch Scheepvaart Museum at Amsterdam

THE BATTLE OF THE DOWNS (OCT. 21ST, 1639)

On the left the firing of the *Santa Tereza*. In the left middle distance De Oquendo's flagship *Santiago* is hotly engaged. In the foreground some burnt-out Dutch fireships.

long before it came to the *Spanyards*, which caused them to fetch up the *Spanyards* before they were as farre as *Douer*, (note this, that the *Hollanders* displayed no Colours till he was past the Foreland) and the *Hollanders* having the advantage of them, by the meanes that their ships did sayl better than the most of the *Spanyards* they battered them exceedingly, but the *Spanyards* neglected not to answer them. For the Spanish Admirall *Don Anthony de Oquendo*, his ship going better than the rest of his Fleet, kept close to the *Portugall* Admirall *Don Lopus de Ossa*, which were two hot ships, and behaved themselves so bravely, that as I was informed from sufficient [*i.e.* reliable] men of *Dover*, not one of the *Hollanders* durst come up alongst their broad side, untill one desperate Sparke in one of the Hollands Pinnesses clapt the *Portugall* Admirall abord, upon the weather bow, amongst his anchors,[1] which intangled him and hindred his way, and presently five of their Fire-ships boarded him on both sides, and fired all on a sodaine and burnt all 7 together.

Don Anthony de Oquendo upon this fearing the like, made all sayle that he could to the Westwards, divers of the rest of the Spanyards they tooke. But of that herafter.[2]

All the Dutch accounts agree that the English ships and castles did "weinig ofte niets", whilst the Spanish versions are equally unanimous in deriding the inability or unwillingness of the English to interfere. Yet no impartial reader can peruse the accounts of Pennington and Peter White without coming to the conclusion that the English admiral did his best under very difficult circumstances. His own sympathies and still more

1 This is a mistake. Evidently Captain Musch's ship is meant. The bowsprit of his vessel was entangled with the lower gallery of the Portuguese "Goliath" as the Dutch sailors called her. This ship was the only one lost by the Hollanders in the battle. Most of her crew were saved.

2 The bravery of the aged Don Lope de Hoces in the *Santa Tereza* is fully confirmed by De Mello, *op. cit.* pp. 567–8. When the Dutch returned to the Downs three days afterwards, Tromp himself told Peter White "how that *Don Lopus de Ossa* the Commander of that ship, and his Company did shew themselves brave Soldiers, for her lower Ordnance continued playing upon them when the fire was at their Top-masts head; also he said that they saved of the *Spanyards* that lept overbord nere 70 men, who did certify him, that *Don Lopus*, albeit he was a man of above 70 years of age, and had his arme shot of in the begining of the fight, yet hee continued above vpon the upper deck, Incouraging of his men to fight it out unto the last, vntill the fire seazed vpon him, whose death he did much lament. Also he said, that the prime Admirall Don *Anthony de Oquendo*, never Cut his Mainsayle nor let fall his Sprit sayle, but continued by his consort *Don Lopus* so long as he could succour him, but when hee see him fired, and past hopes of Reliefe, he made all the Saile that he could and with the Admirall of *Dunkirk* & divers other ships of his fleet, he ran away to the westwards" (Peter White, *op. cit.* pp. 49–50).

those of his crew were undoubtedly with the Hollanders. When the Dutch began the onslaught they were encouraged by shouts of "kill them! kill them!" from the sailors of the English fleet. Nevertheless, even if Pennington did actually effect "little or nothing", it was not his fault that all the great Spanish ships were "incountered, dissipated, and destroyed by the *Hollanders*, though *Englands* Royall Navie endeavoured seriously to protect and defend them". It is clear that he outmanœuvred De With, and after doing so he seized two Dutch ships which had grounded alongside the Spaniards. These he subsequently released, as a council held aboard the *Unicorn* agreed that, if Tromp demanded them to be returned, they would perforce have to comply, which would mean the infliction of an additional humiliation on the King "in his Chamber".[1] Although his firing at Tromp's ships had no appreciable effect on them, this was only because of the "sluggishness" of his ships which could not get up with the Hollanders, "the more wee chased the farther they were from us".[2] His claim to have chased Tromp out of the Road is scarcely very convincing, as in any event the Hollanders were doing their best to get out of it in pursuit of the Spaniards. But Pennington certainly did what he could for the Spaniards after the fight. Of the 23 ships which had gone ashore in the first onset, the majority had done so deliberately. Two of these were destroyed by a Dutch fireship, and four or five others were irreparably damaged, and broken up by the country people. The remainder—of whom the majority were hired Lubeckers and Hamburgers—floated off the shore at the next tide.[3]

Pennington sent Fielding and Peter White aboard these vessels to proffer assistance, but the Spaniards were still hopelessly despondent. They "basely forsook" the superb *San Agustin* (56) of Naples on the plea that the hold was full of water. Peter White, looking down into it, "could perceive the flowre [floor] dry", whilst the ship herself "did swim as jocant now as shee did when she was in the Road". Her cowardly

---

1 Peter White, *op. cit.* p. 46, where the incident is related at length.

2 Which led the publisher of Peter White's account—Andrewes Burrell, one of the Master Attendants of the R.N.—to observe "that *Englands* great sluggish Ships, are not serviceable in *Englands* despicable Navie"!!

3 For details see Peter White, *op. cit.* pp. 45–50; *Cal. S.P. Dom.* 1639–40, pp. 25–63, and Peter Munday, *op. cit.* p. 41.

commander had been the first to run his ship ashore, and was now on land with all his officers, deluging the English authorities with querulous complaints.[1] In view of the example thus set them, perhaps it is not so very surprising that the crews followed suit before long. After thus drifting about for a few days, the *San Agustin* and two other ships were finally wrecked and broken up.

On October 23rd Tromp returned and found 14 sail of Lubeckers and Hamburgers riding in the Road. Peter White, who was soon on board the *Amelia*, informed him (by Pennington's order) that all these ships had been bought by the English, and were now their property. Upon which, Tromp "said he was glad that the English had so much benefit by them, and also, that thereby hee was free from being Ingaged, to fetch them from the shore, and from amongst our fleet, as some of his other Captaines had made a motion to have him doe". In reality, however, this fiction had been given out by Pennington to "divert them from their Resolutions", because, as he told the Spanish Vice-Admiral, if the Hollanders had come and taken them away, "it would have cost him a Bloody nose, at least".[2]

In answer to further enquiries, Tromp told Peter White that De Oquendo had got into Dunkirk. "But said hee, I hope ere long to Burne both him and all his Fleet, as they ride in the Road under the Splinter". Shortly afterwards Tromp set sail with all his fleet, and a few days later the English ships likewise dispersed, "so there was none left but the Winter guard".

When, on October 29th, Tromp related to the States-General the success of the mission with which he had been entrusted, he was able to tell them that of the 53 sail of the Armada which were lying in the Downs on the 21st, "about 40 were either stranded, sunk, burnt or taken, whilst the remainder were harried and scattered elsewhere". The losses of the Spaniards were estimated at 7000 men including 1800

---

1 In fairness it must be said that although the authorities did all they could to help, the inhabitants treated the fugitives "very basely".

2 Peter White, *op. cit.* p. 51. Cf. *Journal* under Oct. 23rd and Peter Munday, *op. cit.* p. 41.

prisoners in the hands of the Dutch.[1] This crushing victory had been achieved with the loss of one ship and a hundred casualties to the victors. Tromp and his men had indeed earned the rewards bestowed upon them by a grateful country.

The day after the disaster, De Oquendo reached Mardyck with his flagship and the *capitana* of Bartelosa. The *Santiago* bore striking evidence of the ordeal she had been through, with 1700 shot holes between wind and water. De Oquendo himself was a broken man, in health if not in spirit. "Now it only remains for me to die, since I have brought the flagship and Standard safely into port", he ejaculated bitterly on entering the harbour. Altogether some 13 storm-tossed and battered fugitives made their way into Dunkirk at one time or another. With these ships and a convoy of eight sail of Dunkirkers, led by Miguel de Orna, who had piloted the *Santiago* to safety on the disastrous October 21st, De Oquendo left the Flemish port in the depth of winter (February 15th, 1640) to return to Spain. The Spaniards preferred to run the risks of this stormy season in these waters, rather than face Tromp again. De Oquendo reached Santander in safety together with his precious freight of four regiments of Walloon soldiery in March. But he came ashore—like his father before him after the Armada of 1588[2]—only to die of a broken heart.

Nevertheless the material losses to Spain in this expedition were not so great as is generally assumed. Of the 12,000 soldiers who had left La Coruña in August 1639 the majority

1 Tromp's figures (from Aitzema, *op. cit.* ii, p. 615) are the lowest of the Dutch accounts, and agree very well with those of Manuel de Mello, the most reliable Iberian authority. In *Epanaphora* iv, p. 570, we read, "Spain lost in this battle six thousand vassals, the majority of them Castilians; forty-three ships; 600 bronze cannon, and a great quantity of senior and junior Officers". Portugal's share in the disaster was "900 Portuguese...and such an excellent ship as was the *Santa Tereza*, which by her design, burthen and strength, apart from ornamentation, was the admiration of the North, as I saw by the numerous people who came from afar to view her". In actual fact the loss of this vessel created a profound impression at the time. In all the numerous paintings, woodcuts, and etchings of the battle, the blowing-up of the *Santa Tereza* forms the chief *motif* of the artist.

2 The great Miguel de Oquendo, who bid Medina Sidonia "load the guns again" when the latter was contemplating surrendering to the English on June 29th, 1588.

were safely landed at Dunkirk at one time or another.[1] Of the original 67 sail which had departed from the same port, about 25 survived to reach their goal.[2] Out of the 25,000 men who were mustered on departure not more than 8000 had perished. It must not be forgotten that in the action of October 21st the vast majority of the Spaniards ran ashore without showing fight, and these were subsequently shipped over to Dunkirk by the English.

But the moral effect of Tromp's victory was far greater. Spain was shamed in the eyes of the world through the defeat of her great Armada under her stoutest admiral by the handful of Dutch ships under Tromp on September 16th and 18th. The long-drawn out agony in the Downs showed clearly to the whole of Europe how low the *morale* of her soldiers and sailors had sunk. The last vestiges of her power at sea—always excepting the Dunkirkers—had been shattered for good and all; whilst the disastrous fate of the expedition had no small share in bringing to a head the smouldering fire of revolt in Catalonia and Portugal, which burst into full flame next year.

The man who had brought this great campaign to a successful conclusion was honoured by friends and foes alike, and I hope that the publication of this *Journal* will serve to bring his outstanding qualities into a clearer light. Those who trouble to read the daily entries, will see for themselves how he planned and thought ahead. The weeks of waiting in the Channel; the blockade of Dunkirk; his tactful diplomacy as regards the difficulties with England; his audacity in giving battle on September 16th and 18th; his subsequent caution before October 21st, when the issue was certain, and there was no sense in running needless risks; his sympathetic handling of superiors, equals and inferiors alike; a study of these things, as exemplified in the *Journal*, will help us to understand why Maarten Harpertszoon Tromp was loved and honoured in the Dutch navy as no other seaman before or since. To what an extent he commanded the unfaltering loyalty and devotion of

1 *I.e.* 3000 on Sept. 22nd-23rd, 2000 from eight English ships in October, and as many more in November.

2 *I.e.* 13 on Sept. 22nd-23rd, 13 on Oct. 21st-Nov. 4th. One of these 13 was wrecked in harbour.

his men, may be gauged from the following extract from a letter written by an Englishman at The Hague, when the news of Tromp's death in the hard-fought battle of Ter Heide (August 10th, 1653) reached Holland: "If they should cast twenty Jan Evertsens and twenty de Ruyters into one, they could not make one Tromp, and to make him alive again that they would yet once more fight the last fight".

DUTCH MEDAL COMMEMORATING
THE BATTLE OF THE DOWNS

PREFATORY NOTE TO THE JOURNAL

The *Journals* of Tromp in the Algemeen Rijks-Archief at The Hague are listed as Admiraliteitscolleges, XLVII, 1.

Some nine *Journals* of Tromp, covering the period between November 21st, 1637, and April 19th, 1646, neatly written on 508 sheets of folio-paper, are bound up in one volume with an eighteenth-century binding. One of these *Journals* (April-October 1638) is a duplicate, thus in reality there are eight.

At the end of the 508 pages of MS. is a superb unfolding copper-plate engraving with descriptive text, depicting the actions at sea in the autumn of 1639, from the first meeting of the fleets until and including the Battle of the Downs;[1] accompanied by a chart which is reproduced in De Jonge, Deel I, and in Dr De Boer's work.

In the front of the *Journal* are two MS. notes as follows:

I. "Bought by me in 1830 at a sale at Scheurleer's. These Journals are clearly those of Lt: Admiral Tromp, as may be seen by the text and writing, this last being from the hand of his Secretary. Some of the marginal notes would appear to be by Tromp himself. J. C. de Jonge".

II. "Purchased for the State at the bookseller Scheurleer's sale at The Hague, on 26th April 1830; originating from the Van Wassanaer family".

Now the writing of these *Journals* in general and that of 1639 in particular is of one and the same hand, and is too even and balanced to have been written up on board ship. The *Journal* then is but a copy, and not always a good copy at that. The number of times that words are omitted is considerable, and other errors are not rare. Thus the copyist has been particularly careless on September 7th. Other examples are: September 1st: "setten stengen op en cruijsten" should read "en cruijsten de raas"; September 2nd: "een pools Engelsman" for "een pools Edelman"; September 10th: "Bevesier zagen wij Z. t. O. van

---

1 The actual plate of the battle of Oct. 21st, 1639, is more interesting than valuable; it had already done duty many years earlier (with a few slight differences in the background, etc.) for a picture of Wolfert Harmenszoon's fight with the Portuguese off Bantam in December 1601.

ons" [in which case the fleet would have been reposing several miles inland!]. Furthermore, two dates, namely April 24th and August 3rd, are omitted altogether.

The *Journal* therefore is obviously not that kept by Tromp himself. Nor, of course, did he keep one with his own hand. His secretary was entrusted with this task, and Tromp dictated or added parts of it at intervals. That this was so, is seen by the use of the first person in many passages, particularly towards the end of the book in the months of September and October.

From the nature of some of the marginal comments, and from other indications, both Captain S. P. L'Honoré Naber and myself are of opinion that the *Journal* was copied for the use and instruction of the Lieut.-Admiral Jacob Van Wassenaer-Obdam (killed at Lowestoft in June 1665). When he was first appointed to command the naval forces of the States-General on the conclusion of the first English war (1652–4), a contemporary Englishman caustically observed that his nautical experience had been confined to sailing on the canals of Holland. As a cavalry officer he must doubtless have felt the need of instruction from some master-mind in his new and unaccustomed sphere. What more natural than that he should turn to the journals of his great predecessor—one of the greatest admirals of all time—for enlightenment? It would have been easy for him to get copies made by the Admiralty Board concerned. The caligraphy of the *Journal* is undoubtedly of the middle of the seventeenth century; the MS. was derived from the Van Wassenaer family; the natural conclusion seems to be that it was copied at the order and for the use of Jacob Van Wassenaer-Obdam himself.

In translating the *Journal* into English, I have tried so far as possible to turn it into contemporary English, and whenever I could think of a correct seventeenth-century rendering I chose it in preference to a modern one. It stands to reason, however, that this is not always possible; and when I felt uncertain as to the correct seventeenth-century equivalent of some of the knotty technical sea-faring terms, I have plumped for a modern word or phrase rather than risk one of whose meaning I was not sure. In this connection I found particularly useful the contemporary *Seaman's Dictionary* of Sir Henry Mainwaring recently ably edited for the Navy Records Society by G. E. Manwaring and W. G. Perrin. Mr R. C. Anderson's invaluable *Rigging of Ships in the days of the Spritsail Topmast* (1600–1720) proved a veritable mine of information, and I have also consulted modern text books such as D. J. Boom's *Zeemans Woordenboek in vier talen* (1888), etc.

Above all, I have to acknowledge the unfailing help and consideration which I have received from Captain S. P. L'Honoré Naber and from Commander J. C. M. Warnsinck, both of the Royal Netherlands Navy. The former not only lent me his scrupulously accurate typed copy of the *Journal*, with its invaluable notes,[1] but went through all the difficult passages point by point. The latter gave me most useful information on many technical terms, etc., which were far from clear to me, and both have saved me from committing the innumerable errors into which I as a landsman would otherwise have fallen. Such faults as remain are my own.

I have also received valued assistance from Mr W. Voorbeijtel Cannenburg of the Netherlands Historical Shipping Museum in the matter of selecting the illustrations. I am further indebted to Lord Monson, and to Messrs Nijhoff of The Hague, for the loan of books; to Commander G. R. Gordon-Broun, R.N., and Mr G. R. Barnes who have kindly read the proofs and contributed many helpful suggestions; to Messrs Halton and Truscott Smith for the loan of the blocks of the picture of the *English, Dutch and Spanish Fleets off Deal*; and last but by no means least, to Mr W. G. Perrin for his constant help, advice and encouragement, which he has so generously given in everything connected with the publication.

---

1 In the *Journal* notes derived from Mr Naber's own notes are marked (N.). In addition he is responsible for the identification of the majority of the place-names.

THE JOURNAL
OF
MAARTEN HARPERTSZOON TROMP
Anno 1639

Journal kept by the Heer Lieutenant- (25)
-Ad(miral) T ROMP on going to sea with
the ship *Amelia* in the Land's service,
Anno 1639.

The 23rd April 1639 we took leave of Their High Mightinesses,
as also of His Highness, and arrived at Rotterdam in the
evening.

The 25 ditto,[1] in the morning, we went to Hellevoet via the
Briel, and reaching Hellevoetsluijs in the evening we found the
Heeren Feltram and De Jong there, likewise our ship, which was
far from ready, and the crew unpaid, as never happened before.

The 26 ditto early in the morning I, together with the directors,
came on board with money, but could not pay out; we were
very busy the whole day with all hands taking supplies aboard,
and fitting out the ship; an hour after sunset we began to pay
out, and had finished most by two o'clock at night, having paid
4 months' wages and one month's prize-money, since our crew
had had 2 months' prize money previously, making a total of
3 months'.

The 27 ditto unloaded a number of boats; the soldiers came
on board, and we made the ship predy[2] as far as we could; the
wind at S.W. with a stiff breeze.

The 28 ditto in the morning the wind was at S.W. with rain,
wind and variable weather; cleaned, heeled and paid[3] our ship
'twixt wind and water. About midday we weighed our anchor,
and in the afternoon we weighed our daily anchor and tried to
beat up to windward, but the main mast[4] fell overboard; we
drifted below the Goeree harbour, and in the evening it was
again fine weather; made taut the stays and shrouds like we did
on the 26th ditto.

1 The 24th is omitted in the original copy.
2 A seventeenth-century term for "ready" or "ship-shape". See Mainwaring's
Seaman's Dictionary, 1644.
3 Laying on of pitch in careening.
4 *groote mast* in original, but probably "groot steng", main topmast, is meant.

Came out of the Goeree Gate:
Lt-Adm. Tromp
Cap. van Diemen.

Lay before the Mase
Vice-Adm. De With,
Colster, Vijch, Brederode, Voornham, Keert de Koe, Halfhoorn, Ringelssen.

Missing.
Muijs who had put into the Maes.

The 29th ditto in the morning before daybreak the wind was east, but gradually shifted to southwards. At sunrise we weighed anchor, as also did Captain Van Diemen, and stood out to sea. Found outside the captains named in the margin, immediately made sail and plied to westwards as best we could, having first dispatched our Secretary Berckelo with a letter announcing our departure to Their H.M. and His Highness. During the day the wind veered S.S.W. with drizzling rain. In the afternoon set our course eastwards and at sunset westwards again, when Westcappel bore S.E. by E. of us 3 miles[1] away; we sailed W.S. west for three glasses. In the first watch it began to blow hard, we took in our main topsail, and sailed under courses,[2] the wind being S. west.

The 30 April the wind at S. with hard weather; sailed still under courses to W.S.W. by W. Our shrouds had eased so much that we had to set them taut, otherwise we would have run the risk of losing our mast. About the time the sun was S.S.E.[3] tacked towards the east, when the tower of Orfordness[4] bore 3 miles W. by N. from us. At sunset it was somewhat better weather and by midnight it was calm.

The first of May, in the morning the wind at S.E. We tacked westwards, sailed S. westwards, and spoke a Dane coming from Setubal,[5] who declared that he had seen no Dunkirkers, neither had he heard anything of ships from La Coruña;[6] we

1 The mile used by Tromp was probably the *Duitsche geografische mijl* derived from Snellius' triangulation of 1617, which is to be estimated at 7155 metres, or a little less than four modern sea miles. (N.)

2 *schooverzeilen* in original. The *schooverzeilen* were the foresail and mainsail together. "A pair of courses" might perhaps be a better translation, but at this time "courses" in England generally excluded the mizzen. See Mainwaring, *Seaman's Dictionary* (N.R.S. 1921 edition), and the article on seventeenth-century rigging by Alan Moore in the *Mariner's Mirror*, III, pp. 7–9.

3 This fashion of reckoning time by the position of the sun was more prevalent amongst the Dutch seamen of the time than their English rivals. A number of other instances occur in the Dutch journals published in the N.R.S. series, *Letters and Papers relating to the first Dutch War,* 1652–4.

4 MS. *Orforsnes.*

5 MS. *St Tubes.* Setubal, a little way south of Lisbon, was one of the chief sources for the supply of salt to Northern Europe.

6 MS. *de Carune.* La Coruña—"the Groyne" of seventeenth-century England—was the chief naval base in Northern Spain, and situated in Galizia.

let him go unhindered on his way. We gave Capt. Ringelsen 2800 lbs. of ship's biscuit, 8 brandywine hogsheads of beer, a tun of oatmeal, a tun of green peas, 200 firebrands; to the Vice-Admiral De Wit 900 lbs. of bread with the sacks pertaining thereto, and 500 loaves of bread. About three o'clock the wind veered S.S.W. We set our course westwards, when the Fore-land[1] bore S.W. b. S. of us 6 miles away, at sunset W.S.W. Sailed S.S.E., the wind at S.W. During the day, we were passed by 4 ships sailing before the wind, although not spoken; when the first watch was over we steered westwards.

The 2 ditto in the morning at daybreak the wind S.W; steered eastwards; an hour after sunrise [?][2] the wind veered to the S.S.E., tacked S.W. About 6 o'clock we saw Calais Cliff and the S. Foreland, set our course to the S.W. Discovered a number of ships in the Narrows and made towards them; the first came up with us and proved to be Captain Muts, the rest were Zeelanders—Jan Evertsz.[3] with his 6 sail. We set our pilot Cornelis Bos ashore, with a written order that if any ships came into the Downs they were to betake themselves as speedily as possible to between Portland and the Casquets,[4] and cruise about there until they should find the flag. Captain Van Diemen was ordered homewards with letters to His Highness, and with orders to touch at Calais and take in the passengers that were there; he was likewise told to hand over as much victuals as he could spare, as he did. After midday[2][?] Captain Van Diemen parted from us and 2 Amsterdammer ships of the College fell in with us, namely Captain Waterdrincker and Jan Geerbrantsz. We were then as in the margin. Set our course S.W., the wind at S.E. Captain Soetendael was a little to west-wards of us with a convoy, trying his best to ply into Dieppe. 7 glasses in the first watch tacked to the south, the wind chopt

Came in the Narrows. Lt-Adm. Tromp, Vice-Admr. De With, Cap. Brede-roode, Colster, Vijch, Diemen goes home; Post, Half-hoorn, Voornham, Ringelsse, Keert de Koe, Muijs.

Find there;— Vice-Adm. Jan Evertsz., Command. Banque, Vlieger, Gloey Oven, Abram Krijnssen, Hollaer.

Join us;— The young Water-drincker, Gebrant Janssen. Somma 20 in total.

1 MS. *Voorlant.*

2 *een uijre op son.* This puzzling expression *op son* occurs very frequently in the *Journal* and from the different contexts might mean sunrise, noon, or sunset. No Dutch authority has been able to give me any explanation whatever of the term.

3 See under his name in list at end of journal.

4 MS. *Kiskassen.* The Casquets are the rocks west of Cape la Hague.

south-west with a squall of rain, when the point of Dungeness[1] bore S.W. of us, a mile off.

The 3 in the morning the wind S.S.W. We tacked to the west about 7 o'clock and when the sun was southerly we tacked off from Fairlight[2] and took in our topsails, the wind being S.W. by W. At south-west sun we stood off from the shore, when Beachy[3] lay $2\frac{1}{2}$ miles west of us. Sailed S. by E., the wind at S.W. by W. with a raw gale.

(26)   *The* 4 *ditto* in the morning at sunrise the wind was S.W. Tacked westwards, when Dieppe bore 6 to 7 miles S.E of us; barely had we tacked, than the wind chopt to S. then S.S.E, so that the sun being S.S.W. it began to blow hard to a topsail gale; we took in our topsails in order to wait for our ships, which we could not see owing to the thick misty drizzle; shortly after this it began to blow a Tempest, we lowered our foresail on the bow,[4] and let ourselves drive under one course; towards evening the wind chopt W.S.W. We drifted northwards.

The 5 *ditto* in the morning the wind at S.W. by W., still with rough weather; tacked southwards under one sail, when Beachy bore 3 miles E.N.E. of us. We were but 15 sail, missed 4 of our ships; at 7 o'clock we spoke a pinnace coming from the West Indies; it was of Hoorn and bound for the Texel, had seen neither friend nor foe to west of us. We secured the rigging of our mainmast, which having done we set our course southwards and our missing ships came up with us again. It gradually became fine weather, so that at sunset we tacked from the French coast, being about 4 miles therefrom, the wind as before.

1 MS. *Cingels.* I suppose this Dutch word is derived from the English "shingle".

2 MS. *Vierley.* Cf. *M.M.* iii, p. 377: "Fairlight in Sussex is generally called Fairlee at sea. Many Sussex names are pronounced differently from what their spelling suggests but Fairlee is never met with ashore".

3 MS. *Bevesier,* as always with the French and Hollanders. Probably a corruption of Pevensey which lies just N.E.

4 *wij namen onse focke opten bouch.* Perhaps this means that the sail was unbent from the yard and was sent down on deck in its brails or buntlines, and stowed in the forecastle so that it could not be blown out of the gaskets.

The 6 ditto in the morning the wind S.W. by W. At sunset we tacked westwards, when Beachy bore about 4 miles N. by W. of us, the wind W.N.W. and the sun S.W.; we stood off from the coast, at which time Cap d'Antifer[1] bore about 4 miles S. and S. by E. of us. Captain Abram Crijnsse[2] signalled that he wished to speak to us; said that Captain Ringelssen had told him to tell us that he had no more fresh water in his ship, wherefore we steered to him and gave him 3 casks of water at sunset. Etretat[3] then bore S. of us 6 to 7 miles. The wind S. west.

The 7 ditto in the morning at sunrise, the wind at S.S.E. with rain after a strong wind; took in our main topsails and sailed S.W. by W. Judged at sunrise that Cap Barfleur[4] bore 8 to 9 miles S.W. of us. Ditto afternoon, again set our topsails, and an hour before sunset we tacked out to sea near the Isle of Wight;[5] at sunset the Needles[6] bore 4 miles N. of us, sailed S.S.W. under courses, the wind at W.

The 8 May in the morning the wind at W., backed to south-wards during the day. About 6 o'clock we plied to westwards until 9 o'clock; fell in with a Spanish prize laden with Canary wines, taken off the island of Grand Canary whilst bound for Angola. Had been captured by Captain Pietge Banckers, privateer of Vlissingen, and had on board his Lieutenant Jan Jansz. Roos to bring the prize to Vlissingen. Had seen neither friend nor foe and asked convoy, but we dared not give him it, but advised him to put in to Antifer, where we thought he would find a convoy, and whither he took his course about southern sun, whilst we steered W.S.W., when Cap La Hague bore 4 to 5 miles S.W. by S. from us, the wind S. by E. with drizzle, which rain continued with very misty and thick weather. At sunset we set our course S. Eastwards, brailed up

Met Pietge Banckers' prize.

1 MS. *Seinhooft.*
2 Probably the father of the Abram Crijnsse who defeated an English convoy off Tangier in the first Dutch war, and captured Surinam in Guiana from us in the war of 1665–7.
3 MS. *Struijsraet.*   4 MS. *Cabo Berchleeu.*
5 MS. *Wicht.*   6 MS. *Westnaelde.*

our foresail and let ourselves drive under one sail; the Casquets then bore 3 miles S.E. by S. of us.

The 9 *ditto* in the morning the wind S. with thick misly rain; at 7 of the clock it cleared up, we set our foresail, and missed two of our ships. About 8 o'clock we tacked to the westwards, steering to the west, judged that Cap La Hague was then 7 miles S. of us; the sun being in the south, we discovered our 2 ships; they came up with us and proved to be the Captains Abram Crijnsse with Gloeijenden Oven.[1] Set our topsails till about sunset, when we cast about to eastwards; judged that Portland was then 3½ miles N. by N.[2] of us; took in our topsails, sailed S.E. by S., the wind at S.W. by S. with a loom gale and dark squalls of rain.

The 10 *ditto* in the morning the wind S. by W. with dark misly weather; at 7 o'clock tacked westwards; judged that Cap La Hague was something more than 2 miles S.S.W. of us, and could however not see it owing to the mist. At 3 o'clock in the afternoon[3][?] Captain Ringelssen signalled us; we gave him 6 tuns of fresh water and to Captain Mus a hogshead of green peas, 2 tuns of oatmeal, 1¼ tun of butter, 1 clew of sail yarn; also distributed most of the rendezvous letters to all our ships. In the afternoon we spoke an Englishman of London coming from the Strait.[4] He had not met with any Frenchmen.[5] At sunset the wind was S.W. We judged that Portland bore then N. by E. of us 5–6 miles off, and sailed under courses W.N. westwards. The same ditto after the first watch we tacked to southwards.

(27)   *The* 11 *May* in the morning the [wind] at west after being at W.S.W., set our course S. by east; about S. by east[sun?] we saw the land of Guernsey[6] S.S. east and Alderney[7] E.S. east of us. We brailed up the sails and set taut our shrouds, signalled all

1 Lit. "Glowing Oven". This captain (and also a ship of this peculiar name) took part in the first English war of 1652–4.
2 *Sic!* Probably N. b. W. is meant. (N.)
3 *op son.*   4 Straits of Gibraltar.
5 Probably Spaniards are meant.   6 MS. *Garnesee.*
7 MS. *Ornaij, i.e.* Aurigny. Cf. Macaulay in his poem on the Armada of 1588, "…Aurigny's isle".

the Captains to repair aboard, and found that a number of them were unprovided with water, wherefore we resolved that Captain Commander Brederode and Captain Ringelssen with all the empty water-casks of the fleet should run under Portland to water, and also to careen their ships. They separated from us at sunset, when the west point of Alderney bore 4–5 miles S.E. by south of us. Stood westwards under courses. Ditto we gave to Waterdrincker 8 and to Jan Gerbrantsz. 4 soldiers from the Heer van Dircxlant.

The 12 *ditto* in the morning the breeze[1] N.W. but calm. Signalled all the Captains to repair on board and held a Court-martial. Jan Doenssen, who had been pilot on board the ships when one was wrecked opposite the Vuijlbaert[2] and the other on the Goodwin[3] (the Captains being Jacques Forant and Symon Cool), was condemned to be ducked 3 times from the yard, keel-hauled and whipt, but owing to his sickness, old age and rupture had this punishment remitted, but instead all his wages confiscated, and declared unfit ever to be employed again in any post of pilot or mate in any of the Land's war-ships, on penalty that if ever he were so found he would be hung, and finally set ashore on the nearest land as a worthless rascal.[4] There was likewise examined Hendrick Steve, Lieutenant of Captain Voorns, concerning whom the Provost-Marshal Steenbergen had sent on board some papers about some insubordination that the aforesaid Steve had committed at Hellevoetsluijs, most of which he denied, and took upon himself to prove the contrary, wherefore that business was held over. There was likewise brought from Captain Halfhoorn's ship and examined by the Court-martial, a certain Heijndrick Janssen of Rotterdam (his father Hans de riffelcramer,[5] living in the Santstraet

---

1 MS. *luchie*. Strictly speaking this implies a very feeble breeze. This word frequently occurs in the *Journal*. "Light airs" is perhaps a better translation.

2 A bank just westwards of the harbour of Dunkirk. The fairway between this bank and the shore was called the Scheur or Scheurtje, the inner road of Dunkirk. The western entrance was protected by a fort called "het houten Wambuis", or "the wooden blockhouse" (*lit.* 'waistcoat').

3 MS. *Goijen*.

4 "Discharged with ignominy" in modern parlance.

5 *I.e.* Hans the Peddler.

in the house called the Roemer) who was charged by the Judge-Advocate ex officio with having struck dead one Hercules Antheunissen, whose father was Claes Domp, at the present time still living at the Sleutelsteech on the Schiedam Dike, which he freely acknowledged without any excuse; the Court-martial therefore told him that they would give him time until another occasion, so that in the meantime something might be found by him or someone else which might tend to exculpate him, or otherwise he would suffer for it, and he was placed in

(27)
Verso
Cap. Hollaer goes
to La Coruña.

irons on the quarter deck. We resolved that Captain Hollaer with the frigate under his command should go to La Coruña[1] to see whether the Spanish fleet still lay there or not, also to get hold of some fishermen from there or elsewhere on the coast, in order to obtain from them as definite information as is possible of the aforesaid fleet, which Hollaer left us at eventide. We gave to Vice-Admiral De Wit 6 tuns of ling, 300 loaves, 6 bundles of lunt, 2 rounds of fresh beef; to Captain Vijgh 6 tuns ling, 200 lbs. stockfish, 1 tun e[illegible] and pots, to Colster and Vijch, and to Captain Mus a half-used main course. At sunset Alderney bore 4 miles S.S.E. of us; sailed under courses to northwards, the wind at W.N. west. After the first watch we tacked towards the south.

The 13 *May* in the morning the wind at W.N.W. with a handsome gale; at 6 of the clock tacked to the northwards, when the west point of Alderney bore 3½ miles S.S.E. of us, our ships being spread out over a distance of 4 to 5 miles. When the sun was in the south 2 shots were fired from our ships right under Portland; it was apparently at a strange ship that we saw near them, which afterwards continued on her course. Tacked S.W., when Portland bore about 3 miles N.N.E. from us. Sailed until sunset to the south and then tacked and stood northwards, the west point of Alderney 4–5 miles S.E. of us; our ships were again assembled together; sailed N. by E. under courses.

The 14 *ditto* in the morning the wind at N.W., at 6 o'clock tacked, being spread out to the west, Portland bearing 3 miles

1 MS. *Carone*—"The Groyne".

N. by E. of us. It was beautifully fine weather. During the day we brailed up all the sails and let ourselves drift to about midway between Portland and Casquets. At sunset the west point of Alderney bore 5 miles S.S.E. of us, stood under courses to the N.N. westwards, the breeze S.W., though a very gentle gale; our ships were still somewhat scattered, but lay with their heads towards each other.[1]

The 15 ditto at sunrise the wind was E.S.E. Alderney bore S.E. by S. 5 miles from us. We set our course to spread out W.S. westwards till southern sun, when we tacked to the west, and judged that Start Point[2] was 8 miles N.N.W. and N.W. by N. from us. Sailed until one o'clock in the afternoon[?][3] to N.E. by N., then stood out to sea; judged that Portland bore 8 miles N.E. by N. of us, the wind at E.S.E., sailed southwards under courses. During the day 10 ships sailing before the wind[4] passed us, mostly English, some of whom were spoken by our ships. After sunset Captain Abram Crijnsse came and hailed us, declaring that he had spoken 2 Englishmen during the day who said that nothing had yet been seen or heard of the enemy's fleet and that no enemy had been sighted.

The 16 May in the morning, light airs from W.S.W. We discovered 16 or 20 ships and made towards them; they were all Englishmen, most of them bound for the Strait and one for the East Indies. They likewise knew nothing of the enemy's arrival, nor had they heard that the enemy had done any damage. Captain Colster with the Vice-Admiral De With[5] said that he had spoken some Englishmen yesterday, who had sailed in company with 6 States' ships till the longitude of Portland, whither we set our course N.E. by eastwards; it was then 6 of the clock, the breeze came N.N.W. The high land of Dartmouth[6] bore 6 miles N.W. of us; at 9 of the clock we sighted 8 ships E. by N. of us, chased after them, and coming up with

(28)
The Lt-Adm. Tromp, Vice-Adm. Jan Evertsz., Vice-Adm. de With, Schout bij Nacht Banque, Colster, Vijch, Ringels, Commander Jan Pouwels, Capn Abram Crijnssen, Capn Adriaen Janssen, Capn Brederoode, Commander Post, Capn Claes Ham, Keert de Koe, Halfhoorn.

Of the College of Amsterdam

Capn young Waterdrincker, Capn Jan Gerbrants.

---

1 *thooft na den anderen toe, i.e.* with converging courses. (N.)
2 MS. *Goutstaert.* Dom Manuel de Mello in his *Epanaphora* also calls it "Gaudestert".
3 *op son.*　　　　　　4 MS. *voorwintseijlders.*
5 See note (2) in List of Captains at end of *Journal.*
6 MS. *Dortmuth.*

Of the College
of Rotterdam
Capn Musch.

Of the College of
the Northern Qr
Capn tjonge Hoen,
Capn Cornelis Meij.

Ships hired at
Amsterdam
from the West-India
Compy Laurens Prs
ship, ship Frederic
Pieters, ship Lam-
bert Henricxsz., ship
Jan Jacbsen Lops of
Medenblicq.

Totalis 24 ships &
Capn Hollaer gone
to La Coruña is
29 vessels [sic!].

them when the sun was S.S.W., we found that they were our water-getters, Captains Brederode and Ringelsen; they had in their company the 6 States' ships mentioned yesterday by the English, which joined us, the ships and Captains named as follows, Captains tjonge Hoen and Cornelis Meij from the Admiralty of the North-quarter, the ship *The Salamander*, skipper Laurens van Bachuijsen, of the West-India Company, with 40 guns, a ship with 28 guns hired from private individuals, skipper Frederick Pietersz. of Enchuijse, yet another similar one with 20 guns, skipper Lambert Henricxs Snip, yet another a fluyt with 28 guns, skipper Jan Jacobsz. Lops of Medemblicq. We made both Captains and skippers come aboard; they brought 3 letters from Cornelis Bos[1] and from Glarges[2] with a copy of one from the Comte de Charost,[3] one from the Ambassador Joachim,[4] and one from Mr Maes. We made the 6 new ships stay with us provisionally, and gave them the list of ordinary and extra-ordinary signals and rendezvous letters. It was calm and everyone fetched his water out of the water-getters. Sent Captain Gloeijenden Oven under Start Point, and Abram Crijnsz. to under Guernsey and west of the Casquets as scouts, so that if it were possible, the expected Spanish fleet should not escape us by hugging the shore;[5] we were then by each other as stated in the margin; at sunset the wind at N., stood westwards under courses, what time Portland bore 3 to 4 miles N.N.W. of us.

The 17 ditto 2 hours before daybreak, the wind still northerly, we sighted 4 strange ships, standing on their course towards the east. We set our topsails and stood after them, and our nearest ships speaking them, cast about to westwards; at daybreak we sighted 3 ships to eastwards of us, and the Vice-Admiral de With with his squadron stood after them and

1 Tromp's pilot (see May 2nd) who, during this cruise, served as agent at Dover and the Downs.

2 De Glarges, the Netherlands agent at Calais who was so prominent in the first Dutch War of 1652–4 (*vide Letters and Papers, passim*).

3 The Governor of Calais.

4 Albert Joachimi, Heer tot Oostende, the Hollands ambassador at Charles' Court, and resident ambassador at London from 1625–51.

5 *heen cruipend.*

coming up with them fired some saluting shots. At 6 o'clock we in the west and Jan Evertsz. in the south discovered two ships close inshore, and coming up with them off Dartmouth,[1] found it was Gloeijende Oven who had separated from us yesterday evening, having with him the Captain Tybout, Privateer[2]-captain of Vlissingen coming from the west. He declared that on the 21st of March in the roadstead of Saffi[3] he had spoken a certain English skipper coming from Cadiz,[4] who stated that 15 English King's ships lay there coming out of Spain, which when he left were laden full of infantry destined for La Coruña and thence for Flanders; but as certain tidings had come there that the Silver fleet was on the point of arrival, the ships were thus careened and victualled for 2 months and sent to Terceira[5] for the aforesaid Silver fleet, since the rendezvous was there. We saw under the shore another 14 sail holding their course to the west; there came on board us Commander Veen and Tjaert, coming from the Goeree Gate, who brought a letter from His Highness, also from Blauhulck[6] and Cornelis Bos; they had sailed from there on the 11th; Captain de Zeeu had met with them at Dover, and come together with them and stayed with the Vice-Admiral de With, giving some provisions over to Captain Halfhoorn. At sunset Start Point bore 6 miles W.N.W. of us, the wind at N., with calm; stood eastwards under courses and collected our ships together in so far as we could with the calm.

The 18 *May* in the morning it was yellow[?];[7] Start Point bore W. by N. 6 miles from us. We held a Council of War and communicated to the said Council His Highness's letter that Captain Veen brought yesterday, which stated that we should

(margin notes) (28) *Verso*

Captains Veen, Tjaert, Lieuen de Zeeu,—all 3 Captains join us.

Hold a Council of War.

1 MS. *Dortmuijden.*
2 MS. *Caper.* Although the Dutch word *Caper* was commonly used by the English up till the Peace of Utrecht, when the word *privateer* took its place, I have generally translated *Caper* by "Privateer" (*vide M.M.* ii, p. 64).
3 Or Safi on the coast of Morocco, a Barbary pirate stronghold.
4 MS. *Calismalis.*
5 MS. *Teresa.* Terceira in the Azores was frequently used as a rendezvous both by the Spanish and Portuguese East- and West-Indiamen.
6 Blauhulck was the *equipagiemeester* or master attendant at Hellevoetsluijs.
7 MS. *geel.* Probably the word should have been "heel" (= very) followed by a description of the weather. (N.)

seize all the King of Spain's money and men that we might meet with coming from Spain to Flanders, in whatever nation's ships they might be; secondly, we were to hire a small English vessel and send it to La Coruña so that after spying out the enemy's fleet it could inform us thereof; thirdly, we were to send scouts out to the mouth of the Channel to spy out the aforesaid fleet. As regards the first point, a written order was at once dispatched to each Captain to the effect that one should visit in the most civil manner all ships coming from the west, to see whether they had any Spanish men or money aboard, and if so to give them over, and in the event of their refusing to do so, to treat them as enemies; as regards the second point, the Council of War considered it impracticable to hire such an English spy as should be able to do us any service, because the English are not and cannot be trusted,[1] and also because it is the custom in Spain whenever the King's ships or Armada lie ready to put to sea, that all vessels for many miles around are seized and detained until such time as the Armada has put to sea and carried out its plans; but to that end, albeit Captain Gerrit Hollaer was already on the 12 inst. ordered by us to proceed to La Coruña, and there to use all available means to reconnoitre the aforesaid fleet and inform us thereon, Captain Gloeijende Oven as Commander and Captain Veen were ordered to go with their two frigates to careen ship in Falmouth[2] in order to proceed to La Coruña as quickly as possible for the above stated reason, to spy out the aforesaid fleet, and in the event of their finding it still there, to lie there and remain cruising in the vicinity until its coming out or until their supplies shall be nearly exhausted; and so soon as the Armada should come out, then one of the two must come and warn us, whilst the other must stay near the fleet until he saw that it was taking a definite course, whether round Ireland or up the Channel, and seeing that, come and warn us thereof, shooting off guns the whole way up Channel in order to enable us to act accordingly. Which Captain Veen to-day went to Start Point in order to give Oven that order, for he lay there cruising.

Send out many spies and discuss His Highness's letter.

(29)

1 An early instance of "perfide Albion"!
2 MS. *Vaelmuth.*

As regards the third point, that we should send scouts to the mouth of the Channel, despite the fact that since the 16th inst. Captain den Oven off Start Point and Abram Crijnsse off Guernsey had lain cruising with their frigates to reconnoitre, yet it is further ordered that not only should Cornelis Meij with his frigate cruise in Captain Oven's place off Start Point, but also between him and Abram Crijnssen the skipper Lambert Heijndricxs Smith, as well as Captain Colster off the Casquets and Captain Brederoode off Portland, whilst we with the main body¹ of 19 ships will cruise in the middle between Portland and the Casquets; these scouts were all in their places by 8 in the evening. Captain Veen had brought with him 2 young noblemen, one called Haersolte, the other Bloemendael, to be landed in France, to which end he had brought a letter from Their High Mightinesses and a private one from the Heer Artsolde,² wherefore we immediately ordered Captain Mus to set them ashore at Cabo Hague, who accordingly at once left. Likewise the criminal who had committed the murder was again examined (having been previously examined on the 12th inst.), who handed in a request wherein he stated that he was winning his case & had every likelihood of pardon, whereon it was resolved to send his request to His Highness asking him whether they could pardon him or no.³ At southern sun Portland bore N.N.E. from us. Sighted 4 ships to eastwards of us. Sent Captain Colster's shallop to them; they proved to be skipper Hans Lanchorst of Hamburg, ship in ballast bound for San Sebastian,⁴ also skipper Michiel Roeloffs of Hamburg, skipper Jurien Scholten of Lübeck,⁵ skipper Lourens Peters, likewise of Lübeck, all three laden with seed and bound for Lisbon; they declared that on the 16th inst. between Wight and Beachy Head they had seen (tho' not

Brederode and Captain Colster go cruising, one off the Casquets and the other off Portland.

(29)
Verso

1 MS. *gros*. This word was always used by Tromp for the main part of his (or any other) fleet.
2 Should be "Haersolte".
3 This is the best that can be done with the ambiguous and obscure original text.
4 MS. *St Sebastiaen*. San Sebastian lies in the Province of Guipuzcoa close to the French frontier.
5 MS. *Luijbecq*.

spoken) 50 to 60 sail close to the shore; said their course was eastwards, which caused us great amazement that we had not seen anything of them; to-day we went aboard the hired ships, inspecting their guns, ships, and men, which we found all in order. At sunset the breeze westerly; ran E.N.E. under foresail.

The 19 *May* in the morning [wind?] at N. & N.N.E.; at 9 o'clock Portland bore 4 miles N. by E. from us. Tacked northwards, the wind chopt N.E. and E.N.E.; still had sight of Captain Tijbout as also of our scouts, Brederode to northwards and Colster to southwards, besides 2 other strangers to the north, another small English ship to the east and a ship to northwards. Sent our boat aboard to visit him and it proved to be an Englishman, skipper Thomas Gips of London, coming out of the strait from Zante[1] island, laden with currants; was 6 weeks out of Gibraltar[2] and had spoken nobody nor did he know any news in the world; he had gone out of his course in the new Channel.[3] In the evening at sunset Portland bore 2 miles N.E. of us, light airs at west S.W. tho' very calm. Lay head on to the south. 3 glasses before sunset we heard 4 shots in the S.W., and 2 glasses after sunset we brailed up our fore and mizzen courses and so drifted. The wind at N.W. by N.

The 20 *ditto* in the morning light airs E.N.E. Portland 5 miles N.E. of us. Saw three strange sail and rowed with our shallop[4] to two of them. The first was a little English vessel of Dover, Skipper Willem Willemsz. of Leijden,[5] coming from the bay of St Vincent in Biscay[6] with fruit; declared that he was 5 weeks out from there, and that when he had left there

1 MS. *Sante.* Zante island is west of the Morea peninsular in Greece.
2 MS. *Jubaltar.*
3 Meaning the Bristol or St George's Channel (?).
4 MS. *saloup.* Captain N. Boteler in his Sea Dialogues of 1634 defines a shallop as follows: "the peculiar service of itt is to rowe, speedily, upon all occasions from one place or shipp to another; and it may, alsoe with more safety and conveniency be brought to a shipp's side att sea, when ye sea is somewhat rough, than the Longbote can" [*M.M.* 1, p. 239].
5 William Williamson of London is presumably meant.
6 S. Vicente de la Barquera, near Santander.

8 or 9 men had been pressed and sent to Guetaria[1], where
2 galleons lay, as also 2 in the Passages,[2] in order to help bring   (30)
the galleons into La Coruña, to be used in the expected Spanish
fleet that still lay in La Coruña; he had not heard that there
were any more ships arrived in La Coruña other than those from
Flanders. The second was of London, skipper Milteriniuy[?!],
coming from Malaga;[3] declared that he had seen off Start
Point 8 French ships with white flags and about 20 smacks,
apparently French fishers with their convoy: both of them
declared that our scout bound for Start Point had been
aboard of them, as also of the French. At 7 of the clock we set
our course S.S.E. At southern sun tacked again to the north,
the Casquets being 2 miles south of us and Captain Colster
2 miles S.E. by E. At sunset Captain Mus rejoined the fleet,
having set the noblemen on shore after parting from us on
the 18th. Took in our topsails, light airs at N., though
variable and calm; Portland bore 5 to 6 miles N.N.E. of us.
Saw Captain Brederode betwixt Portland and us—he being
our No. 1 scout.

The 21 *May* in the morning the wind was at N.E. by E.
We discovered a fleet of about 26 sails to eastwards of us and
made up to them; it was a Zeeland fleet coming from the
Wielingen, bound for Rochelle, convoyed by Captain Bastiaen
Tijssen of Ter Veer, who brought a letter to me from the
Admiral of Zeeland, requesting that if a homeward-bound
Zeeland warship should chance to pass by, it should put into
Falmouth in order to pick up the ship *de Witte Flessche* which
was lying there laden with wines. After we had spoken that
fleet, they continued on their course, and we tacked northwards;
we further fell in with 2 ships bound for New Netherland[4]

1 MS. *Gateria*. The place is west of San Sebastian.
2 Pasajes or Pasages in Guipuzcoa was then a great shipbuilding centre, and
the port where the Spanish Newfoundland fishing fleet wintered. The *Santa Anna*
of the Armada of 1588, as also the *Santiago*, the flagship of the 1639 Armada, were
built here. For a contemporary plan of the port see *Navegantes Guipuzcoanos*, by
D. Ramón Seoane y Ferrer, Madrid, 1908.
3 MS. *Malgum*.
4 MS. *Nyeuwnederlantse Lantsvaerders*, carrying colonists for Nieuw-Amster-
dam, or New York as it became after its capture by the English in 1664.

laden with cattle, horses, & peasant men and women; one was called *de Haen* of Amsterdam, the other was of Hoorn and brought a letter from the West India Company asking us to convoy the ships till clear of the Channel. Captain Joris likewise joined us from the Goeree Gate, together with Captain Abraham Crijnsz., who had wrongly cruised off Start Point instead of off the island of Guernsey. Immediately sent Tjaert as Commander besides Captain Joris Pieters with the oared yacht[1] to act as convoy to the ships bound for New Netherland as far as the longitude of Falmouth, and then to put in there to careen, on completion of which they were to rejoin the flag forthwith, bringing in company with them the above named *Witte Flessche* in order to convoy her homewards. During the day some Englishmen were spoken, one of them from London. He was called Thomas Graff, bound for the Virginis [= Virginia], laden with women, children and provisions; he declared that 3 weeks previously 10 tall ships had been hired in London to go to La Coruña in order to fetch the Spanish men and money, but the Admiral Melord Van Noort[2] had opposed this affair and it was dropped; he further stated that His Majesty of England had left for the Scottish frontier with his army.[3] Towards evening skipper Adriaen Domens joined us and came aboard; had been hired at Amsterdam for 500 guilders a month, mounted 32 guns and was manned with 87 men; the ship was 137 Amsterdam feet long, 29 in beam, 14 in draught; had put to sea on the 2nd and put into the Texel owing to bad weather, and set sail again on the 12th. After we had given him both the ordinary and extra-ordinary lists of signals he went his way. During the day the wind was variable with calm; at sunset Portland bore 5 miles N.E. by E. from us, light airs at S.E. We sighted two ships coming

Margin notes:

Capn Joris joins us with the oared yacht.

Capns Tjaert and Joris go to Falmouth to careen.

(30) *Verso*

Adriaen Domens joins us.

---

1 MS. *roeijjacht*. A word difficult to translate, as yachts were not introduced into England until the Restoration of Charles II, 1660. Perhaps the contemporary English *Whelps*, which were fitted to use sweeps, closely corresponded to this class of vessel. See *infra* under October 14th.

2 *Sic.* I presume Milord North (the Lord High Admiral, Earl of Northumberland) is meant.

3 Quite correct. For Charles I's inept proceedings on the Scottish Border see S. R. Gardiner, *Fall of the Monarchy of Charles I*, i, pp. 200–45.

towards us from the east. After the first watch, tacked northwards, the wind N. east.

The 22 ditto. In the morning the wind N.E. with a fresh breeze. We saw a ship plying to eastwards of us, but could not get up to her. We were joined by the 2 ships which we saw yesterday to windward; they were Captain Sluijs and Matthijs Gillisz. who had sailed from Texel on the 16 and Dover[1] on the 10 [*sic!*] and were victualled for 4 months. A fluyt[2] came sailing through our fleet; sent Sluijs thereto who went aboard him and drove along beside him until he was out of sight. At southern sun we tacked northwards, when the west point of Alderney bore south from us 2 miles off. Captain Colster came on board us, and stated that he had spoken a certain Arent Pouwels of Vlaerdingen, captain of a small ship of Dover, which he had left the day before yesterday bound for Rochelle,[3] who said that the army of His Majesty of France lay between Dunkirk and Saint Omer, burnt down everything wherever they went, and that they had returned from Flemish soil on Saturday or Sunday. At sunset Alderney bore from us S.E. by E. 6 miles off; we brailed up all our sails and drove with the calm; at 2 glasses in the first watch we began to hear gunfire which lasted until 5 glasses were run out. Counted 74 or 75 shots from heavy ordnance. It was E. by S. from us whither we laid over towed by our boats, whilst the yacht fired guns as signals.

The 23 May in the morning, light airs from the west, dead calm; saw Captain Colster eastwards of us, & plied towards him. He declared that he had met an enemy frigate in the night, which had outrowed him owing to the calm. We held a Council of War and signalled all Captains on board; ordered them all to draw up a statement showing, that in the event of the enemy not coming and the Supreme Authorities[4] deciding that we should remain at sea till the end of October or mid-November, what provisions or stores they would still stand in

Capn Sluijs and Matthijsz. Gillis join us.

(31)

1 MS. *Doevers.*   2 Or flyboat.
3 MS. *Rochel.*
4 *de Ho. Overheijt.* This means the Government in the sense of the States-General and the Prince of Orange, Frederick Hendrik, together.

Capn Vijch goes
to the bay of La
Hougue to spy out
facilities for careen-
ing & watering.

need of. Dispatched Captain Vijch to La Hougue[1] on the French coast, to see whether or not one could careen or water there, which we may be obliged to do. At sunset after we had plied to and again, Portland bore from us 2 miles. Also dispatched Captain Halfhoorn to cruise in Colster's place off the Casquets, and a written order to Post commanding him to relieve Captain Brederode off Portland. Hauled up our sails and tried with a main course. The wind at N.W. with handsome weather.

The 24 *ditto* in the morning, the wind at north, sighted a fleet of 24 to 28 sail. Bore up to them and coming up with them found that they were ships bound for the fatherland, coming from Bordeaux, Rochelle, Nantes. Had with them 2 convoyers from the Maas, Captain Marinus Juijnbol and Pieter Breeck. We commanded them—albeit their written orders directed them to sail to the Maas—that after first bringing safely home the ships destined for the Wielingen and Maas, they should likewise bring those of the Texel home in safety, and thus they parted from us. We signalled all Captains aboard, who brought with them their lists of necessaries.[2] Captain Post bore away after the afore-mentioned fleet; declared that the French Armada still rode off St Martin,[3] preparing to put to sea on the 25th, but knew not whither. Likewise visited an Englishman of London coming from Bordeaux, who had been in Falmouth and had sailed thence yesterday morning; said that three of our frigates lay ready there. There was another Englishman named Jan Jansz.,[4] in his company, coming from Bordeaux and bound for the Texel. At sunset the wind at west, took in our topsails; we were then between Portland and the Casquets; after the first watch we tacked northwards. During the day we had seen Captain van Diemen beating up from leeward.[5]

1 A haven well protected against westerly winds just S. of Cape Barfleur, which nevertheless proved unsuitable for the end in view (cf. May 30th). The famous battle of 1692 was fought near here.

2 *cedullen van behoeften.* Lists of provisions of which they stood in need are meant.

3 Saint Martin de Ré near La Rochelle. (N.)   4 *I.e.* John Johnson.

5 *van Lije.* It is just possible that this means from Lyme Bay, but it is unlikely.

The 25 May in the morning at daybreak, the wind S.S.W., set our topsails and there came a squall of rain which forced us to take them in again. Captain Van Diemen joined us, bringing a written order from His Highness, and he had set ashore under the Cape d'Antifer 40 persons in the service of His Majesty of France; he also brought a duplicate of his Highness's letter concerning the attacking of foreign nations [' ships] having on board Spanish money or troops. About 8 of the clock tacked to the west, the wind veered N.N.W. Portland bore N.E. by N. 2 miles off; shortly after midday we sighted a fleet of ships in the S.W., chased after them but could not weather them, but observed that 3 of them clapt upon a wind, which joining us proved to be our scouts, Captain Lambert Halfhoorn, Captain Abram Crijnsz. and skipper Lambert Heijndricksz. Snip, whom we spoke; they said that they had spoken the fleet we had seen, and that it was a fleet coming from the Maas bound for Bordeaux. We ordered them to keep a sharp lookout and told them they would find us on our station, whither we set our course at sunset, steering away N.E. under courses; judged that Portland was then N.W. from us 11 or 12 miles off, the wind N.W. During the chase Captain 't Jonge Hoen's main top-mast went by the cap.

The 26 ditto in the morning the wind N.W. with a fresh gale. Portland N.N.E. from us 5 or 6 miles. When the sun was S.E. we sighted 3 strange ships coming from the west, who, joining us, proved to be Captain Tjaert and Joris Pietersz. coming out of Falmouth, where they had careened by our orders. Declared that Captain den Oven together with Veen had left for La Coruña;[1] they had in their company the fluyt *de Witte Flesse*,[2] which we immediately sent homewards under convoy of Captain Mus. Gave him letters to leave at Dover, Calais, Zeeland and Holland, together with the lists of necessaries for all our ships to Their High Mightinesses. They left us after midday, having declared that they had [blank] Englishmen, who had said that the French Armada had set sail from St Martin with about 100 sail, including many fireships, for an unknown destination.

Captain Van Diemen joins us.

(31)
Verso

Capn Mus goes home, in company with the *Witte Flesse*. Schedules of supplies wanted sent homewards.

---

1 See under May 18th for their orders.   2 See May 21st.

We ordered the Vice-Admiral de With to give his main top-mast to Captain 't Jonge Hoen, as he did; we plied to and again, and at sunset saw the west point of Alderney S. by E. from us 4 or 5 miles. Sailed under courses N.N.E. with squally weather. At western sun we had sighted 2 tall ships under Cabo Hague firing 2 shots.

The 27 *May* the wind was N.W. Saint Andrew's Land[1] bore S. by W. from us. We cast about to westward and set our topsails; about 6 o'clock we sighted a fleet of ships and chased after them; coming up with them, proved to be a French fleet, mostly merchantmen,[2] between 60 & 70 sail strong; our oared yacht, Captain Joris, spoke them. Said that the French Armada had left Saint Martin. We clapt upon a wind to the west. About 9 o'clock tacked northwards, when Cabo Hague bore S. from us 2 miles off. We steered away N. by E. and N.N.E. until 2 of the clock, then hauled our wind again to the west, the Needles of Wight bearing N.N.E. from us and the point of Saint Andrew's Land[3] N. by W., with a hard top-sail gale and rainy weather. Shortly before sunset Captain Halfhoorn came in the fleet on our weather-bow and kept by us without speaking us.

The 28 *ditto* in the morning the wind was N.W. The coast of Saint Andrew's Land bore from us N.N.W., $2\frac{1}{2}$ miles distant. We tacked westwards and sailed S.S.W. At 8 o'clock we set our main top-sail, in a hard gale; at about 6 in the evening, we brailed up our sails and set taut the shrouds. Fetched water out of Captains Tjaert and Joris Pietersz.' ships. Ordered Tjaert to sail as scout to the Casquets and Captain Joris to Portland to take over from Captain Post, whilst Captain Halfhoorn remained with us. At sunset the west point of Alderney bore from us S.E. by E. 3 miles off, steered away under courses to the N.E., the wind N.W. by north.

(32)

1 The high land behind St Aldhelm's or St Alban's Head in Dorset, now known as the Isle of Purbeck; but the bearing of S. by W. is obviously a copyist's error and should be N. by E.

2 *grande partie vaerders* in the MS. What the *grande partie* was I do not know, but suspect the ships trading to Bordeaux and the Garonne for wines, etc.

3 St Aldhelm's Head, commonly but erroneously called St Alban's.

Photograph of a contemporary engraving in the Nederlandsch Historisch Scheepvaart Museum

TROMP'S FLAGSHIP *AMELIA* C. 1639

The 29 *ditto* in the morning at daybreak the wind at N.W. by N., we tacked westwards, Alderney bearing S.E. by S. from us 4 or 5 miles. A strange fluyt fell in with the fleet; her boat came alongside and it proved to be Jan Pietersz. Bonstee, laden with foodstuffs for 4 or 5 months for Captain Brederode and Captain Post. At half-past eight we tacked eastwards with the ebb-tide. We saw another 2 sail S.S.W. from us, supposed that one was Tjaert and the other plied to westward; a Hoorn fluyt bound for Rochelle was spoken by Captain Colster. At 4 of the clock signalled all Captains to repair on board and resolved that Captain Brederode as Commander with Captain Post, should, after careening the provision-boat, take over the provisions; also sent Captains Ringels and Keert de Koe to careen in addition. The reasons for sending these to Guernsey were (1) because the fluyt could not be unladen and ballasted again at sea, (2) owing to the N.W. and N.N.E. winds, 3rdly the strong tide,[1] 4thly to get clean ships, and 5thly to survey the fairway and to water. At sunset Portland bore N. by W. from us 4 miles off. We sailed under courses W. by N., the wind at N. by west.

1 There is a great disparity between the rise and fall of the tide on the English and French coasts, as may be seen from the following table:

TIDAL INFORMATION

Place	Lunitidal intervals		Height above datum of soundings		
	H.W.F. and C.	L.W.F. and C.	Mean H.W. springs	Mean H.W. neaps	Mean tide level
	h.　m.	h.　m.	feet	feet	feet
Jersey (St Helier)	VI　24	XIII　07	$35\frac{1}{4}$	26	19
Guernsey (St Peter Port)	VI　37	XIII　18	$26\frac{3}{4}$	$19\frac{1}{2}$	14
Portland	VII　01	{XI　43} {XV　00}	7	6	$3\frac{3}{4}$
Falmouth	IV　57	XI　18	17	$13\frac{1}{2}$	$9\frac{1}{2}$
Dover	XI　24	XVIII　50	$18\frac{1}{2}$	$14\frac{1}{2}$	$9\frac{1}{4}$

Extracted from Admiralty Chart No. 1598.

The 30 *May* in the morning the wind at N.N.E. with a hard gale. Sailed N. westwards. We signalled Captain Post alongside and told him to follow Captain Brederode to Guernsey and that his orders were in Brederode's ship, wherefore they all set their course to Guernsey and left us. We were left as per margin with our 19 sail; Captain Tjaert fetched up with us from astern. About 9 of the clock tacked eastwards, when Start Point bore W. by N. from us 2 miles. During the day it gradually became fine weather; set our topsails; 2 sail[1] passed us to windward bound to the west; saw a tall Englishman with a little ship in company; we told Captain Tjaert to return to his station off the Casquets, whither he immediately sailed. During the day we passed a number of Englishmen (of whom we spoke 2) coming from the Downs bound for the west, who knew nothing of any enemy. At sunset Portland bore N.E. by E. about 6 miles distant. Captain Vijch joined us from the bay of La Hougue which he had found unfit to ride in and brought a deer with him from there. The wind N.N.E. with calm.

The 31 *ditto* in the morning it was calm. We were becalmed. Portland bore N.E. by N. from us. We repaired the cap of our mainmast, saw a number of English ships something to westwards of us; our other vessels likewise heeled and scrubbed their ships. About noon light airs sprang up from the W.S.W. Sighted a ship coming from the west. It was an Englishman, skipper Jan Ja: [*sic*] coming from Genua;[2] he knew nothing else other than he said that eleven weeks ago off Cabo de Lopo Gonçalves[3] he had been in company of the West India Company ships *Walcheren*, *de Robbe*, and *Nassau* bound for Brazil with slaves. We set our course northwards to Portland, and about evening came up with Captain Joris Pietersz., our scout off Portland. He had no news. We sent him a sailor for strengthening his crew. At sunset we lay over to westwards under courses, the wind at W.N.W., when Portland bore N.E. from us 2½ miles off.

(32)
Verso

To Guernsey:
Capn Hollaer,
Capn den Oven,
Capn Veen.

Scouts between Start Point and Guernsey:
Capn Abram Krijnse, Corn. Meij, Capn skipper Snip. Capn Tjaert off the Casquets. Capn Joris off Portland.

The main body between them:
Adm. Tromp, Vice-Adm. De With, Vice-Adm. Jan Everts, Comm. Bancke, Capn. Colster, Ham, de Zeeu, Halfhoorn, Van Diemen, Sluijs, M. Gilissen, Comm. Jan Pouwels, Cap.'t Hoen, Cap. Waterdrincker, Cap. Jan Gerbrants.

Skippers:
Lourens Pietersz., Fred. Pietersen, Jan Jacobs Lops, Adr. Domentsz.

Cap. Vijch to La Hougue

In Guernsey:
Cap. Brederode, Cap. Ringers. Cap. Post.

Homeward bound with letters:
Cap. Mus.

---

1 MS. *mijlen* but obviously *zeijlen* are meant. (N.)
2 *Sic* in MS. From the context Guinea and *not* Genoa is intended. (N.)
3 MS. *Loop Consalva.*

The first June in the morning the wind N. Sailed W., about 8 of the clock tacked eastwards, when Start Point bore W. by N. from us 4 miles. In the afternoon we chased a sail and coming up with him found it was Abram Crijnsz. who had water for 9 days and victuals for 3 weeks only. We gave him 6 hogsheads of water, and towards evening he steered away to his station and we lay over to N.E. by eastwards with very little wind yet what there was at N.W. Guernsey bore S.E. from us 6 or 7 miles.

The 2 ditto in the morning the wind N., Portland N. by E. from us 4 miles off. We brailed up our sails and held a Court-martial; keel-hauled 3 sailors, each 3 times, and whipped them with wet bums[1] before the mast, mulcted of their wages and discharged the fleet; they had run away from Captain Sluijs; one was called Thomas Andriesz. of Anslo, on board skipper Adriaen Domensz., the others being 2 brothers, Swen and Andries Andriesz. of Gottenburch in the *Grooten Christoffel* under skipper Frederick Pietersz. t Hovelinck of Enchuijsen; yet another of our men was ducked three times from the yard-arm and whipped with a wet bum before the mast, who had run away from the ship of Potbreecker and was called Jan Jansz. of Edenburch. Skipper Snip joined us, bringing with him a Lübeck[2] man, a vessel of 140 tons laden with salt, figs, and oil; he came from Tavira in the Condaet;[3] stated he had sailed from San Lucar[4] about a month before and that 3 great English merchantmen were freighted there to go to Cadiz,[5] as also 4 similar English merchantmen, including a skipper named Mr. Leums "the fat man", in order to fill their ships with soldiers and thence to sail straight to Dunkirk with their

(33)

1 *met het natte gat.* Cf. note under August 25th.
2 MS. *Lucqstad.*
3 The Condaet, Condado, or El-Condado, as it was variously known to Dutch and English seamen, comprised the greater part of Huelva in Spain, and specially from a commercial point of view, Huelva, Palos and other seaports in the deltas of the Rivers Odiel and Tinto (see *Letters and Papers*, II, p. xviii). In this case it seems to have included the Portuguese province of Algarve in which Tavira is situated.
4 San Lucar de Barremeda near Cadiz. MS. *St Lucas.*
5 MS. *Calis.*

Tidings received of
English merchant-
men filled with
soldiers, expected to
go for Dunkirk.

7 English ships; that furthermore a number of Easterlings[1] lay at Cadiz and San Lucar ready to go full of soldiers to La Coruña; it was because they hoped that the English would be let go free by us, they sent them to Flanders. In the evening Alderney bore S. by E. from us and Portland north. At sunset Snip left us to scout again on his station; the wind W., sailed S.W. under courses.

The 3 in the morning the wind was N. with good weather. Skipper Snip came from windward bringing us an English skiff of 60 tons of Dover. The skipper named Thomas Lovell[2] had left Ribedeo[3] on the 20 of the last month and had in his ship a Galego[4] named Alonso Doriges, servant of a merchant at Ribedeo named Diore Remonde, trading to Madeira; he was only sent to England by his master with letters for 4 English skippers at London whose ships his master would load with salt at Ribedeo, to carry it to San Lucar, whilst he, the servant, should learn the language in England. This skipper Lovell declared that 2 days before he left he had come from Cedeira[5] where he had stayed with a Spanish Alferez[6] who was in command of 700 soldiers that had come from the islands[7] with 2 ships, one an Englishman from Madeira, the other an Easterling from the other islands, which had disembarked them in La Coruña and again left for the islands; these troops had been embarked besides many others who had come there from all parts of the land. It was honestly believed that at least

(33)
Verso

5–6,000 infantry in 20 Dunkirk Royal ships, 3 Royal fluyts and 2 Hamburgers arrived from Lisbon fully laden with wool and sugar and bound for Dunkirk, which had been driven into La Coruña by strong N.E. gales, would avail themselves of the King's convoy and go therewith, taking in as many infantry as they could carry: furthermore that this fleet in all probability had set sail 2 or 3 days after his departure, and he

1 *I.e.* Baltic traders. Especially Danes and Lübeckers.
2 MS. *Louvel.*
3 MS. *Ribadeus.* Ribadeo lies on the boundary of Galicia and Asturias on the north coast of Spain.   4 Native of Galicia.
5 MS. *Siberus.* Cedeira lies S.W. of Cabo Ortegal.
6 MS. *Alpheres.* An Alferez was an Ensign.
7 *I.e.* the Azores.

felt certain it had got as high as Ushant.[1] He also said that the afore-mentioned Alferez the day before his departure had left Cedeira for La Coruña with 150 thousand pieces of eight and a vast amount of copper money, in order to pay the expenses of his soldiers with the copper money and to ship the silver on board with him; furthermore that many mules and horses laden with money had arrived in La Coruña overland from Castile, and this was likewise shipped in the fleet. We took out the aforesaid Galego and let the skipper go on his way unharmed, after which we at once signalled all the Captains on board and related these tidings to them, charging each one to keep continually a good look out, and make everything ready, so that in the event of meeting it, each one should comport himself as a manly and honourable soldier. Dispatched skipper Snip to his allotted station between Guernsey and Start Point, with orders forthwith to look for Captain Meij off Start Point and Captain Abram Crijnsz. off Guernsey and warn them of the above and command them to do their duty in scouting to the utmost; he was likewise to look for Captain Matijs Gillisz., northwards of us, and off Portland. [Sent] Captain Joris Pietersz. with the oared yacht and Captain Sluijs to the Casquets southwards of us in order to seek Captain Tjaert, the scout there, to warn him of all these tidings, with orders to carry out his mission with all diligence and dispatch. Each Captain returned aboard his ship, and made all necessary preparations such as bending new sails and so forth. The weather became very thick, with an E.N.E. and E.S.E. wind. It cleared up about midday. We cast about to the north. At sunset it was dead calm, we launched our shallop and paid our ship. Brailed up all our sails and so drifted. Portland N.E. by N. from us 3 to 4 miles.

The 4 June in the morning it was dead calm. We lay and drove with sails hauled to the mast, Portland N.E. by N. from us 4 miles. We saw 2 ships below Portland, apparently our scouts. Some of our ships were careened and paid. Towards midday it became very thick, with the wind at W. At 3 o'clock it was

1 MS. *Heijsant.* Ouessant.

clear[er?] tho' driving mist. At sunset cloudy sky. We drove
with sails brailed up.

(34)   *The 5 June* the wind was S.W. and W.S.W. with calm, and
dark weather, there was a ship E.N.E. from us. Captain Van
Diemen bore down to him but after chasing a little, the chase
fired again, it was apparently Mathijs Gillisz. our northernmost
spy. Before noon also sighted a ship S.E. from us, being a fluyt
standing on its course to the west, which plied about us in
short tacks, through the variable wind with misly rain and
driving mist; also sighted a ship S.W. b. S. from us, lay with
the head to the west with sails brailed up, being apparently
Captain Teeus our southern scout. At sunset, the wind S.E.
and calm. Drove with sails hauled to the mast with the head
to the south, it rained hard most of the night.

The 6 ditto in the morning the wind east with a scant breeze,
made sail, sailed close hauled to the northwards; there passed us
3 English ships sailing before the wind who were spoken by one
of our ships. About 7 o'clock the Vice-Admiral de Wit forced an
Englishman to strike, we saw yet another eastwards and another
northwards of us but apparently our scouts. We tacked to the
south, Portland N.E. by N. from us 3 miles, set our course
S.S.E. At southern sun we sighted our scouts stationed off the
Casquets, spoke Captain Tjaert who had no news. Captain Jan
Teeue came on board us, stated he had spoken an Englishman
in the afternoon, skipper Jan Prenis of Yarmouth[1] who had
left Yarmouth the 9 May, laden with wool, bound for Hâvre;[2]
he said that 15 new Royal galleons had left the Pasajes for
La Coruña to join with the Dunkirk ships lying there, and that
some 60 sail are riding there, including the aforesaid new
galleons, which he the skipper together with his men had
helped to bring out of the fairway of Pasajes. Also stated that
the French Armada was expected at San Sebastian, and therefore
he knew for certain that the French Armada and Spanish had
not yet left La Coruña,[3] neither would it leave before knowing

1 MS. *Jarmuth*.   2 MS. *Habel*. Hâvre de Grace.
3 He could not have known that the French Armada was off La Coruña, which
in fact it did not reach until the 9th.

what end the French Armada has in view. 2,000 armed men had likewise arrived at San Sebastian. Says also that within 8 or 10 days there must come a small French ship of 8 guns, being a Dunkirker, the skipper a young man on his first captaincy, laden with wool and money, bound for Dunkirk with a number of passengers; in this man['s ship] was a son of David de Lange, sailmaker of Briel, named Jacob Davidts with a person from Delfshaven who likewise confirmed the same. We parted from each other, the scouts for their stations. 2 hours before sunset, the wind veered N. by W. We tacked to the east. At sunset we cast about to the west, what time the centre of Alderney bore S.S.E. from us 3 miles, the wind N. by east. Captain Halfhoorn visited an Englishman examined previously today by Captain Sluijs as related above.

News of a French vessel laden with wool.
(34)
Verso

The 7 June the wind was N. with a fresh gale, our course was W.N.W. We saw a ship to windward of us, thought that it was one of our scouts. We bought his catch from an English fisher, who said that a warship lay in Falmouth which had taken a Turk and thrown the crew overboard. We signalled the Captains aboard; requested that 200 lbs. of stale bread should be taken out of Captain Vijch's ship in exchange for 100 lbs. [fresh] bread, which was granted. I went in Arie Domensz.'s ship to visit it. We sent our shallop to another ship and brought the skipper thereof on board Arie Domens' ship. He was called Thomas Fort of Yarmouth[1] and had sailed from San Sebastian 20 days since, and 3 weeks ago last Sunday he had helped to bring out of the Pasajes 3 galleons, 3 Holland ships[2] and a frigate bound for La Coruña. There was also an order given that if those ships could not warp out they should be burnt. There were likewise another 5 ships at Bilbao[3] destined for La Coruña where a mighty Spanish fleet lay assembled, though whither they were bound he knew not. 20 miles off Sein[4] he had met a private Dunkirker, put to sea in despite of the

News from San Sebastian.

1 See June 14th. MS. has *Jaermuijden*.
2 *I.e.* Holland-*built* ships.   3 MS. *Bilbaeu*.
4 MS. *Seems*. The Isle de Sein, in 48° Lat. lies off the west point of Brittany and in the seventeenth-century sea atlases is usually called Seyms, Ceyms, etc. (N.)

owner's wish; the Captain named Tifart den IJersman.[1] At sunset we hauled our sails to the mast and so drove. During the day we heard some shots, but knew not from where.

The 8 in the morning, the wind at N.N.E. At daybreak we sighted a fleet of 35 or 36 sail to eastwards of us. We beat up to them. It was a fleet bound for the Gulf,[2] which had left the Texel on the third. They declared that His Highness had marched out and that today was a day of prayer in Holland. Declared that a convoyer from the Maas had been sunk and 3 boyers[3] taken by the enemy's frigates. In the afternoon we sent our shallop to Captain Mathijs Gillisz. our northern scout, to tell him that a French vessel from San Sebastian[4] was expected with wool, money and passengers on board, bound for Dunkirk, which he should narrowly watch for and advise Captain Joris thereof. Our shallop spoke 7 ships coming from the Texel besides the aforesaid fleet, the skipper Adriaen Syvertsz. of Hoorn, Jacob Bartels of Edam who was only bound for Setubal, Pieter Syvertsz. of Amsterdam, Willem Hendricksz. from the Maas, Dirck Cornelisz. of Enchuijsen, Dirck Jansz. of Nyeuwendam, Gerrit Adriaensz. of Amsterdam, all 6 bound for the Strait. When the sun was west we saw two sails in the wind, the nearest clapped upon a wind and we chased after him. Our three ships coming from Guernsey[5] joined us. Captains Cornelis Ringelsz., Keert de Koe and Post had careened, whilst Brederode and Post had discharged the victuals from the younger Bonstee,[6] and Captain Brederode in accordance with our order had accompanied Bonstee to the longitude of Ushant. These careeners declared that it ebbed and flowed 4 fathoms with the spring tide and afforded a good anchorage for 4 or 5 ships; also that they had sailed in on the first and out again on the fourth having done everything. Towards evening it became calm and misty, brailed up our sails, and

Meet a fleet from the Texel.

(35)

---

1 Irishman.   2 Bay of Biscay.
3 Kind of bluff-bowed fishing vessel; now only used as barges and wherries on inland waterways. There were then sea-going boyers.
4 That mentioned under June 6th.
5 See May 28th.
6 Skipper of the victualling flyboat. See May 29th.

fired many signal shots. We likewise heard a number of heavy ordnance shots.

The 9 June in the morning the wind west with handsome weather. At daybreak we saw 10 sail to southwards of us, bore away after them and coming up with them found they were 7 Hollanders coming from Pernambuco[1] laden with sugar, bound for the fatherland. The skipper named Pouwels Jansz. of Amsterdam, the ship *de Barquelonge* Admiral, the Vice-Admiral Thijs Cornelisz. of Dorth to whom I gave letters for the Recorder[2] Musch and Bonstee, Jan Cornelisz. of Medenblicq Rear-Admiral, Jan Jacobsz. of Enchuijsen, Jan Evertsz. of Groeningen, Willem Dircksz. Cromsteven, Jacob Cornelisz. of the Maas. They declared that affairs in Brazil were in excellent posture, and that there was a large quantity of sugar there, and that only ships were lacking; they said that the Spanish Armada had arrived in the Bay[3] though so weakened by sickness that they could effect little or nothing against us. There was also in company a laden fluyt which we sent Captain Tjaert to visit. They were in company with both our scouts the whole night long, who had fired 7 shots with their great guns in the night; these were Captain Sluijs and Tjaert. After we had taken leave of them they continued on their course. We discovered 2 or 3 sails north of us and chased after them, what time it was very thick weather. We brailed up all the sails and so drove. Portland bore N.N.E. from us 3 miles off. In the mist an

Meet with Pernam-buco traders home-ward bound.

(35)
Verso

1 MS. *Phernambucque.* Pernambuco, or Recife, in Brazil was captured by the Hollanders from the Portuguese in 1630, and was the capital of Netherlands Brazil until the expulsion of the Dutch in 1654 when the place capitulated. The Dutch named it Mauritstaad originally.

2 Secretary of the States-General.

3 *I.e.* Bahia de Todos os Santos in Portuguese Brazil. This Hispano-Portuguese Armada of 80 vessels had been fitted out in Lisbon and Cadiz for the reconquest of Pernambuco. It was commanded by D. Fernando Mascarenhas, Conde da Torre, who with the Lisbon squadron had left Portugal in October 1638; whilst awaiting the Spanish contingent at the Cabo Verde islands, the Portuguese lost 1000 men from disease, including the Almirante Francisco de Mello e Castro. For the subsequent proceedings of this fleet see Quintella, *Annaes da Marinha Portuguesa,* ii, pp. 332–5, Lisboa 1840, and S. P. L'Honoré Naber's sumptuous edition of Caspar Barlaeus' *Nederlandsch Brazilië onder het bewind van Johan Maurits, Grave van Nassau,* 1637–1644, pp. 217–37, Hague 1923.

Englishman came sailing through our fleet whom we sent to visit; he came from Malaga with oil and wool, bound for London; said that when he had left Cadiz above 5 weeks since, a great fleet lay ready with many infantry embarked to go to Biscay; also stated that the Spanish silver fleet[1] had not as yet arrived. Captain Jan Teeue brought on board the memorandum concerning various Englishmen that he had visited, item one on the 4 ditto that came from Rotterdam; he declared that on the 3rd he had heard 500 great cannon shots when off Dunkirk, and spoken several other ships and sailed in several directions but had no news. On the 7th he (Captain Sluijs) had spoken the Hamburger bound for Nantes; said that east of the Narrows he had met 10 frigates sailing together which he presumed were all Dunkirkers since they did not come and visit him. Ditto, spoke another two Hamburgers, laden with grain and Scandinavian cargo bound for Viana and Porto,[2] their skippers Fredric Pietersz. and Ebbert Andree, who confirmed the foregoing about 10 ships east of the Narrows, [but] presumed them to be States' ships because they were wearing prince-flags. 3 hours before sunset it cleared up; another Englishman sailed through the fleet; he had come from Virginia and was Mr. Barry of London laden with tobacco; these last 6 days he had had winds between N. to S.W. and had spoken Captain Meij. At sunset Portland bore from us N.E. 5 miles off, the wind N.W., laid over to the south under courses, [then] brailed up the foresail and drove.

The 10 *June* in the morning the wind mostly W. and west by S. At daybreak we made sail and ran southwards; at 8 of the clock Ringelsz. fired 2 shots; we tacked northwards, when the Casquets bore S.S.E. from us 2 miles off. At southern sun we saw Portland but could not discern our scouts, the Captains Matijs and Joris Pietersz. Discovered in the wind 12 ships, which were Englishmen, Luibeckers and Hamburgers, that Captain Brederode stopped and visited. We spoke an Englishman coming from Lisbon and bound for London; he

(margin note: hear much news also of the enemy's frigates.)

1 The yearly fleet from America (Havana).
2 MS. *Viane en Port a Port.* The Scandinavian cargo for the Portuguese ports was timber, etc. for masts.

said that 2 carracks had arrived at Lisbon from East-India, and knew no other news; his name was Sr Pering;[1] the rest were Michiel Schot of Danzig,[2] Andries Jonas of Bergen in Norway, Hans Visscher of Danzig with another Dane coming with an Englishman from Lisbon without knowing any news of importance, further Matheus Meijes and Wm. Robijn of Hamburg coming from Viana with sugar, bound for Amsterdam. After visiting them, allowed them to continue their voyage since they had no fresh news. In the afternoon we spoke yet another Englishman, Jan Scheer of London, with Caspar Bartels of Hamburch, both coming from Porto, the Englishman bound for London and the other for Amsterdam, who declared that there was a great press in Portugal, whence all were being shipped to La Coruña. Captain Meij passed to windward of us with 2 ships coming from the islands[3] which he visited; in the evening Captain Meij came on board us. We gave him an order for Snip, to the effect that he, Snip, should replace the watch of himself and Captain Abram Crijnsz. until Abram Crijnsz., after having careened in Guernsey, should relieve him and that he—Snip—should then go. Captain Abram Crijnsz. came on board and complained of the foulness of his vessel, whilst Captain Brederode came to make report of the careening of the ships under his command in Guernsey and of the convoying of the victualling fluyt of Bonstee to Ushant which he had performed. At sunset the wind N.N.W. Portland bore N.E. from us 3 miles, we tacked under courses eastwards.

The 11 *ditto* in the morning at daybreak we signalled all our Captains on board, the wind N., Portland bore N.E. by N. from us 3 miles. Resolved that Captain Colster as Commander over Captains Vijch, Diemen and Jan Gerbrantsz. should go to Guernsey, in order that after having careened and watered for the fleet there, they should rejoin us, whilst Captain Abram Crijnsz. should likewise careen in Guernsey and then go to relieve Snip. About 7 of the clock the careeners left us; Captain Colster had spoken an Englishman at daybreak coming

Marginal notes:

(36) speak many ships.

Captain Brederode joins us from Guernsey.

Captain Colster goes with a squadron to Guernsey to careen.

---

1 Perrin?   2 MS. *Dansicq.*
3 The Azores.

from St Andree[1] with fruit. He declared that there the rumour was that not more than 15 sail lay in La Coruña, to go with the infantry to Dunkirk. Captain Mathijs Gillisz. and Captain Joris Pietersz. joined us; owing to chasing they had been somewhat eastwards of their station off Portland; they brought on board a list of whom they had visited. Matijs Gillisz. had on the 9 spoken an Englishman coming from San Lucar, who said that he was 9 weeks out from there, and that 4 English ships were to go to Cadiz to ship soldiers and money for their pay, in order to go with 7 or 8 ships all straight to Dunkirk. Had heard of many other troops, some for Genua,[2] others for Biscay, in fine there was a great commotion everywhere. At sunset it was calm; brailed up the sails and drifted. Portland N.E. from us 5 or 6 miles off.

The 12 *June* in the morning the wind was N. and N.N.W. We made sail and bore westwards, at 7 of the clock tacked eastwards, when Dartmouth bore west N.W. from us about 2 or 3 miles off; an Englishman passed us, whither the Vice-Admiral de With had sent his shallop alongside. We saw a ship making towards us from the S.W. We sent our shallop alongside her and it was Commander Snip, who said he had spoken an Easterling coming with salt from Saint Martin where there also lay a hundred ships waiting for a favourable wind to set sail. We told him—Snip—to keep a good look out on his station, whither he returned. We saw Captain Tjaert to southwards visiting an Englishman. At E.S.E. we saw another 2 sail making towards us; it was Adriaen Domensz. who brought an Englishman on board us named Jan Hesse of Newhaven,[3] coming from Laredo in Biscay with fruit, who said that 6 vessels from the Pasajes, 4 from Bilbao, and 4 from Santander, all King's ships, had sailed to La Coruña. He had sailed from Laredo on the 10 May, when it was said that the Spanish Armada in La Coruña was 60 sail strong; on the 4th inst. he had met the French Armada in about 45° Latitude, Belle

---

1 *Sic* in MS. Probably Santander is meant.
2 *Sic* in MS. Probably Coruña and *not* Genoa is meant.
3 MS. *Nijeuhaven.*

Isle[1] 45 miles N.E. by E. from him, 90 sail strong including 30 fireships. They had on board as many infantry as they could hold and were well supplied with everything. After visiting him we let the Englishman continue on his voyage to London and Adriaen Domensz. return to his watch. Towards evening, light airs at W.S. west, saw another 2 sails N.N.W. from us, that were visited by Commander Snip. At sunset Start Point bore W. and W. b. N. from us 5 to 6 miles off. We set our course under foresail E.N. eastwards, tho' calm.

The 13 *ditto* in the morning, the wind N.E. We saw 2 ships steering towards us from the north; coming up with us it was Captain Marcus Jansse and Hans Arents, the privateer frigates of Middelburg, sailed from the Wielingen. They had no news other than that His Highness was on the march with siege train, and that on the first of the present Captain Soetendael had been sunk by 2 Dunkirker frigates outside the Steen-bancq;[2] that the half of his topmast could be seen from Walcheren; he had 3 boyers[3] in company, 2 laden with horses and one with piece-goods, the boyers' crews had rowed away in their boats and reached the Walcheren shore, not knowing whether any of Soetendael's men had been saved; the enemy had likewise taken the boyers with their boats. Further, that the skippers of Houtebeen[4] had had their swords broken on the 6 of the present. Captain Marcus was short of men, asked some from our fleet but could get none tho' we had landed Cornelis Bos at Dover to hire men for us if he could get them, to whom we dispatched the Captain, so that if he had got any men he could send them aboard ditto Captain Marcus. Therewith the frigates left us taking their course eastwards. During the day

1 MS. *Bolin.* Belle Isle lies off the south coast of Brittany west of the mouth of the Loire.

2 A bank N.W. of Walcheren, off the Roompot. Steen Bank in Admiralty Charts.

3 There were sea-going boyers at this time. Nowadays their use is restricted to acting as wherries on canals.

4 "Wooden leg". The nickname of the West India Company's Admiral Jol, some of whose skippers had not supported him during an attack on the Spanish silver fleet in 1638. See the Dutch edition of Barlaeus' *Brazilië* (pp. 111 ff.), and Aitzema, *Saken van Staet en Oorlogh*, II, pp. 589, 591.

(37) we sighted various other ships here and there, whereof some were our scouts. At sunset it was calm, light airs at E.S.E. Sailed N.E. and north towards Portland.

The 14 *June* in the morning the wind E. to N.E. Portland bore N.E. from us 3 miles. We sailed northwards and saw Captain Mathijs Gillisz.—our scout—to westwards and Captain Joris eastwards with yet another small sail under Portland. We signalled Captain Joris to repair on board but he did not come, wherefore we sent our shallop with our Captain Barent on board him,[1] to run on ahead a little and buy on shore 250 lbs. grease wherewith to pay our ship, as also a knee for Captain Ringels' bowsprit. Signalled the Court-martial to repair on board. The Lieutenant of Captain Voorn's ship was sentenced to be mulcted 4 months' wages. and to go in place of the Lieutenant of Captain Mathijs Gillisz., so that Voorn's [other?] Lieutenant, Hendric Steur, might take his post. We ordered the suspended Lieutenant of Captain Keert de Koe to provisionally go to Captain Ham [unintelligible], Keert de Koe to Captain 't Hoen.[2] Captain Mathijs Gillisz. brought on board 4 Zeelanders, taken out of an Englishman coming from San Sebastian, who confirmed the tidings received on the seventh of the present from Skipper Thomas Fort of Yarmouth,[3] which 4 Zeelanders remained serving with Captain Gillisz. We drifted the whole day with calm until the evening when there came a shower of rain with thunder, light airs at N.N.E. We brailed up the sails and drove.

Confirmation of tidings of 7 present.

The 15 *of this present,* in the morning light airs at E. by N. with rain. Portland bore 2 miles north from us; about 8 o'clock set a pair of courses and chased after a small English ship which was visited by Captain Jan Teeue. It was a barque of Poole,[4] first taken betwixt Belle Isle and Cardinals[5] by

1 Tromp's flag-captain, Barent Barents Cramer. He had served as Quartermaster under Schapenham, Boatswain under Verburch, and Master under Van Dorp. At the end of 1644 he was still acting as Tromp's flag-captain (see *Kronijk Hist. Gen. te Utrecht,* xxviii, 1873, pp. 141 ff.). (N.)

2 This is a plausible translation of the original Dutch which is so obscure as to mean almost anything—or nothing.

3 See June 7th.   4 MS. *Poel.*

5 Probably Cordouan, at the entrance to the Gironde. (N.)

Biscayers, being laden with fish and bound for Nantes and by this reason that fish declared good prize at San Sebastian; the barque being given back free, left San Sebastian on the 19 May; he confirmed those tidings heard yesterday from the 4 Zeelanders and also gathered from an Englishman on the 7th inst.; yet added thereto that he had spoken the French Armada off Belle Isle, which, according to the master of the said barque named Richard[1] Dobble, said that it was bound for La Coruña in order to burn the Spanish fleet there; therefore he says he is certain that the Spanish fleet will not come out before they see what end the French fleet has in view. Towards evening Captain Joris brought Captain Barent on board, who brought with him $2\frac{1}{2}$ hundred pounds of horse-fat for our ship at 29:[2] 14 stivers a stone [?], a few vegetables, and the knee for Captain Ringelsz.'s bowsprit. Captain Joris had spoken an Irishman yesterday come from Laredo the 15 May who said that there lay then in La Coruña 97 or 98 Spanish warships, awaiting an order from the King to go to Fuentarrabia;[3] as stated above he had also met the French Armada on the 1 inst. off Belle Isle that said they were bound for La Coruña. At sunset a breeze at west. Set our course S. by W. Portland bore E. by N. from us 2 miles off with handsome weather.

Tidings of the French Armada.

The 16 *of this present* the wind east with misly and thick weather with little wind. At 7 o'clock we sighted some ships which bore down upon us; it was Commander Cats who had sailed from the Goeree Gate on the 10th inst. together with Captains Forant, Dorrevelt and Pieter Pietersz. They brought a letter from their High Mightinesses in answer to my letter of the 25 May, stating that in order to save time they had sent the original lists of wants and provisions sent by me to them, to the Directors, but they still retained the five hired ships and would likewise carefully look after the food supply for the frigates and exhort those of Vriesland in respect of the maintenance of their ships.[4] They likewise left it entirely to our

Commander Cats, Forant, Pieter Pietersz. with Dorrevelt join us.

1 MS. *Ritsert.* 2 Guilders probably.
3 MS. *Fonteribie.* Fuentarrabia lies on the French border.
4 All this of course refers to Tromp's previous letters, the contents of which were not given in the *Journal.*

discretion whether to dispatch a squadron to the North Sea or not.[1] We held a Council of War on this matter. It is resolved that the Vice-Admiral de With with Captains Sybrant Barentsz., Jonge Waterdrincker, Pieter Pietersz., Dorrevelt and Captain Commander Jan Pouwels under his command, should go to careen as speedily as possible in Guernsey, who thus left us forthwith. After this, the letter of Their High Mightinesses being duly deliberated upon, it is decided that the Commander Bancker should follow to careen in Guernsey, and this done go to the North Sea between Texel and the Narrows in command of 5 sail, and there remain until the 18 or 20 of the next month, viz.—Captains Commander Bancque, Colster, Farant, Post and Tjaert. Bancker immediately left us. During the day it became calm, 2 hours before sunset Start Point at W.N.W. from [us]. Brailed up our sails and bore away N.E. under foresail. At sunset our ships were S.E. from us, out of sight of those that were making for Guernsey; with the dusk we brailed up the foresail and drifted. It rained nearly the whole night long.

The 17 *ditto* in the morning it was calm, with rain and misly weather; about 7 o'clock we spoke an Englishman coming from Plymouth,[2] bound for Weymouth and thence to London; he had no news. At 8 o'clock there came a small wind, the breeze being at S.S.W. We sighted 7 ships to southwards and tacked towards them; coming up with them it was a squadron of merchantmen coming from La Rochelle, to wit Jan Fransz. and Jan Arentsz. of Vlissingen bound for Zeeland, with Jan Dircxsz. 't Kint of Rotterdam and Dirck Jansz. of Amsterdam bound for the Texel; there were also bound for Le Hâvre, on account of the "grand partie",[3] Leendert Hertoch of Schiedam with Cornelis Sterreman of Rotterdam and Anthony Splinter of der Veer. Those who were bound via the Narrows asked for convoy which we could not refuse them, but [told them they] must perforce wait until Commander Bancque again returns from Guernsey when he could then convoy them unto the Texel inclusive, whereon they decided to consider it, and thus

Marginal notes:
Ditto. Commander Bancke. All go to Guernsey.

(38)

---

1 To keep an eye on the Dunkirkers who might be tempted to fall upon Tromp's fleet from the rear.
2 MS. *Pleijmut.*   3 See note under May 27th.

everyone repaired aboard his own ship. We judged Alderney
S.E. by E. from us 4 or 5 miles off; at evening we brailed up
the sails and let drive with the calm.

The 18 *June* the wind at N.W. We made sail northwards,
but sighting 4 sail tacked towards them. It was Commander
Colster coming with his 3 careened ships from Guernsey.
Alderney bore S.E. by S. from us 4 miles off. Cast about to
the north. We yet saw the 3 "grand partie" traders which were
standing on their course to Hâvre, but the other 4 ships being
wishful to go for Zeeland and Holland remained with us.
Captain Colster declared that an Amsterdamer lay in Guernsey
that had spoken on the 1st inst. in the Texel a Hamburger
coming from La Coruña, who had said that at his departure
only 15 or 16 sail of Royal Flemish ships lay in La Coruña,
and there was no preparation made to go to Flanders; that
another trader coming from Guernsey said that he was expecting some money with the fleet out of Spain, and that this
was not now coming but that there were already 8 English
Royal ships gone for Spain to bring over the Spanish money
and soldiery; furthermore that 8 ships were to cruise off Land's
End to unite with the expected Royal ships and so sail
all together for Flanders. Ditto in the evening Captain Abram
Crijnsz. joined us; he had spoken a Hamburger in the morning
named Jacob Verdoncq bound for Dieppe with salt, who
declared that on the 13 inst. he had sailed from St Martin,
where a French frigate had arrived out of the French Armada,
mounted with 6 guns, that had sprung her foremast on the
8 off Cabo Ortegal[1] whilst with the Armada, which stated that
it should sail straight into La Coruña; 3 of their stoutest ships
being ordered to bombard the castle and the remainder to
spoil and fire the [enemy] ships; which the aforesaid skipper
Verdonck has heard the Captain of the said frigate affirm with his
own mouth in the presence of some merchants of Rochelle; and
besides him (Verdoncq) 2 galleons had sailed from Saint Martin
to La Coruña. During the day there fell in with us from Bordeaux
skipper Leendert Jansz. with Skipper Symon Joppe and Claes

(38)
Verso

Hear further news of
the French Armada.

1 In Galicia.

Pietersz., all 3 of Rotterdam, with 3 Zeelanders namely Teeu Tams, Willem Metaelman, Abram Witboom bound for the fatherland; and since Commander Bancque was to go with his squadron to the North Sea at the earliest opportunity and keep strict watch over the enemy in the Narrows, they therefore were resolved to remain with us until Bancker's departure. Some Englishmen were spoken by our ships, but allowed to continue on their voyage. At sunset Portland bore N.N.E. from us 3 miles off; the wind at N.N.W. We brailed up all sails and drifted.

The 19 *ditto* in the morning the wind at N. Portland bore from us 4 miles off. We made sail, saw 2 sail in the wind of us that we waited for, and they were the Pernambuco traders that had fallen in with us on the 9, and had rejoined us through fear of the enemy. We helped them with foodstuffs and water, giving the *Eendracht* of Dort 600 lbs. of bread on receipt, the others were supplied by the Chambers to which they pertained. We gave Captain Colster 2,000 lbs. of bread, 300 cheeses, 3 tuns of meat, a hogshead of grey and another of green peas with 3 tun oatmeal; to Captain Vijch half a cask of butter, 2 tuns of meat, 200 lbs. of cheese; the rest got from Captain Van Diemen what they wanted.

About 4 of the clock cast over to the north when Start Point bore N.W. from us 6 miles, we bore away N.E. by N. Towards sunset Portland bore N.E. by N. from us 4 to 5 miles, brailed up the sails and so drifted; there further joined us the ship *de Gulde Zon*, skipper Willem Ariens of Schiedam, bound from Nantes to the Texel; he also said he would stay with us until the squadron left. At southern sun Captain Vijch left us to relieve Captain Tjaert off the Casquets and at sunset Captain Tjaert came aboard us, but brought no news; there likewise came aboard us Skipper Jan Cornelisz. Opperdoes of Medenblicq of the Company's ship the *Groenwijff*, whom Captain Zeeu had not been able to help, & to whom we gave a further 500 lbs. of bread.

The 20 *June* in the morning, the wind N.W. We set sail northwards and at 7 o'clock tacked westwards, Portland bearing 2 miles from us; a Hamburger joined us, Skipper Hans

Pernambuco traders join us.

Skipper William Adriaens of Schiedam joins us.

Pietersz., coming with 184 barrels of powder on account of His Majesty of England, whereof he showed the passport of His Majesty's Resident at the Hague dated 3 June; had still other goods on board such as [illegible] bread and powdered sugar, house-tiles and so forth & bound for Dublin, whither he was allowed to continue on his voyage after the Council had visited him. In the afternoon we sighted a fleet of ships whose numbers we could not count; steered towards them and coming up with them it was Captain Hollaer who had been sent by us on the 12 May to Coruña as scout; he had taken 2 Biscay ships off Cape Ortegal on the 5 inst.; one of 180 tons burthen laden with Biscay iron, barrels of nails, coulters and similar iron ware, the skipper named Quantus de Roblesse, the ship *San Paulo*; the skipper having been shot dead at the taking thereof; it was manned with 32 men so that there were still 31 prisoners. The other was of 100 tons burthen partly laden with iron ware as above, besides several thousand pounds of black and yellow resin, both coming from the Pasajes though hailing from San Sebastian, bound for Cadiz; they were in company with 2 Hamburgers and an Englishman who had escaped; the crew of the smallest ship had escaped in their boat save 2 men only. The remainder were the Holland fleet coming from Rochelle, bound for the fatherland and thus to the eastwards. Their wafters were Commander Magnus in the ship *Zeelandia*, Captain Jan Aetjens and Captain Nijeuhoff. We immediately ordered that the Pernambuco merchantmen remaining with us should go under convoy of a squadron of 5 sail, viz. Commander Colster, Farant, Post, Hollaer and Tjaert de Groot with orders to waft them safely home, each one wheresoever he will, for which purpose I also gave Commander Magnus a written order. At sunset the fleet parted from us, 150 to 160 sail strong. We cast about N.N. eastwards under a pair of courses. Sent by Colster letters to Their High Mightinesses and to His Highness.

The 21 *June* the wind at W.N.W. with a stiff topsail [gale]. At sunrise we tacked westwards, when Portland bore from us N. by west 2 miles. We were still together as per margin.

Margin notes:

Captain Hollaer joins us with 2 prizes. The Holland fleet joins us.

Cap^n Colster goes home with the fleet & Post, Tjaer[t] and Hollaer.

(39)
Verso

Adm. Tromp, Vice-
Ad. de With, Rear-
Adm. Cats, Brede-
roode, Jan Teeue,
Diemen, Lieven de
Zeeu, Halfhoorn,
Ham, Keert de Koe,
Ringelsz., Jan Gar-
brantsz., Thoen.

Hired ships
Bachuijsen, Lops,
Fredrick Pieterssen,
Adriaen Domens.

*Left yesterday with
the Fleet*
Command. Colster,
Farant, Post, Hollaer,
Tjaert.

*Still careening in
Guernsey*
Vice-Adm. De With,
Command. Bancque,
Jan Pouwelssen, Pr.
Prsz. Dorrevelt,
Jonge Water-
drincker.

*Still absent scouting
off Coruña*
den Oven, Veen.

*Likewise scouting off
Portland, Guernsey,
Start Point, and
Casquets*
Com. Meij, Snip,
Abram Crijnssen,
Vijch, Matijs Gilli-
sen, Joris Pieters.

Summa—36 sail.

About southern sun cast about to the northwards, at sunset tacked westwards, when Portland bore N. from us 1 mile, the wind at N.W. with courses weather.[1]

The 22 *ditto* in the morning the wind was N.N.W. with a stiff gale; did not see a single strange sail, we tacked with a pair of courses to the north, and about noon tacked westwards. Portland bore 2 miles from us; in the afternoon we bent our old sails to the yard, and the fore-topsail having been set a little time was rent from the bolt ropes, so that we bent another fore-topsail. We sighted Captain Abram Crijnsz. who spoke an English[man] coming from London, bound first to Plymouth and thence to Newfoundland. We laid over to the north, & Abram Crijnsz. westwards; at dusk we tacked S.W. with a pair of courses, when Portland bore N.E. by E. from us 3 miles, the wind W.N. west.

The 23 *ditto* in the morning the wind at S.W. with cloudy weather. We cast about to the W.N.W., & discovered 6 sail in the wind of us, sailing under shortened sail,[2] that bore down to us; it was the Vice-Admiral de With with his squadron and Commander Bancque coming from Guernsey where they had careened. We at once dispatched Commander Bancke to the Maas, there to find Commander Colster with the squadron which Bancker was to command for the security of the North Sea until the 12–15 July when he was to rejoin us. We brailed up the foresail and so drove. When the sun was about S.S.E. we sighted a fleet ʃf 30 or 40 sail, which fetching up with us was Bastiaen Tijssen of der Veer, coming from Rochelle bound for the fatherland; had sailed from Rochelle on the 16 ditto, had no news other than that the rumour went that the French Armada had sailed to La Coruña. At southern sun we tacked out to sea, the wind at W.S.W. when Portland bore N.N.E. from us 3 miles off. When the sun was S.W. the wind chopped with a great squall of rain N.E. About 4 of the clock,

1 This is perhaps a rather literal translation of *schoverzeilsweder*. A "hard gale" is what is meant; "blown into courses" was also used in seventeenth-century England. The topsails were furled.

2 Probably meaning "with the bonnets reefed".

two hawses¹ and a half-port being open we shipped a deal of water, so brought the ship by the lee and closed the hawses; shook off the bonnets and sailed westwards with a hard gale.

The 24 ditto in the morning tacked north, the wind at N.W. with courses weather, we discovered a ship among our company, which was now 23 sail strong; in the afternoon we saw Portland and at 5 o'clock came right under Portland, where we saw 7 or 8 ships lying in the bay, whither we sent Captain Jan Teeue to visit them. On his return he said they were all English. We stood out to the offing so that at sunset Portland bore 2 miles from us, the wind at west with fickle courses' weather; we were 22 sail strong, the 23rd man remaining in the wind of us, being apparently one of our scouts. We sailed S.S.W.

The 25 June in the morning the wind was S. and S.W. with hard courses weather [= hard gale] and thick rain; tacked westwards and at 10 o'clock tacked southwards again when we judged that Portland bore N. by east from us 4 miles off; at 3 o'clock tacked west again, and an hour before sunset 4 or 5 ships stood towards us; we thought they were some of our scouts with a non-Dutchman² that were sailing past Dorrevelt. At sunset tacked to the S.E., the wind at S.S.W. with weather as before. Judged that Portland bore 3 miles from us.

(40)

The 26 ditto in the morning the wind S. by W. with hard courses weather [= hard gale]; at 4 o'clock tacked westwards; we were joined by Captain Veen, who had been sent to La Coruña on the 18th May to spy there under the command of Captain den Oven; he hailed us saying that the enemy had sailed from La Coruña on the 19th inst., tho' owing to the strong wind blowing we could not understand him very well. The wind shuffled slowly round to S. and south-south-east with thick rain and a hard storm so that we were forced to tack at about 2 of the clock after noon, what time Portland bore N. by E. from us 4 miles. Sailed E. by S., [and] east-south-east. When the first watch was ended we saw to windward on our

Captain Veen joins us from La Coruña.

---

1 Or hawse-holes.   2 MS. *een onduijts.*

quarter some blue-lights amongst our ships, having apparently been enforced to repair something through the hard weather.

The 27 *ditto* in the morning the wind at S.W. at 3 o'clock tacked to the west with courses weather; judged that Cape La Hague bore S.S.W. from us 4 miles. Before noon we launched our shallop and sent aboard Captain Veen to ask him about the enemy in La Coruña; he first said that he had been before La Coruña and counted 30 ships there, 2 or 3 uncertain, and had been there again on the 10th when he had counted 27 sail riding before La Coruña, whereof 3 or 4 were under sail; on the 12th ditto Captain den Oven had been off La Coruña and had seen nothing, wherefore they had returned hither; he added that Captain den Oven was to leeward of us and had spent his main yard to pieces. We caused his (Veen's) journal to be brought on board wherein we found what is said above, and could not gather from the journal that there was ever a wind with which the Armada carrying all the soldiery to Flanders could have set sail, from the 10th (when according to Veen they still lay there) until the 12th (when den Oven missed them), which caused us no little wonder; and moreover since it was previously reported to us on the 18th inst. that the French had been off Cape Ortegal, and Captain Hollaer on the 8th of the same had likewise seen a great fleet off Ortegal, haply the French Armada can have put in there on the 9th and Captain Veen may well have seen some of them riding outside on the 10th.[1] At 3 in the afternoon tacked to southwards; just before noon 3 ships passed us sailing up Channel which were spoken by some of our ships, viz. Captains Matijs Gillisz. and Vijch. Ditto towards evening we met 2 ships of Danzig coming from San Lucar, [the skipper of] one called Hans Scholte being visited by us declared he had sailed from San Lucar the 23 May, and that 5 days out from Cadiz he had met 60 miles out at sea thwart of Cabo da Rocca[2] 5 great English ships full of foot-

(margin note, left:) Captain Veen's journal brought on board.

(margin note, left:) News from Danzigers of English ships laden with soldiers.

1 This conclusion was perfectly correct. The French fleet under De Sourdis had actually appeared off La Coruña on June 9th (De la Roncière, *op. cit.* v, p. 51). Cf. Introduction, Ib.

2 In Portugal; known to English sailors as "The Rock of Lisbon". MS. has *Roxeijnt.*

soldiers, and each one mounting between 30 and 40 guns. He thought that the said English ships must needs reach here tonight, or tomorrow morning at the latest. There also came 3 other ships from windward that were spoken by Captain Pieter Pietersz. in the evening. They were 3 Hollanders coming out of the Strait, skipper Jonas of Enchuijsen from Genoa, de Jonge of Amsterdam, Jan Gerritsz. of Hoorn, both from Livorno, all of whom we let go on their course.

The 28 *June* in the morning the wind S.W. we saw 2 great ships, fetching up with them they were the 2 Englishmen mentioned yesterday, coming from Cadiz in Spain laden with soldiery. We made the Admiral come by the lee by threatening to clap him on board, and the Vice-Admiral de With [did the like to the English Vice-Admiral]. We sent our shallop alongside with a request that the skipper [= master] or some other of the chief officers should come on board, as one Master Fisher did, who was evidently the supercargo. We said that we must have the Spanish soldiery out of their ships whether peacefully or by force; he answered that such was their freight, whereby the skipper and crew had their livelihood, and that therefore he would defend those people together with his own for so long as he could, and we must reckon upon this. We therefore sent the aforesaid Mr. Tom Fisher accompanied by the Heer Vice-Admiral Jan Everts,[1] Commander Cats and the Judge-Advocate, aboard the English Admiral with a friendly request that he would hand over the Spaniards to us, but got

1 This is a mistake. From the preceding and following paragraphs, it is clear that it was not Evertsen but De With who was the Vice-Admiral in question. It can be definitely stated that Evertsen was not even in the fleet. Where he was is not certain. In the fleet-list in the margin of May 30th he is shown, but is omitted from that of June 21st; so that it can be confidently assumed that on June 16th, when the Rear-Admiral Cats joined the fleet, he was sent away on a secret mission (perhaps even to Holland). He had rejoined by July 3rd. But the fact that it was De With, and not Evertsen, who acted on this occasion, is definitely proved by the entry in his "record of service" copied by his son-in-law Walter Breeman Van der Hagen which runs: "in the year 1639 I brought 2 English ships carrying 700 soldiers by the lee, each mounting 30 guns, and captured them". See the *Leven en Bedrijff van Vice-Admirael de With, Zaliger,* published by S. P. L'Honoré Naber in the *Bijdragen...van het Histor. Genootschap te Utrecht,* 1926, XLVII, p. 159. (N.)

no answer other than that if we wanted the men we must come and fetch them with cannon, and he threatened the Vice-Admiral with a pistol against his chest, who again came aboard us and made report thereon. Meanwhile the Englishman made sail to steer his course to the Isle of Wight, when we set sail and began to shoot at him, with order that so far as was possible— since the sea was running high—our men should shoot at the hull and flag as little as they could; thus it happened that after 28 shots had been fired at him, he, the Admiral, named Jan Crouter of London, in the ship *Rainbow*, struck. He had again fired three blank shots in a vain show, and we then took out the soldiery. He declared that he had taken in 4,000[1] men at Cadiz, some of whom had died, whilst the Vice-Admiral had shipped 370 men which he now yielded up without resistance. The Admiral had 3 coffers of silver, each worth 5,000 guilders, on account of his freight, and he was to have drawn on the money when he had brought the Spaniards to Dunkirk; he had a further 6 coffers of silver aboard for merchants at Dover and at London. In the Vice-Admiral's ship were 3 similar coffers for his freight on the same condition, with another 3 coffers of merchants' money, whereon we held a Council and it was decided to leave each of them 3 coffers for the freight, and since we could find no proof that the remainder was Spanish money we left all this bullion in the ship and let them continue on their voyage unharmed; at their request we gave them a certificate thereof in the name of the said Council of War, whilst they gave us one in return stating that we had not taken any of their merchandise or money and let them go further unharmed.

During the same day at two o'clock we met an Englishman named Master Dammas, one of the five carrying 300 Spanish soldiers, whom he let us take out without any trouble, and continued on his course unharmed; he had no money on board, hailed from Lübeck and came from Setubal with salt. We cast about to the south at nightfall, the east point of Wight N.W. by N. from us 3 miles.

(41)

Both these English also laden with salt and wine besides soldiers.

1 For 4,000 read 400.

The 29 *June* in the morning the wind was S.W., made sail to northwards, sighted 4 ships, coming up with them they were Easterling Hamburgers laden with salt, coming from Setubal, who declared they had no news other than that they had certainly had some ships in their company previously, both Easterling as Hollanders. They continued on their course after having been visited by our ships. We plied to and again; towards evening sighted 17 sail, [coming up] with them it was Abram Crijnsz. with the afore-mentioned ships from Setubal, with a Schiedammer in company, the ship's captain being nick-named "Za the Frenchman", bound for the Maas, to whom we gave a letter for Their High Mightinesses, and one for the Heer de Reus, concerning what befell in the taking of the 1,070 Spaniards out of the three Englishmen which took place yesterday.[1] After visiting them allowed them to continue on their course. Captain Joris Pietersz. with the oared yacht joined us; he declared that he had been forced to come to anchor west of Portland on the night of the 25 ditto through a storm, where he had ridden until the 28 ditto, losing three anchors, cut $2\frac{1}{2}$ fathoms of the cable and then the weather being much improved got under sail and above Portland, where, his taffrail being smashed in he put into Weymouth road where he found Captain den Oven lying. With the evening we tacked out to the offing under a pair of courses.

(41)
Verso

The 30 *ditto* in the morning the wind at S.W. We tacked westwards. An hour after sunrise we signalled Captain Abram Crijnsz. and Captain Joris to repair aboard; dispatched Captain Crijnsz. to Calais and Dover with letters for Glarges[2] and the Ambassador Joachimij[3] concerning our encounter with the English and the taking of the Spaniards out of their ships. Ordered Captain Dorrevelt to hand over a cable with an anchor to Captain Joris. We gave Captain Ringels some victuals; at 10 o'clock Captain Abram Crijnsz. left us and we plied to and

Captain Abram
Crijnsz. goes to
Calais and Dover
with letters.

1 *I.e.* 400 men aboard the Admiral, 370 in the Vice-Admiral and another 300 in the third ship taken on that same day. The fourth ship put into the Isle of Wight, whilst the fifth landed her soldiers at Helford near Falmouth. *Vide* under July 1st, 4th, 12th, 17th, and 19th, *infra*.

2 Agent at Calais. 3 Ambassador in England.

again off Selsea Bill.¹ At sunset we tacked out to sea under a
pair of courses, the wind at N.W. with misly rainy weather.

The first July in the morning at daybreak little wind yet
what there was S.W. by south. We tacked to westwards, the
wind chopped to south by west with misly rain. When we tacked
judged Dunnose² to bear north-west from us 4 or 5 miles off.
About midday it cleared up, we tacked out to sea, when
Dunnose bore out of the north from us 3 miles; after the sun
was in the south-west Captain Cornelis Meij came out and
joined us from the island, wherein he had run for shelter from
the storm; there likewise joined us Skipper Jan Teunisz. of
Groeningen, who had come from Pernambuco with the ships
gone for the fatherland with the great fleet on the 20, and
Harman Cornelisz. of Schiedam laden with salt and bound for
Rotterdam. Brought tidings that the remaining 2 English
ships with Spaniards aboard lay at Cowes; they asked us for
convoy and we requested them to remain with us for some days.
In the evening Captains den Oven, Snip and Vijch joined us
2 hours before sunset. Held a Council of War. Resolved that
Commander Brederode with Arent Domensz., skipper Lops and
Fredrick Pietersz. should take that opportunity to set the
captured Spaniards ashore in the Bay of La Hogue, providing
each of them with 6 ships-biscuits, and that for three reasons,
viz., that they should not infect our ships with sickness and the
bloody flux which was ravaging them,³ and to save our victuals
who have few enough, and not to quit the sea untimely; and
(42)   because we do not know how strong the Spanish fleet shall
come we cannot approve of detaching 4 of our ships to carry
the aforesaid Spaniards to the fatherland. In the evening we
cast about to the offing.

The 2 ditto in the morning the wind was S.S.W. with misly
rain. Tacked to the westwards. At about 6 o'clock the misly
rain cleared up and the wind veered W.N.W. The Groeninger
Pernambuco trader⁴ had silently absconded during the night.

---

1 MS. *Weenbrugge.*   2 MS. *Wolfferhoorn.*
3 Tromp apparently thought that the French peasantry were not so liable to
infection from the *roode loop* as his own men!
4 See under July 1st.

We signalled everyone to bring his Spaniards into the allotted ships to be set ashore. They left us about 10 o'clock.[1] We summoned the Council of War to repair aboard, as well as Captains den Oven and Veen and understood from them the information they brought about the enemy, from which we could gather little or nothing of certainty; we therefore determined to await what tidings Abram Crijnsz. shall bring from Calais,[2] in order then to resolve upon what the service of the Land shall require. Dispatched the skipper Snip under St Helens to keep watch on the 2 remaining Englishmen full of Spaniards that had put into Wight on the 29 of this present, to inform us if they came out; and Captain den Oven was likewise sent to Cowes,[3] with orders at once to bring us advice of what course they took with the soldiers. At southern sun we steered away E.N.E. towards Beachy Head, and at evening Jan Pietersz. de Jager joined us coming from Zante, laden with currants and bound for the fatherland. We laid south under a main course; thwart of Arundel[4] we were three miles from the land, the wind at W. by south. We saw Harman Kees [= Cornelisz.][5] who went on ahead not wishing to wait.

The 3 July in the morning the wind was at W. by N. with good weather. We borrowed the Vice-Admiral's long-boat wherewith to careen and ballast our ship. We rounded Beachy Head, which bore E.N.E. from us 3 miles, with the Vice-Admiral Jan Evertsz. and Pieter Pietersz.; astern of us came Captain Sijbrant Barentsz.—being the young Waterdrincker, and Lambert Halffhoorn; passed another Englishman to eastwards who had been visited by our ships. At about 8 o'clock came to an anchor in 6 fathoms offshore from Beachy, the point S.W. by W. from us. Our cable broke asunder, whereon we stopped the ship with the sheet-anchor; we fished our anchor up again, got 6 boats and shallops with ballast and careened our ship. At sunset we had nearly finished when Captain

1 See July 10th. Not all the prisoners were landed.
2 He had been sent there on June 30th.
3 MS. *Koe* (cow).   4 MS. *Orendeel.*
5 See previous date.

Set the Spaniards ashore near La Hogue.

Abram Crijnsz. (as we thought) came beating up towards us from the east, but it proved to be Captain Mangellaer.

The 4 ditto in the morning the wind at S.W. Before daybreak we fired a signal-gun and got under weigh and lay seawards. When it was day Captain Mangelaer came aboard bringing three letters, one from His Highness dated the 20 June in the camp before Philippine¹ in Flanders, the second from Their High Mightinesses in the Hague of the 7 June, the third from Middelburg from the Admiralty [of Zeeland] of the 20 June as before. The 2nd letter [of Their H.M.] mentioned the capture of Soetendael and the sinking of his ship, adding that the enemy was wreaking havoc in the North Sea and preparing to do still more, but that nevertheless they left the question of detaching a squadron to free the North Sea to our own discretion. The news from Middelburg was that a few days previously eleven enemy frigates, 5 miles off the Foreland, had discovered this Captain Mangelaer coming from London with 10 small vessels of Vlissingen and Middelburgh, and had taken all the boats, only Mangelaer escaping; and since they were still expecting the Zeeland fleet from France, they therefore begged us to keep a vigilant look-out for them. At 9 o'clock we tacked to westwards and at noon we discovered 15 sails that ran before the wind towards us. It was the Vice-Admiral de With with our 15 ships; he came aboard us and declared that yesterday he had spoken an Englishman coming from Rochelle who stated that he had discovered that 30 French warships had arrived there from their Armada, all tattered and torn, which 3 weeks ago yesterday had been off La Coruña and missed the remainder of their Armada, as also the great ship;² we therefore immediately signalled the Council of War to repair aboard and having duly pondered over all our advices, we finally resolved for the best service of the Land that we with the main body of our fleet should proceed through the Narrows

1 In Zeeland Flanders, a few miles N.E. of Sas van Gent, and not far from Ghent.

2 This probably refers to *la Couronne,* the great French ship which had been built as Richelieu's reply to *The Sovereign of the Seas.* She was certainly in this fleet, and her condition was "avarié" (see De la Roncière, *op. cit.* pp. 51, 52).

for a turn of 10 or 12 days' cruising between the Maas, Orfordness, Dunkirk and the North Foreland; and that Commander
Brederode, who was meanwhile setting the Spaniards ashore
with his squadron, should cruise between Wight and Beachy
on the 2 Englishmen lying off the island full of men and money;
and should he discover that they had crossed or sent the money
overland to Dover, to remain cruising with the squadron under
his command, and meanwhile to send Skipper Snip, who lay
at anchor as a scout off St Helens, to come and warn us if the
English leave Wight, for the protection of our trade in the
Channel and to ascertain news of the Spanish fleet; he was
likewise to send on to us the frigates of den Oven, Abram
Crijnsz., Veen and both the oared yachts, besides all other ships
in quest of the flag; Captain Cornelis Meij was to cruise
between Wight and Beachy in order to give Commander
Brederode his written orders, and having done this to proceed
to Dover forthwith in order to hand over our letter to Cornelis
Bosch,[1] and then to rejoin the flag. At sunset Captain Meij left
us and we spooned afore to the E.N. eastwards, when Beachy
bore W.N.W. from us 8 miles, the wind at W.S.W. with a hard
following gale blowing and thick misly rain; we were strong
as per margin.

(43)
Adm. Tromp, Vice-
Ad. De With, Vice-
Ad. Everts, Rear-
Adm. Cats, Diemen,
Vijch, Sluijs, Mathijs
Gillisz., Ham, Keert
de Koe, Zeeu, Halff-
hoorn, Ringelsz., Jan
Poulus, Pr. Pietersz.,
Sybrant Barents, Jan
Gerbrants, T. Hoen,
Salmander, Mange-
laer.

The 5 July in the morning the wind at W.S.W. at daybreak
we were off Cape Grisnez,[2] signalled Captain Vijch who was
going to Dover for news of the enemy. We stood over to Calais.
We sent our shallop ashore for news as aforesaid, when de
Glarges came aboard in person and had no news other than
that the French Armada was destined to fight the La Coruña
fleet whether they found them at sea or in La Coruña, and
having destroyed it or missed it, to cruise for the silver fleet;
whilst no news of the French Armada had been received at
Calais, still less of the Spanish. Driving off Calais at about 9 of
the clock we discovered eleven sail in the offing and made chase
after them; they were all enemy frigates and set their course
outside the Goodwins. Captain Vijch came out of Dover and
followed astern; coming off the north end of the Goodwins

1 Cornelis Bos, Tromp's pilot, still at Dover. See under May 2nd.
2 MS. *Swartenes.*

some of our ships fetched up so close with them that they fired on each other, but it falling calm the enemy thus escaped by rowing.[1] We followed them the whole night long; in the evening the wind blowing fresh from the southward; we held on our course to the north.

The 6 in the morning an hour before daybreak there came a breeze from northwards, so that the enemy were then 2 half-cartou shots[2] in the wind of us; we tried our best to fetch up with them, but through their divers plyings to and again, and owing to the calm, they escaped us by rowing. The sun being at W.S.W. a small ship with a black topsail passed betwixt us and the enemy. We bore down towards our leewardmost ships and signalled all Captains to repair aboard; gave each of them a station to cruise on until the 15–16 of this present between the Maas, Orfordness, Dunkirk and the North Foreland, and on the expiration thereof they were to rendezvous under the Castle of Hythe[3] if it was a weather shore, but if a lee shore then in the Vlacke[4] Sea; the North Foreland W.S.W. from us. We communicated to all the Captains the decision taken by the Council of War on the 4 inst. concerning the abandoning of the Channel and making a tour in the North Sea and asked their opinions thereon, which they all unanimously confirmed as being the best seamanship in view of our information, wherefore they all signed the resolution. At sunset we saw 6 sail right in the wind of us, first steering towards us and then standing on the same tack as us with the darkness. We did our best to fetch up with Maas, Schouwen and Walcheren, the wind being at E. by N. We gave our letters to Captain Mangelaer with 2 sailors from our ship, Jan Soetendael and Sijmon

(43)
Verso

1 By using sweeps.

2 *cartou schoten*. In a document of 1624 published in Aitzema, *op. cit.* i, pp. 492–3, *heele kartouwen* (= cannon royal?) are rated at 4,000 lbs. weight, Dutch ½ *kartouwen* at ± 4,000, new type ½ *kartouwen* at 3,000 lbs., as also French ½ *kartouwen*; with a charge of respectively 10, 10, 4.5, and 8 lbs. of gunpowder. (N.)

3 MS. *Casteel van Ida*. This probably refers to Saltwood Castle at the north end of Hythe, and still inhabited. It may however refer to Sandgate Castle.

4 The Vlacke Zee is the southern part of the North Sea. The identification of it in *Letters and Papers*, ii, p. 139, is wrong. (N.)

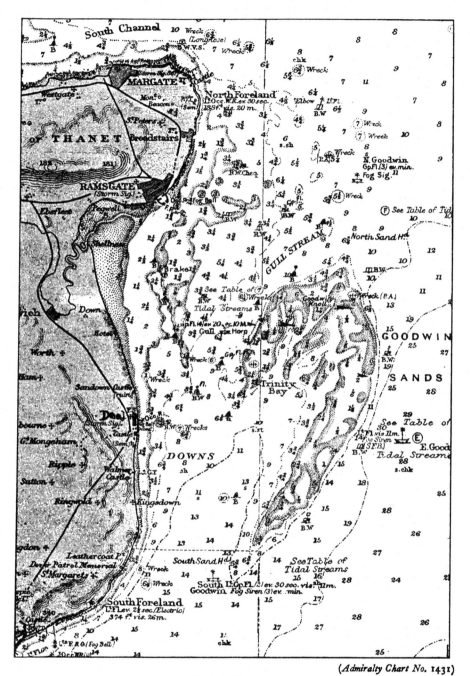

THE DOWNS

(*Admiralty Chart No.* 1431)

Kerckhoven, one being sick and the other to carry our letters, though Mangelaer still remained with us.

The 7 July in the morning the wind at N.E. by E. with a fresh gale. At break of day we saw 3 or 4 small sail S. of us apparently Flemish fishers. Nieupoort bore S.E. from us and Dunkirk S. b. W. Tacked out to sea off from the banks and saw in the wind some small sail as before. At southern sun we likewise discovered 7 sail to leeward of us, with a small sail on our lee bow which we spoke; was an Englishman of Yarmouth with fish, said he was bound for Southampton and declared that 7 sail had been near but not spoken him, he presumed them to be Dunkirkers, after whom we chased until the sun was W.S. west, when seeing there was no hope of fetching up with them we bore up round thus having Nieupoort bearing 3 miles from us; 3 ships sailing before the wind passed us to seawards, apparently Englishmen coming out from the Wielingen. We sailed N. by W., the wind at N.E. with a stiff breeze, took in our fore-topsail and mizzen.

Chase 7 frigates.

The 8 ditto in the morning at daybreak the wind was E. by N. Lay over to the south. At 7 of the clock Nieupoort bore E.S.E. from us 3 miles. We tacked out to sea and first discovered 2 sail, seeming first to run before the wind N. westwards. Saw another fleet of ships and coming up with them it was an Amsterdam convoy which had left the Texel at noon yesterday 40 sail strong bound for Rouen with 2 convoyers. Knew nothing in particular. At southern sun we tacked to southwards and 2 hours afterwards 2 rainbows appeared; the wind variable; 2 hours before sunset we tacked out to sea, Ostende bearing S. by W. from us 2 miles off; when it began to rain we took in our topsails and hove out the main topsail with the darkness.

Texel fleet spoken by us.

(44)

The 9 July in the morning at daybreak it was calm, with little wind yet what there was at N. by W. Tacked to the E. About 8 of the clock we made signal to scatter and shaped our course E.N.E. then east. About one o'clock we saw the land of Schouwen and when the sun was in the S.W. we came off the Maas where we found Commander Bancque with his squadron, viz. Captains Colster, Post, Farant, and Tjaert de Groot.[1] We sent our shallop thither to tell them to make sail which they accordingly did. Plied to and again until sunset when it became calm so that we had to stop the flood tide in 10 fathom, the Tower of Goeree bearing S.E. by S. from us.

The main body

Adm. Tromp, De With, Jan Everts, Rear-Adm. Colster, Diemen, Sluijs, Matijs Gillissen, Post, Keert de Koe, Halfhoorn, Zeeu, Jan Pouwelssen, Sibrant Barents, Jan Garbrants, Backhuijsen, 't Hoen, Pr. Pieterssen, Farant, Tjaert.

Off the Maas

Bancker, Ringels, Vijch.

In the Channel

Brederode, Adriaen Domens, Lops, Snip, Fredric Pieters.

We expect to join us from the Channel

Veen, den Oven, Abram Krijnsse, Corn. Meij, Joris Pieterssen, Dorrevelt.

Hollaer is away with his prizes.

The 10 *ditto* in the morning before daybreak the wind was W. by S. afterwards W. by N. We weighed our anchors with the beginning of the ebb tide and stood out to sea. At 7 o'clock Gravesande[2] bore S.E. by S. 3 miles from us, we then lay with our head to the south and signalled all the Captains to repair on board. Ordered Captain Vijch to put into the Maas with the Spanish officers and their servants, who totalled 71, in order to hand them over to the Admiralty. Commander Bancque showed a letter dated the 30 of June sent him by Their High Mightinesses stating that on the request of Admiral Tromp they had already shipped divers victuals, both in the Maas as in the Wielingen, for our fleet, whilst he (Bancke) was to wait until the victualling ships came out to convoy them to under the flag; we therefore told Commander Bancke to ride before the Maas with Captain Ringelsse, whilst Captain Vijch having discharged the Spaniards should come out with the victualling ships, under the command of the aforesaid Bancque and together with him should bring those victualling ships into our fleet whilst the other ships were to remain with our main body, viz. Colster, Farant, Post and Tjaert; our main body was then as per margin. At half past 4 of the clock Vijch left us and we tacked to the N.W., 's Gravezande S.E. by S. from us. At sunset Bancke and Ringels left us. During the day we had seen 2 sail, one steering to the S.S.E., the other eastwards. We sailed north-west, the wind N.W. with a fresh gale.[3]

The 11 *ditto* in the morning wind slight and variable. At sunrise judged the Hook of Holland to bear 11 or 12 miles S.E. from us; owing to the lack of wind we continued to drive, and everybody washed and paid their ships. At half past four

1 See June 20th and 23rd.
2 MS. *Gravesent*. This South Holland town should not be confused with Gravesend in England.
3 *Sic* wind at N.W. and course N.W.! Another copyist's error obviously. (N.)

there came light airs from the east; we saw a sail to south-wards of us after whom we chased until sundown when we lost him and we sprang our luff under courses and sailed S.E. by southwards. Another ship came down from windward astern of us; apparently an Englishman shaping his course for Yarmouth.

The 12 *July* in the morning the wind was E.S.E. When it was daylight, we discovered 2 sails in the W.N.W. and chased after them. Coming up with them it was Captain den Oven with Joris Pietersz. coming from Beachy. Captain den Oven had been sent by us on the 2 inst. to Wight to inform us of the state of the English ships which had put in there with the Spaniards. He declared that on the 28 of last month Skipper Thomas Witting of London had arrived at Cowes with the ship *Swan*, having 335 Spaniards on board; he had been warned off Portland by a ketch from Dover that we were cruising in wait for them, and therefore had put into the Isle of Wight, but he knew nothing of his consort and feared he had been lost. He was resolved not to put to sea with the Spaniards until he had a Royal convoy, and failing that he was going to haul his ship up the creek because the Spaniards were not allowed to land. They[1] had left our squadron off Beachy, with Brederode in command thereof, and had had Cornelis Meij in company for a while, who had later sailed away from them. On the 7 they had seen 7 ships under the Old Man[2] steering to the S.W. apparently enemy frigates. They had not discovered Abram Crijnsz. Today in the morning a small English vessel passed us, which was visited by one of our ships, and in the afternoon another one coming from Plymouth, who had met 6 States' ships off Beachy. During the day the wind was variable and at sundown mostly from at S.W. We tacked S.S. eastwards under courses, when Orfordness bore W. 6 or 7 miles from us.

Captain den Oven and Joris Pietersz. join us.

---

1 *I.e.* Den Oven and Pietersz. The Spanish soldiers in the *Swan* were landed at Portsmouth at the end of July and sent to London overland (*Cal. S.P. Dom.* 1639, p. 391).

2 Captain Naber, R.N.N., says that *den ouden man* was the nickname for a Dunkirk privateer, but is not certain as to whom the nickname was applied. I myself have not been able to trace him.

The 13 *ditto* in the morning the wind at S.W. by S. We discovered 2 sail shaping their course eastwards, we chased after them E.S.E. & found that our vanward ships had spoken them both and we sailed close hauled again. Captain den Oven spent his fore-topmast. About 10 o'clock tacked out to sea, when Westcappel bore S.E. by S. from us 3 miles off. In the afternoon 5 sail passed us to leeward, apparently shaping their course to the Maas, the wind gradually shuffled S., at sundown mostly S.W. We judged that Orfordness then bore N.W. from us about 11 or 12 miles distant.

Veen, Dorrevelt and Meij join us.

(45)

The 14 *ditto* in the morning at daybreak the wind at S. Discovered 3 sail E. of us; steered towards them & found they were our frigates, viz. Veen, Dorrevelt, and Cornelis Meij who brought letters given by Glarges to Abram Crijnsz., who had missed us, and on his return to Calais had sailed to the Wielingen with some small vessels at Glarges'[1] request; we also got a letter from the Ambassador Joachimi.[2] We ordered them to stay with us and then we luffed and steered eastwards, till 10 o'clock when we laid over to the west. An hour afterwards some of our ships chased to the east, whereon we followed them, and coming up with the ships it was Commander Bancque and Ringels, having 2 victualling ships in company, Job 't Kint of Rotterdam and Gerrit Senten of Schiedam; the third, Cornelis Albertsz. of Rotterdam, was still riding at anchor and would probably come with Captain Vijch since he was not yet ready. We forthwith ordered Captain Colster to sail to the Maas to await Vijch and the victualling ship to convoy them to us, whilst Commander Bancque, Ringels and den Oven were to go to Vlissingen to fetch their victuals. At southern sun the Maas bore E. by N. from us 5 or 6 miles; the wind grew to a storm so we took in our foresail and so drove. Towards evening Bancker and Colster left us under courses, the wind at S. by west.

Job t Kint and Gerrit Senten join us.

The 15 *July* in the morning the wind at W. by S. we set our foresail, the wind shifted to N.W. by N. About 5 o'clock

1 The agent at Calais.
2 Netherlands Ambassador in London.

we lay over to the west sailing under a pair of courses S.W. by west and W.S.W. until 5 in the afternoon. Then it became calm and the wind shifted W. by S. when we judged the Maas to be S.E. from us 12 miles off. Sailed until sundown 3 miles S. by E. and sailed close hauled. In the morning about breakfast time 4 laden ships came up with us coming from La Rochelle, bound for the Texel, and at sundown we saw three sails S.W. from us, apparently our oared yacht [Captain] Dorrevelt with Middelburger privateers; saw from the topmast 2 sail in the wind's eye, not knowing who they were.

The 16 *ditto* in the morning the wind was W.N.W. Sailed S.W., saw north of us 3 sail who were steering away N.E. Saw from the topmast another 2 sail right ahead which we pursued. At 9 o'clock judged Dunkirk S. by E. from us 9 miles. When the sun was in the south we came off Nieuport which bore S.S.E. from us 3 miles, and stood out to sea. Towards evening the ship of Post came to speak us; said that the 2 ships chased by us this morning were the 2 Zeeland privateers which had said that 12 or 13 ships lay in the Scheur[1] and presumed them to be enemy frigates. At sundown we judged the North Foreland to be 9 miles from us, the wind having backed to S.W. When the 1st watch was over we tacked in 12 fathom. In the evening after sunset Adrian Jansz. alias the East India Voyager died.

The 17 *July* in the morning the wind at W.S.W. Sailed southwards. There was a small ship with a black topsail in the wind of us; at S.E. sun we saw a King's ship with a flag at the fore-topmast plying to and again apparently trying to get into the River of London [Thames]. At 1 o'clock we came to an anchor in 15 or 16 fathom, the North Foreland bearing S.W. by S. from us 5 miles off. We brought our victualling ship (skipper Gerrit Senten) on our quarter[2] like the Vice-Admiral de With did to Job Cornelis t Kint and began to discharge them. The English King's man likewise anchored. We saw still some other sails to N.E. of us, besides 5 sail south of us which

(45)
Verso

1 Dunkirk road. See note under May 12th.
2 MS. *achter aen*, but it could not very well have been literally astern.

steered towards us. It was Commander Brederode with the squadron wherewith he had been cruising betwixt Wight and the Narrows. Commander Brederode who joined us on the 17 brought with him skipper Adriaen Slateij coming from San

Advice of the enemy. Antonio[1] with a small barque, laden with apples and lemons, taken by Fredric Pietersz. 't Hovelinck on the 12 ditto 4 miles south of Dunnose, bound for Dunkirk, where the skipper declared he dwelt; he had further said that when he had left San Antonio on the 4th instant the enemy's Armada, 30 sail strong, still lay in La Coruña, and he was sure that it would not cross until October; whilst the French Armada had lain off La Coruña, and over 3 weeks ago had landed 3,000 men

A parcel of warships. there, who had been forced to retire again to their ships with the loss of 400 men,[2] and at his departure they still lay cruising off La Coruña.

Commander Brederode had understood from Jereen Leeuwen, coming from La Rochelle, that on the 4–5th instant a part of the French Armada had arrived off Belle Isle whilst the rest still lay before La Coruña. He added that the Englishman carrying Spanish troops lying in Wight was still lying there and that in the meantime he had sent the Spaniards overland to Dover;[3] that on the 10th instant he had spoken the last Englishman carrying Spaniards, who had landed the Spaniards in Helford,[4] with the exception of a padre whom he (the Commander) had taken out of the ship. We determined to distribute all the fruit

(46) amongst the fleet in order to refresh the men amongst whom were many sick, and that the prize and crew together with the captured padre should be sent home at the first opportunity, whilst we with the main body of our fleet should proceed to between Portland and the Casquets, the more so since the Heere de Charost advised me that the enemy's ships in this month July with Spanish foot-soldiers, which they had shipped

1 Close by La Coruña.
2 See the Introduction for a summary of these operations. This news was the first really accurate information Tromp got about the state of affairs in North Spain.
3 London to be exact (*Cal. S.P. Dom.* 1639, p. 391).
4 Near Falmouth.

in the flyboats [blank], in short all the advices confirmed that the enemy still lay in La Coruña, as did the tidings from Dover.

The 18 *July* in the morning the wind was S.E. Weighed anchor at the turn of the tide and sailed S.S. westwards and beat up to 2 miles off the Foreland. We caused Vice-Admiral de With with Commander [Brederode?] to divide up the lemons and apples out of the prize, and distribute them amongst the whole fleet, to wit 35,000 apples and as many lemons. Just before the tide began to ebb we weighed anchor and got under sail and sailed S.E., the wind S.W. with handsome weather, and at midday at the turn of the tide, we stopped the flood in 20 fathom,¹ the point of Dover bearing S.W. by W.

The 19 *ditto* in the morning the wind at W. Weighed anchor with the turn of the tide and got under sail. We plied to and again, and were joined by Captain Hollaer on his way from Vlissingen to Calais, who brought us from Calais 2 letters from His Highness, one concerning the attacking of all kinds of ships carrying Spanish men and money, the other about keeping a watchful look-out for the East India men which are expected "north about",² as also some missives from the Admiralty of Zeeland. The wind about the turn of the ebb tide shifted S.S.W. with a hard topsail [gale]. We could not weather the Goodwins, wherefore we stood over to the Vlacke Zee³ and anchored in 10 fathom, the North Foreland bearing S.W. by south from us 2 miles off. We held a Council of War, and, since Captain Hollaer brought tidings that 7 enemy frigates had taken the Amsterdam Rouen convoy, viz. 5 boyers, 2 square-rigged ships, and 2 convoyers, their Captains Jacob Anteunisz. with the ship *Rooboontje* [and—? omitted], we resolved that the Vice-Admiral Jan Evertsz. should cruise between Texel and Portland on the aforesaid 7 enemy frigates with a flying squadron,⁴ namely the Captains Jan Evertsz., Farant, Brederode, Pieter Pietersz., the ship[s] of Post, Hollaer and Jan Pouwelsz., whilst we should

Marginal note: Today died Jan van Utrecht and Jan van Oosten, both sailors.

Marginal note: The Flying Squadron Vice-Adm. Jan Evertsen, Comm. Brederode, Captains Farant, de Wint, Hollaer.

---

1 So as not to be driven back on the English coast by the flood tide.

2 Round outside of Ireland and Scotland, and so home via the Shetlands; this was the usual route taken by homeward-bound East-Indiamen in times of actual or threatening danger.

3 See note under July 6th.   4 *een vliegent Esquadre.*

proceed to our rendezvous off Portland, and since Jan Evertsz. and Jan Pouwels must needs go to Vlissingen at the beginning of next month, Brederode shall then take command. The padre taken by Brederode out of the Englishman,—having still been left aboard when the above-mentioned Spaniards had been landed at Helford through the warning of an English King's ship—was likewise ordered to be sent to Zeeland with the Vice-Admiral Jan Evertsz. to be confined by the Admiralty, together with the 20 Spaniards whom Captain Dorrevelt still had on board; who had joined us this evening having missed us owing to the departure of Commander Bancque; the 19[1] in the evening Hollaer sailed for Vlissingen to set the passengers ashore there.

The 20 *ditto in the morning* the wind was N.W. We weighed our anchors and got under sail, the Vice-Admiral Everts left us after firing some salutes, and shaped his course for the Flemish banks, and we through the Narrows. We dispatched an order to Cornelis Bos by Captain Joris who was likewise to set ashore Piero and Verschuyr with another Dol[metsch].[2] Coming into the Narrows the wind backed S.W. and at $2\frac{1}{2}$ of the clock we came to an anchor betwixt Folkestone[3] and the Castle of Hythe[4] in 14 fathoms; 2 hours before sunset we discovered a fleet of six brave ships coming out of the west. We made signal and weighed our anchors and gave chase. Coming up with them, they were 6 Brazil traders coming from Pernambuco and bound for the fatherland. The skippers were Marten Pietersz. in *de Robbe* of Amsterdam, the Vice-Admiral Joost Mast of Middelburg in the ship *Walcheren*, the Rear-Admiral Skipper Meijndert in *De Bul* of Edam, the ship *Goeree* skipper Abeleevens, the ship *de Leeuwin* skipper Arent, and skipper Halfhoorn. After firing several guns in salutation they continued on their course and we laid over close hauled to the north; they had seen no one up Channel and had no news.

The 21 *July* in the morning it was stark calm; we anchored $\frac{1}{2}$ mile from Hythe Castle and most of our boats went ashore

---

1 MS. has 14th—which is absurd.
2 *I.e.* interpreter.   3 MS. *Folston.*
4 Saltwood Castle. See note under July 6th.

for water. During the day we discharged the rest of our victuals out of the ships of Skipper Senten and Job Cornelis 't Kint, save only the beer; also there came out of the Downs 6 or 8 English ships that were working to westward, whilst another 3 or 4 were steering from west to east; towards sundown and turn of the tide we weighed anchor and beat up to westwards, the wind at S.S.W.

Ditto; died in our ship Corn. van Gent and [ ].

The 22 ditto in the morning the wind at W.N. west. Dover bore N. from us 2 miles. We lay over to the west and plied to and again, and about southern sun discovered 3 sail coming out of the west. Lay over towards them and came up with them off Dungeness beacon, one being an Englishman coming from Zante laden with currants, in company with Jonge Schieman of Amsterdam and a small boat. The skipper was Arent Domensen's brother-in-law. In the afternoon it became thick misly weather. During the day when the sun was in the S.W. our Judge-Advocate, Mr Nicolaes van Beverwijck, jumped overboard, although the shallop towed astern picked him up again to everyone's amazement.[1] We lay over to the S.S.W. At 9 o'clock Dungeness bore N.W. by N. from us 3 miles off.

(47)

The Judge-Advocate jumps overboard.

The 23 ditto in the morning the wind at W.N.W. at 10 of the clock stood off from the French coast; saw a small sail inshore; we gave over some victuals to Captain Joris; at 6 in the evening we tacked from Beachy Head, being close inshore; a small vessel lay under Beachy which was $\left[\frac{\text{spoken}}{\text{visited}}?\right]$ by Captain Joris. At sundown there came a ship out of the west, with a Prince-flag at the main; Adriaen Domensz. spoke him; he was a Hollander coming from W. Indies, and declared that the silver fleet which Houtebeen had met[2] had passed through the Bahama Channel 10 weeks ago; the wind at W. we sailed S. westwards. Seven glasses in the first watch the wind shifted

1 According to Witte de With, the Judge-Advocate (*fiskaal*) had suffered a "gnawing in his conscience" over an unjust prosecution against De With, in which he (the J.-A.) had allowed himself to be involved! See p. 111 of the *Leven en Bedrijff*, *op. cit.*

2 *I.e.* the Spanish Silver fleet unsuccessfully attacked by Houtebeen off Cuba in 1638. See Duro, *op. cit.* IV, pp. 192–5.

southwards with heavy rain; we tacked and set our course W. by southwards.

The 24 *July* shortly before daybreak the wind again veered W.S.W. About 6 of the clock we tacked southwards and sailed S.S.W. Saw the land west of Newhaven;[1] at 2 of the clock we again tacked northwards and at sundown again out to sea, the wind W., what time we judged Beachy bore N.E. from us 6 miles off.

The 25 *ditto* at 5 o'clock the wind was west; tacked to the north; at 8 o'clock the *Groote Christoffel*, skipper Fredrick Pietersz., signalled he wished to speak us; we hove-to and sent our shallop alongside; he complained of general want of provisions, wherefore we helped him. And since a prize captured by him Fredrick Pietersz. was very leaky we therefore ordered the Vice-Admiral de With and Catz to divide the fruit that was still in it amongst the fleet, whilst Fredrick Pietersz. who lacked firewood should break up the barque and make use of it. To-day we gave many victuals to divers who had need thereof; during the day it was calm; at sunset judged Beachy was N.E. 8 miles from us.

(47)
Verso
Captain Dorrevelt
goes to St Malo.

The 26 *ditto* in the morning the wind was S.E. with a fresh gale, after sunrise we signalled Captain Dorrevelt to repair on board; dispatched him with a letter to the merchants and to Captain Cornelis Evertsz[2]. with his skippers at St Malo, wherein we offered that if they would come and cruise under our flag, we should when the opportunity arose provide them with a good convoy to bring them home in safety. Wight bore north from us about 7 miles off; shaped our course S.S. westwards, until about 10 o'clock when the wind of a sudden chopped W. by S. We lay over to the northwards until southern sun when we tacked southwards, which time the Needles bore N. by E. from us 4 or 5 miles. At 3 o'clock we discovered a sail S.W. from us, we tacked towards it, it was a Frenchman from Barches d'Olonne,[3] the skipper named Rumaelde; come from

1 MS. *Nyeuhaven.*
2 See under his name in List of Captains at end of *Journal.*
3 MS. *Barsalone.*

the Newfoundland Banks 13 days since, laden full of fish wherewith he was bound for Hâvre de Grace;[1] he had spoken no
ships and thus knew nothing fresh. After sundown we stood
out to sea, when Portland bore N.W. by W. from us 5 miles
off, and St Andrew's Land[2] N.W. We sailed S.S.W. the wind
at W. About 2 o'clock it had been misty, though by sunset it
became clear.

The 27 July in the morning the wind W.N.W. At daybreak
Alderney bore S. from us 4 miles off; we discovered 4 sail to
the N. of us; coming up with them it was a fleet of 10 sail,
without convoy, from Nantes. The skippers were P. Franck
t Kint, Frans Joppen, Job Aertsz., all 3 of Rotterdam, Jan
Pietersz. Bonstee of Schiedam, Gerrit Peij, Roelant Dircxsz.,
Pieter Claesz. Kat, Symon Schuijr, Maerten Bontekoe and Jan
Claesz. Crijger of Hoorn, all of whom asked for convoy. We
replied that we had summoned the St Malo convoy, whilst our
victualling ships likewise required convoy, but that if they
would wait we would provide them with a sufficient convoy,
whereon they said they would consult and repaired aboard their
ships, yet they continued their voyage, without speaking us
again; wherefore we sent Captain Tjaert after them with a
written paper warning them once more what peril they ran,
and offering that if they would but wait for the convoy summoned from St Malo to arrive and until our victuals were
discharged, then we should provide them with sufficient convoy,
so there was no need for them to continue their perilous course,
whilst we should not fail to write as much to both the Exchanges
at Amsterdam and Rotterdam. Ditto resolved that we with our
ship and Captain Halfhoorn, Lieven de Zeeu and the oared
yacht, Captain Joris Pietersz. and skipper Gerrit Senten should
go to Falmouth to careen, to take our victuals over there; whilst
the Vice-Admiral de With should run under Portland with the
main body of the fleet to discharge his victuals out of Job 't Kint
and likewise to careen the ships, and buy fresh meat and other
refreshments for the sick men since there were many of them
in the fleet. At south-western sun we parted from each other,

10 Nantes traders
join us, but go on
against our will.

The Squadron
Adm. Tromp, Cap[n]
Ham, Halffhoorn,
de Zeeu, Cap[n] Joris,
Gerrit Senten with
victualling ship.
*The main body under
Portland*
Vice-Ad. de With,
Cap[n] Cats, Diemen,
Sluijs, Gillis, Keert
de Koe, Veen,
Ferant.

(48)

The Adm[t] of Hoorn
Cap't Hoen, Jan
Meij.
*The Adm[t] at Amster-
dam*
Cap. Waterdrincker,
Jan Gerbrantssen.

1 MS. *Habel de Graes.*   2 *I.e.* Isle of Purbeck, in Dorset.

Hired ships
Backhuijsen, Adriaen
Domenssen, Thove-
linck, Lops, Snip,
victualling ship of
Job 't Kint.

Flying Squadron
Comm. Brederode,
Capn de Wint, Capn
Post, Capn Farant,
Capn Hollaer.

We stay 3 with the
victualling ship
Capn Colster, Capn
Vijch.

We expect from Zee-
land
Commander Banc-
kert, Capn Ringels,
Capn Crijnssen,
Capn den Oven.

After this spring[tide]
Capn Frans Jans,
Comm. Jan Poulus.
Dorrevelt to St Malo.

Totalis 36 ships.

Ditto. Joachim
Stevensse, sailor,
died.

the Vice-Admiral ran under Portland, that bore N.N.E. from us 2 miles, whilst we plied to westwards as best we could, the wind being at S.W. At sundown Portland bore east from us 5 miles off. We laid over to the offing S. by E.

The 28 *ditto* in the morning 3 hours before daybreak the wind was S.W. with a raw gale, we laid over to the north, and at 6 of the clock stood out to sea again on the fore ebb, and at southern sun again towards the land, whilst it rained extreme hard until S.W. sun, when it cleared up, at 5 of the clock stood out to sea, when Start Point[1] bore W.S.W. from us 5 miles off, the wind at W. by S. Sailed S. by westwards.

The 29 *ditto* in the morning the wind was W. laid over to the north; at about 7 of the clock we gave chase to a ship, coming up with her after Captain Joris had forced her to strike. It was a St. Malo man coming from the Newfoundland Bank. We let him go unharmed, stood off from the English coast, and signalled all Captains to repair on board, and determined that if the wind prevented us from coming into Falmouth we should put into Guernsey to carry out what we ought to have done in Falmouth. At 2 o'clock we again laid over to the land, the wind backed S.W. in the afternoon. At sundown we tacked out to sea again, when Start Point bore 5 miles from us. When night fell a ship sailed past us in the offing with a red flag abroad, apparently an Englishman, whilst another small sail sailed close hauled towards Start Point.

The 30 *July* in the morning the wind was W. and since it was new moon today and a spring tide, and not possible to fetch up to Falmouth with this present wind, and moreover it was highly needful for our ships to be careened and their crews refreshed, we thus in accordance with the resolution adopted yesterday steered for Guernsey, and when the sun was in the S.W. came to an anchor in 20 fathoms in the fairway off the mole;[2] we forthwith sent the Captains to the Castle so as to be able tomorrow, being Sunday, to warp in 2 of our ships, viz. Captains Ham and de Zeeu. The wind at N.N.W. with fine

1 MS. *Exmutstaert.*   2 MS. *Moulie.*

clear weather. Captain Joris Pietersz. warped into the mole
with the oared yacht.

The 31 *ditto* in the morning it was calm. Captains Ham and
Lieven de Zeeu with the victualling ship warped into the mole,
we careened our ship and made the carpenters caulk her
between wind and water. Captain Lieven's ship was hauled
down too much on her side, and the oared yacht of Joris
Pietersz. being pulled over by her on to her wrong side, the
gunwale was spoiled; during the day the wind at S. b. W. and
in the evening at E.N.E. with handsome calm weather. During
the day our shallop went sounding in the northern fairway; the
mate Pieter Pietersz. declared that it was a fit channel.

(48)
Verso
Some of our ships
paid in Guernsey.

The first of August in the morning little wind yet what there
was S. after having been N.W. Captain Halfhoorn also warped
within the mole. Captain Joris with the oared yacht warped
out from the mole alongside us, we placed in the yacht 12 heavy
cannon, 7 swivel guns;[1] we found a splendid brook ½ mile
north of the town, whither we sent to fill our casks; we again
careened our ship and the carpenters examined her between
wind and water. In the evening at high water Captains Ham
and Lieven de Zeeu with the victualling flyboat of Gerrit
Centen came out from the mole on the tide, whilst we kedged
to within a cable's length of the shore.[2] After sundown the wind
was little, yet what there was W.N.W. with mist.

The 2 August in the morning the wind S.W. with fine weather.
At daybreak we paid our starboard side, and at about 9 o'clock
we sailed out from the mole into the roadstead and laid out
2 anchors there.[3] During the day the wind was southerly, we
cleared out our battery so as to discharge the victualling ship,

1 The guns of course were temporarily unshipped to facilitate careening. They
were replaced on Aug. 4th, *q.v.*

2 See Mainwaring's *Seaman's Dictionary* (N.R.S. edition of 1922, II, pp.
170–1) for a description of this operation.

3 The following quotation from Mainwaring, *op. cit.*, will make this clear:
"whenever we come to an anchor where there is tide, we lay out two anchors,
so as that, upon the turning of the tide, the ship may wind up clear of either anchor"
(p. 89). One at the bow and one at the stern.

and in the evening at high water Captain Halfhoorn came out from the pier into the roadstead.

The 4 ditto[1] in the morning little wind, yet what there was westerly with thick misly rain; at daybreak we got the oared yacht alongside and took out our cannon. At 9 o'clock we cast loose the oared yacht and got the victualling ship of Skipper Gerrit Senten alongside again and discharged therefrom, for so long as we could see, 51 pipes of beer and 30 kegs of brandy and a great quantity of firewood. During the day we had also fetched a great deal of water; in the afternoon the wind north-west with a raw gale and misly weather.

Take in victuals in Guernsey.

(49)

The 5 ditto in the morning the wind was at N. b. W. with clear weather and a steady gale. We unladed out of the flyboat 60 cheeses, 11 kegs of vinegar, 5 tuns white biscuit, 4 half-hogsheads of wine that were leaking, another 6 Leiden cheeses and 2 sheep's cheeses.

Joris Pieterssen goes to La Coruña.

We dispatched Captain Joris Pietersz. with the oared yacht to La Coruña to spy out once more for the enemy's Armada;[2] at 11 of the clock he weighed anchor and sailed outside of Guernsey. The victualling flyboat cast off after we had today unladen 30 pipes and 22 hogsheads of beer with a quantity of firewood.

Leave Guernsey Adm. Tromp, Ham, Halfhoorn, de Zeeu, Skipper Gerrit Senten being our victualling ship.
[A financial expression follows which I cannot understand. C. R. B.]

The 6 ditto in the morning it was calm. The boats of all our ships went to fetch ballast for the victualling ship of Gerrit Senten. Fired a gun as signal to get under sail and the men aboard from the shore. At 9 o'clock there came a little wind W. and W.N.W. and at 2 o'clock with the fore ebb we set sail and ran out of the southern fairway of Guernsey. We beat up to windward until sunset when the North rock bore north-east from us. Lay over close hauled under a topsail N. westwards, the Captains L. de Zeeu and Halfhoorn being a long way astern.

---

1 In the MS. Aug. 3rd is omitted—a clear proof that the *Journal* is a copy (albeit a contemporary one). (N.)

2 He returned to report on Aug. 27th when Tromp lay before Dunkirk. See under that date.

The 7 *ditto* in the morning 2 glasses in the middle watch[1] the wind became foul first W. by N. then N. b. W. At sunrise we saw some ships ahead of us which tacked towards us at about 7 o'clock and stood for us. Coming up with us it was the Vice-Admiral de With with 20 ships and frigates and 2 victualling ships, viz. Job 't Kint left with him (the Vice-Admiral) and Cornelis Albertsz. who had come out of the Maas with Captain Colster and Captain Vijch; the Commander Bancque had also joined him. We immediately signalled all Captains to repair on board; received letters from Their H.M. that within 6 weeks time victuals for both the hired and victualling ships would come from the Admiralty. Likewise understood that the enemy was fitting out 17 or 18 sail in Dunkirk, with their aim on the great fishery,[2] wherefore we resolved that Commander Bancque with 5 ships should join Captain Brederode, and pick up on his way,—if he should

---

1 MS. *Hondewacht*, but this is not to be translated literally as "dog watch". Captain Naber, R.N.N., writes:

In seventeenth-century Holland, the following two watches were distinguished:
    (1) The Night watch (*Nachtwacht*), from the night gun (*dagschot*) until the day gun (*dagschot*).
    (2) The Day watch (*Dagwacht*), from the day gun until the night gun.

Witsen (1676), p. 413, defines the watches as follows:

Eerste Nachtwacht	First watch	From day gun	till	midnight
Laatste Nachtwacht, or				
Hondewacht	Night watch	„ midnight	„	breakfast
Eerste Dagwacht	Morning watch	„ breakfast	„	dinner (noon)
Tweede Dagwacht	Afternoon watch	„ dinner	„	night gun

The terms *eerste wacht* as an abbreviation of *eerste nachtwacht*, and of *dagwacht* as an abbreviation of *eerste dagwacht* become clear from the foregoing.

The modern division of watches

Achtermiddagwacht	From midday	−4 p.m.
Platvoet	„ 4 p.m.	−8 p.m.
Eerste wacht	„ 8 p.m.	−midnight
Hondewacht	„ midnight	−4 a.m.
Dagwacht	„ 4 a.m.	−8 a.m.
Voormiddagwacht	„ 8 a.m.	−midday

I found for the first time in C. de Jong, *Reize naar de Middelandsche Zee*, 1777–9, p. 3.

2 *I.e.* the North Sea herring fishery. See the Appendix on this in Edmundson, *op. cit.* pp. 158–161.

140 THE JOURNAL

Ringels or Frans Jansz. and that we would send Dorrevelt on
to join him, so that he could blockade the harbours of Dunkirk
and the Scheur with 14 sail and keep the enemy inside, and
subsequently to do whatsoever the service of the Land should
require; yet we should first run under Portland to discharge
Skipper Cornelis Albertsz., whilst the two victualling ships,
't Kint with Gerrit Senten, should be brought home in safety
by Commander Bancque on his way; the wind at N.N.W.
Lay over to the north-east and when the first watch was over
we tacked.

The 8 August in the morning, the wind N.W. There passed
us a parcel of English merchantmen, shaping their course
westwards; our main body was S.E. from us. About 12 of the
clock we came off Portland with Captains Colster, Diemen,
Bancker, Vijch, Tjaert, Adriaen Domensz. and Snip with the victualling ships of Gerrit Senten, Job 't Kint and Aelbert Cornelisz.,
last arrived, who was immediately brought alongside Captain
Colster and discharged not only victuals to him (Colster), but
fetched [?ballast] with the boats from Captains Diemen and
Vijch as much as he could; at 4 of the clock Captain Teeue
joined us from the main body, having on the previous night
carried away Captain Halfhoorn's beakhead, which could not
be repaired at sea.[1] About sundown the ship of Captain den
Oven joined us, the skipper came on board and declared that
he had been off Calais with Captain Everts, and that the agent
de Glarges had written that the English in the Downs had cast
three States' Captains into prison,[2]—the reason whereof he
knew not,—but had let the ships go; during the day there came
some other Englishmen to an anchor by us under Portland;
the wind W. by south.

The 9 ditto the wind W.N.W. with a stiff gale. During the
day variable with hard squalls of rain; the victualling ship
skipper Cornelis Albertsz. was discharged in like manner as

1 See under Sept. 1st for the sequel.
2 Exaggerated. For what really took place see *Cal. S.P. Dom.* 1639, p. 411,
where the names of the Captains concerned, their ships, guns, etc., are given in
full. Cf. also Introduction, II B.

Ditto. Colster com-
plained of Captain
Vijch taking a hostile
flyboat off Dover,
and omitting to
bring the same to
him as Commander.

(49)
Verso

Captain den Oven
joins us with 2 letters
from His Highness.

yesterday, and towards evening brought a cable on board of Adriaen Domensz. and during the day he was filled with as much ballast as he could hold. In the afternoon we sent the ship of Snip out to sea, to search for the Vice-Admiral and bring him to us. At sundown Commander Bancke left to unite with the squadron of Brederode to blockade Dunkirk together, and likewise take the victualling ships, viz. Gerrit Senten and Job 't Kint, to convoy them safely into the Maas; the wind was northerly but variable; a parcel of Englishmen got under sail bound for the west.

The 10 *August* in the morning the wind was N.E. with a fresh gale. Adriaen Domensz. got the victualling ship alongside, and discharged, like as we also did and gave him as much ballast as we could. During the day a number of ships passed us, now as formerly bound for the west; so far as we could see they were mostly English and towards evening we thought we saw some of our main body thwart of us in the offing. At sunset the victualling ship was unladen and casting off from Adriaen Domensz. came to an anchor, but it still lacked a great quantity of ballast, the wind N. by west with fine weather.

The 11 *ditto* in the morning the wind was N.E. by N. with variable squalls with rain. At daybreak we issued an order for all boats to fetch ballast for the flyboat. About 3 hours before noon we weighed our anchor and got under sail, stood out to sea, and came to an anchor with our ships shortly before sundown near the Vice-Admiral de With, having been joined by Captain Dorrevelt from St Malo who brought with him an Amsterdam flyboat bound for the Texel. We signalled all the Captains to repair on board, ordered Commander Cats to go to Guernsey with Veen, Matijs Gillisz. and Cornelis Meij, in order that having careened and made ready they should come and find us forthwith, which Commander Cats left us in the afternoon. We drove with our heads to the west and with foresail hauled to the mast, the wind N. by E. with a fresh gale, when Portland bore W.N.W. from us $2\frac{1}{2}$ miles.

(50)
Go to careen in Guernsey;— Cats, Gillissen, Thoen, Meij, Veen, Brederode.

The Vice-Admiral de With declared that he had met

Some Captains of his Squadron had been guests of Pennington's, then seized and brought into the Downs, though sailed out of the Downs last Saturday, having been released. They asked particularly after the Admiral of Holland. Had something to say to him.

Capn Keert de Koe goes as convoy with Corn. Everts to the Seine.

The main body
Adm. Tromp, Vice-Adm. de Wit, Ham, de Zeeu, Halfhoorn.

Waterdrincker, Jan Gerbrantsz., Backhuijsen, Lops, Frederick Pietersz., Adriaen Domens, Snip, Dorrevelt & the St. Malo flyboat.

(*50*)
Verso

Pennington[1] yesterday, whose boat had been alongside him, and who would gladly have had him out of his ship but he would not go.

The 12 *ditto* in the morning the wind at N.N.E. Skipper Adriaen Domens, with Cornelis Alberts and the victualling fly-boat that had been ballasted, joined us from Portland. We dispatched Captain Keert de Koe, to go with the victualling fleet to the Seine,[2] who left us at 9 of the clock shaping their course westwards, whilst we with the main body steered eastwards; a small sail passed us, to wit an Englishman who was spoken by Dorrevelt. In the afternoon 2 Zeeland West-Indiamen joined us, viz. skipper Lucifer in the ship *Toolen*, with the flyboat *de Hoop*; they had sailed on the day before yesterday morning from the Wielingen; declared that Bastiaen Tijsz. our convoyer should follow with the Zeeland French traders; at 4 o'clock we discovered a fleet of ships to northwards of us; tacked towards them; coming up with them they were 4 empty flyboats, apparently Hoorn passport carriers bound for Setubal.

Two hours after noon we saw a ship lying becalmed off Portland with topsails hauled to the mast, foresail brailed up, with a flag at the stern, a big jack[3] at the bowsprit, with a small sail in company. We considered it to be an English King's yacht with a ketch; when we tacked to the east he made sail and we ran together to south-westwards. At sundown the Needles bore N.E. by N. from us three miles off, the wind at N. by E. Sailed E. by N. Four glasses in the night watch a fleet of ships sailing before the wind passed us, being spoken by some of our ships.

The 13 *August* in the morning the wind N. by E. Sailed E. by N. whilst Dunnose bore N.N.W. from us 2 miles off; about 9 o'clock tacked northwards and at 11 o'clock the wind shifted N. by E. tho' variable. Tacked to the E.N.E., 2 hours after noon the wind veered W.S.W. We hove to and waited for our sternmost man, and exchanged victuals. At sundown

1 MS. *Penneton.* Pennington was the Admiral of the English fleet for the guard of the Narrow Seas. He had arrived in the Downs from Scotland on the evening of July 7th/17th. (Cf. Mainwaring, *op. cit.*)

2 MS. *Senes.*   3 MS. *Groote geus.*

Beachy bore N.E. by north 5 miles from us, the wind at N.E. by N. Sailed E. by S. with fine weather.

The 14 *ditto* in the morning the wind at N.N.E. sailed east. Beachy bore N.N.W. from us 5 miles off; about noon it became calm, stopped the ebb tide in 17 fathom. Beachy as before 4 miles off; at 2 o'clock there came a breeze at W.S.W. We sailed westwards to W.N.W. At sundown Beachy bore N.W. from us 4½ miles; set our course N. eastwards, and sent Captain Dorrevelt to Dover.

The 15 in the morning at sundown the wind was W.N.W. We were between Dover and Cap Grisnez. Shaped our course N.E. by N. About 9 of the clock sent our shallop ashore at Calais, and about southern sun Captain Dorrevelt joined us from Dover, bringing 2 letters from Cornelis Bos, who wrote that tidings had been received at Dover that the fleet still lay in La Coruña with 36 ships; withal there was still no likelihood of its coming over before October, whilst there was a great mortality in their ships, 7 men having died in one night in a King's ship.

He also wrote that the enemy's frigates[1] were making ready to ravage the fishery; that a flyboat had been fetched out from Ostend to Dunkirk so as to be sent to La Coruña with letters, as she was an excellent sailer. He added that Banker had sailed from Dover yesterday with his 6 sail for Dunkirk and had handed him all his letters likewise, whilst Brederode had been detained in arrest in the Downs for three days, having then been released and sailed from the Downs on Wednesday last.

Our shallop coming alongside brought a letter from Glarges, in answer to mine; declared that the coming of the Spanish fleet still tarried, and that the latest advices from Dunkirk stated that 18 frigates lay ready there to put to sea in two squadrons, albeit they had employed all the crews against the French,[2] who had marched on Gravelines and taken 3 guns from the enemy besides 200 prisoners and some killed, but had to beat a retreat again since the ford[3] over the river was so

[margin notes] Arrive off Dover, Calais and Dunkirk.

Letters from Glargius.

---

1 At Dunkirk.   2 On shore.
3 MS. *de pas*, so perhaps "bridge" is meant. Anyway it was a narrow passage of some kind.

strongly held. We steered along the shore towards Dunkirk, off which we came to an anchor at 5 o'clock in the evening, finding 5 Englishmen in the Scheur[1] with 12 or 13 ships and frigates ready in the harbour; also found inside the Brake[2] 5 buoys with anchors, some whereof were fished up by our ships, for we saw that they were frigates' anchors, wherefore we presumed that Commander Bancque who had sailed yesterday to Dunkirk, must have chased and pursued some frigates lying at anchor in the Braeck, the more so since those of Calais had heard heavy firing; the wind W.S. west.

The 16 *August* in the morning the wind W.S.W. with hazy weather. At daybreak we sent Captain Halffhoorn to Calais to bring the boats and passengers in the Brake, and at the same time bring the St Malo trader.[3] There was a small sail eastwards of our bank which we lost to the east. In the afternoon an English Royal convoy 5 sail strong came into the Scheur, one of which grounded near the Mardyke bank; there passed outside the bank Cornelis Evertsz. coming from Cap d'Antifer and had also taken with him in passing the [above-named?] boats; to whom Halfhoorn spoke saying he should go again to the Admiral, so he forthwith joined us; at nightfall came Captain Ham who had found the victualling ship, as per margin, and anchored near us.

The 17 in the morning the wind W. by S. Signalled all the Captains to repair aboard and ordered that as many Captains as possible should take their victuals on board. About noon Skipper Thomas How of Yarmouth came aboard, being skipper in an English King's yacht, *de Roode Bocq*[4] lying in the Scheur; he asked whether since we now lay here we would let his convoy, being 18 sail, come out of the harbour of Dunkirk, to go with him (Anthony Woolward)[5] to the Downs, or if the

(51)
Blockade Dunkirk. Adm. Tromp, Vice-Adm. De With, de Zeeu, Halfhoorn, Jan Gerbrantssen, Waterdrincker, Bachuijsen, Lops, Adr. Domenssen, 't Hovelingh, Snip, Dorrevelt, the St. Malo flyboat, Cap^n Camp the Convoyer of the victualling ships, Ham, Cats, M. Gillisz., Brederode, Post, Janse, Dorrevelt, 't Kint, Waterdrincker, Salamander.

1 The inner road of Dunkirk; see note under May 12th.
2 The Braek of modern charts—the outer road of Dunkirk.
3 See under Aug. 11th.
4 *I.e. Roebuck.* In the lists of the English fleet for the guard of the Narrow Seas 1639 (*vide* Mainwaring, *op. cit.* 1), the *Roebuck* is rated as a pinnace and commanded by Anthony Woolward.
5 MS. *Willaert.* How was presumably the mate of Woolward's ship.

aforesaid merchantmen should have to stay within, whilst he should have to go to the Downs alone. We answered him that hitherto we had no orders to hinder their convoys of merchantmen, save only contraband goods such as Spanish men and money, wherefore their convoy could come out by day, but not by night, because we treated as enemies whatsoever came out at night.

The same skipper also declared that there were four frigates, one of them with 24 and the other 3 with 20 guns each, which would have come out before daybreak this morning had there but been a [favourable] wind, and would still continually try to get out, though the other frigates of which the harbour was full made as yet no preparation to come out. Towards evening we sent a written order to Commander Ham, to follow the enemy, should they come out, with the Captains de Zeeu and Halfhoorn and the oared yacht of Dorrevelt; and if only 2 came out Lieve de Zeeu should remain lying. After sunset the wind shifted S.E. The yacht crept close under the harbour, and the Vice-Admiral de With's shallop on the watch.

(51)
Verso

The 18 *August* in the morning the wind was W.S.W. Captain Ham and his victualling skipper came aboard us and complained about much stinking beer, wherefore we formally instructed Captains de Zeeu and Halffhoorn to test the same and to discharge the most undrinkable into the victualling ship and take over the good. At 7 o'clock we saw about six ships coming out of the west, it was an English King's convoy. The merchantmen having entered into the Scheur, the convoyer clapped on a wind and beat up westwards again; with the flood tide the merchantmen ran out of the Scheur into the harbour.

The 19 *ditto* in the morning the wind was W.S.W. The enemy still lay as before. At about 8 o'clock a French privateer bore up under our stern, and had no news, neither had he sighted any States' or enemy's ships. We asked him if he met any States' ships at sea to tell them to come and join us. In the afternoon it became dark with misly rain; on the flood tide came 2 small boats, 1 ketch with 2 boyers and 3 small boats out of Dunkirk all English save one Scot; our shallop went to

Some English and
Scotch merchantmen
come out from
Dunkirk.

them but not being able to regain us rowed to Captain Halffhoorn. Towards evening our shallop came alongside. The Scot declared that 4 frigates were lying ready, which had intended to come out had we not have arrived, but that the Pagador[1] had forbidden the same, whence they would not come out until they were 20 strong, albeit little trust can be placed upon what the Scotch and English say. [Hoity-Toity!]

The. 20 *ditto* in the morning the wind at W. with a raw gale and thick misly weather; the enemy lay kedged within the Oostcartey, [as also were] 3 English, viz. 2 square-rigged ships and a smack sail. Towards evening one of the 3 ships that lay behind the Oostcartey[2] warped into the harbour again, as likewise did the Dunkirkers lying with their stems against the boom, for they had towed further in, tho' whether to come out to form a squadron as the Scotchman who came out of Dunkirk yesterday said, the time will yet show. At sunset the wind mostly southerly with handsome weather.

(52)

The 21 *ditto* in the morning the wind was S.W. At sunrise 4 Englishmen came out of the harbour, who declared that when we arrived here there were 4 frigates on the point of setting sail, but these were now determined not to come out before a squadron was formed; they also said that there were no frigates at sea, whilst the last (being a small frigate) had arrived at Ostend 3 days since. One of the skippers named Sr Christopher Wilton living at Wapping said that Captain Mouweris[3] of Dover was expected to come out, having a flyboat of about 300–360 tons with a gallery, having on board some metal cannon bound for Spain; that there was also a flyboat expected out bound for the west, with a top, but without a beakhead, with a blue strake.

At about 10 o'clock a small ship passed by us, being the *Hasewintje* of Vlissingen; said that on the day before yesterday he had sailed from Falmouth with Captain Keert de Koe, and he had sailed close-hauled from Beachy. In the evening with

1 Paymaster.
2 Some pier or mole is meant, I suppose.
3 Morris (?).

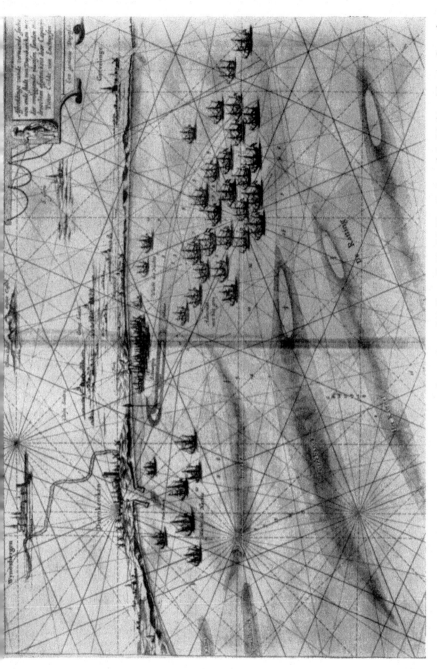

Photo taken and kindly supplied by Mr Van Nouhuys of the Maritiem Museum, Rotterdam

THE BLOCKADE OF DUNKIRK

(Showing usual dispositions of the Dutch blockading squadrons.)

high water yet another Englishman came out of the harbour, who was visited by Skipper Adriaen Domens; was in ballast and bound for Newcastle, and at nightfall Captain Keert de Koe came to an anchor before Mardyke; the wind at S.W. with a stiff breeze.

The 22 August the wind was N. with fine calm weather. Captain Keert de Koe came driving with the flood within the Brake and did his best to discharge his victualling ship. During the day the wind shifted N.E. with a fresh gale; the English King's ship sent his shallop with a King's flag to before the harbour, and 20 or 22 English merchantmen came out therefrom, of whom part sailed straight through the Scheur, and a part outside Vuijlbaert[1] to the King's convoy in the Scheur. We also dispatched the Commander in the Scheur (Jan Jacobs Lops) to set ashore [unintelligible] at Dover for the Hon. Directors of Enchuijsen so as to prepare the salved goods,[2] and thence to proceed to under Portland to bring the victualling smacks under the flag, so as they could be convoyed with a warship to the Downs; after doing this he was to pick up the aforesaid goods [at Dover?] & bring them in safety whilst he (Lops) on his way should take under his protection as far as Portland the victualling ships discharged by our ships, namely Leendert Jansz. and Jan Dircxsz. of Rotterdam, with Jan Gerbrantsz. Abbas, skipper of Enchuijsen.

Lops goes to Portland with the victualling ships.

The 23 ditto in the morning the wind east, with a steady breeze; three English fishers ran out from the harbour into the Scheur, whilst another small vessel and a flyboat in the harbour made ready to come out, but the little vessel on reaching the outermost "duc dalba"[3] turned back again, though the flyboat came to an anchor near us.

1 A bank on the outer edge of the Scheur or inner road. See note under May 12th.

2 The whole of this sentence is extremely confused in the original MS. The "salved goods" presumably refer to those saved from the *Eendracht* (perhaps an East or West Indiaman) which is often referred to elsewhere in the *Journal* as having been wrecked, though how or where is never stated. See September 13th.

3 *I.e.* harbour poles, or mooring poles. This (says Captain Naber, R.N.N.) is probably the oldest place in literature where the word *ducdalf* occurs. It is apparently derived from the Duke of Alba, but in what manner is unknown.

We fetched the skipper on board; he was William Barbeets of Yarmouth who had brought deal to Dunkirk and was now ballasted with sand; he said that the little vessel which had put back into the harbour was full of piece-goods, and bound for Dover, there to collect an English pass and to go with his lading to San Lucar; the skipper was from Deal in the Downs, whilst most of the remainder were Englishmen. He added that there were also 25 frigates small and great lying within the harbour, whereof 5 were new ones which had never been to sea; as yet 8 of that total were ready, with sails hoisted, fitted out and victualled, which meant to come out at the first opportunity; they were mounted with 18, 16 and 10 guns; whilst the remainder were on the point of being fitted out. These were all the frigates which sailed from Flanders, save only a frigate arrived at Ostend. He added that there were men enough within to bring the said frigates out to sea, but they were of all nations; he said that the enemy was expected to come from La Coruña with 50 sail carrying 11,000 foot and a great quantity of money.

In the afternoon the English convoy made sail out of the Scheur 25 sail strong which were visited by our ships, though finding nothing but ballast therein we let them go. The victualling ships Skippers Leendert Jansz. and Abbas[1] left us, whilst the convoyer Lops remained hove-to so as to wait for Gerbrant Jansz., who was discharged by noon and then followed them, tho' when all the victualling ships were out of sight we still saw Lops.

Cap^n Camp joins us.

Towards evening the wind came S.W. Captain Camp joined us having brought the St Malo flyboat to the Texel;[2] he had no news other than that he had spoken the Commander of Enchuijsen sailing amidst the busses off the Texel, who had met with no difficulties of any kind.

Today we gave orders that all tides in the flood notwithstanding,[3] 2 ships with the oared yacht should keep under sail close to the harbour, whilst at night another three boats should

---

1 *I.e.* Jan Gerbrantsz.; see under Aug. 22nd.
2 See under Aug. 11th and 16th.
3 *Sic.* MS. *alle getijden inde vloet can....*

be with them. We summoned Captain Halfhoorn from before Mardyke, who joined us. In the evening an English hooker of Dover came out of the harbour, which continued its course after being visited by us.

The 24 ditto in the morning the wind at W.S.W. A ship warped up to the east pier, being an enemy frigate which was paid during the day; at about 4 o'clock the ship of Captain Ringelsz. joined us, the Captain having remained ashore; came from Dover yesterday where she had left Captain Van Diemen's ship and had no news. During the day we issued orders concerning the pursuit of the enemy should they come out, and laid the clean ships close before the harbour. At sundown we saw 6 sail coming from the west, who signalled us. The wind at west with calm weather.

Ringels joins us from home.

(53)

The 25 August in the morning it was calm weather, the wind at S.S.E. with thick mist. Captains Keert de Koe, Camp, Adriaen Domensz. and Dorrevelt were under sail with 6 or 7 shallops and boats. At about 8 o'clock the mist lifted; the enemy lay as before except a frigate that lay on the careen. 3 shallops came and tried to run into the Scheur, and fired upon our boats both with great cannon as with muskets, and the enemy retired into the harbour. 't Howeling had sailed to Mardyke during the day to relieve Ham and de Zeeu. The 6 sail discovered to westwards yesterday evening weighed their anchors and stood towards us, and anchored off Mardyke, whilst Ham and de Zeeu joined us. During the day we were joined by 2 French privateers whilst the enemy paid those 2 frigates that lay in the harbour.

There was sentenced today in our ship a sailor of the ship *Wassende Maen* of skipper Lambert Snip; this man had struck and threatened the skipper, breaking out into mutiny with a bare knife, broke the locks of his irons asunder, and other things besides; he was keel-hauled 3 times and whipped with a wet bum[1] as much as he could bear, his wages forfeited, and discharged

Wm. Claessen van Blocqziel keel-hauled.

1 *met het nat gat gelaerst.* The *laars* was the thick end of a rope with a whipping of tarred sail yarn wound round it, with which the severe corporal punishments were inflicted. In the nineteenth century the *laars* was about 10 cm. thick in circumference, and about 1 metre long. The end with which the blows were

Yet another 2 sailors from the yard-arm.

the fleet. Another 2 sailors of Captain Keert de Koe, namely Pieter Jacobsz. quarter-gunner and Jan Meinertsz. sailor, both of Hoorn, who had cut each other in the cheek,[1] were also sentenced, viz. the gunner to be ducked 3 times from the yard-arm; as also the other; and they were both to be whipped by the men of their watch in Captain Keert de Koe's ship. At sunset the wind east with a fair breeze.

Commr. Cats joins us from Guernsey, and Jan Teeue from Wight. Joris Cats, Matijs Gillisse, Thoen, Meij and Veen.
From Wight. Sluijs, Bancque, Lt. Bagijn.

(53)
Verso

Snip and Veen go to look for Bancque.

The 26 *August* in the morning the wind at N.W. The Rear-Admiral joined us with his squadron; towards noon the ship of Captain Van Diemen joined us; he declared that he had separated from Commander Bancque outside the Flemish banks on the 15 ditto, with orders to bring the 2 victualling ships into the Maas in safety, whilst Commander Bancque who was 11 strong on uniting with Brederode, sailed northwards to cruise about the fishery on the enemy, whom Jonkheer Brederode was certain was out since he had only seen 4 or 5 English merchantmen lying in the harbour, yet was he deceived because the enemy lay ready in the harbour; we therefore sent Commander Snip along the coast of Flemish Zeeland and Holland, keeping a kenning[2] off the land, over to the

inflicted was usually free of the tackling, whilst the end of the part held in the hand was crowned by a heavy knot (see note on p. 10 of S. P. L'Honoré Naber's *Piet Heyn*, Utrecht 1928). As the man's breeches were wet from the keel-hauling, the pain was considerably increased; it was quite as painful as the cat.

1 *I.e.* "Snicker-sneeing", as the fighting with knives amongst the Dutch was called. Nares in his Glossary derives the word "Snick-a-snee" from the Icelandic *snikka*, "to nick, cut". In Norfolk a sort of large clasp knife is still called "snickersnee". Fryer in his account of Surat, *c.* 1673, refers to the "snicker-sneeing amongst the Dutch; ripping one anothers Bellies open with short Knives". [See the Hakluyt Society edition, vol. xix of Series ii, 1909, of his *Travels*, i, p. 299 and note 1, whence the above is taken.]

2 According to Captain S. P. L'Honoré Naber, R.N.N., the mean worth of a kenning is 6·18 Km. or 3·34 modern sea miles, though other estimates vary from 6·1 to 3·2 modern sea miles. In the seventeenth century, however, the kenning was a measure entirely left to the caprice of individual skippers to determine, and its actual value varied greatly. See *De Mijl voor het jaar* 1617, by Timeeis (= S. P. L'Honoré Naber) in the *Koninklijk Nederlandsch Aardrijkskundig Genootschap*, 2 Serie, deel 37, 1920. T. W. Fulton in his book *Sovereignty of the Seas*, London 1911, states that a land-kenning (in England and Scotland) was 14 miles, 2 kennings = 28 (pp. 222–3). On p. 545 a kenning is stated to be "the range of vision from sea to land, determined from the maintop of the vessel", and this seems to me to be what Tromp meant here. The distance would vary

Dogger Bank, and Captain Veen along the English coast a kenning off the shore, as far as the Well Bank[1] and thence to the Dogger, to look for Commander Bancke and bring him here; both of them set out in the evening. Captain Elbertsz. with his convoy came to an anchor west of Gravelines so as to stop the flood tide. During the day we gave orders that Cats, Gillisz., and Sluijs should take over the victuals sent them with skipper Willem Ariensz. of Schiedam. We also victualled for 6 weeks by borrowing from our other ships, Captain Veen, t Hoen, and Cornelis Meij. At sunset it blew a hard gale, the wind at W.S.W. During the day at low water the enemy had paid 2 frigates in the harbour.

The 27 *ditto* in the morning the wind at S.W. by W. with fine weather; the enemy again paid a frigate in the harbour. During the day we gave orders that all the cleanest and best-sailing ships should pursue any of the enemy's ships that came out. Towards the evening there arrived Joris Pietersz. Broeck, who had been sent by us to La Coruña on the 5th instant; he declared that on coming off La Coruña on the 10th inst. he had discovered 3 galleons & three pinnaces[2] with white Admirals' and Vice-Admirals' flags which ran into La Coruña; he had also been close inshore on the 13 ditto, when he saw a fleet of 59 ships over the spit beyond the fishing-village; amongst them two Admirals' flags, viz. one Burgundian[3] and one white, apparently the Flemish and Spanish Admiral[s]. 7 ships of this fleet were lying out in the mouth of the harbour, and he had not been able to get any more information; furthermore since it was such foul weather, and he could not well ride out the storm, he has therefore returned hither. During the day the victuals of Captain Brederode and Post were distributed amongst our ships. At sunset the wind shifted N.N.W. We ordered Captain Claes Ham to go as Commander before

with the conditions of visibility, etc., but the ship was to keep just within sight of land.

1 The Well Bank, east of the Wash.

2 MS. *patassen*, from the Sp.-Port. *Pataxo*.

3 *I.e.* the diagonal red cross on a white ground—"the ragged Staff", as the English sometimes called it.

Mardyke over Captains Halfhoorn, Camp, and Fredricq 't Hovelingh.

About midnight the wind was S.S.W. by south; our boats that lay on watch signalled that 2 frigates were coming out, who were followed shooting by our oared yacht Dorrevelt and by Captain Keert de Koe; but Captain Cornelis Meij remained lying at anchor, since he had not yet read his signal book which had been given him at S.W. sun.

(54)

The 28 *August* in the morning the wind was S.W. by S. with fine weather. Captain Dorrevelt with the oared yacht and Captain Keert de Koe lay anchored ½ mile eastwards of us. Dorrevelt came on board, and declared that he had seen 2 small frigates which he had chased, but he had lost sight of them of a sudden; we also missed the galliot out of the Scheur.

Miss the galliot with 2 small frigates.

During the day we signalled all Captains to repair on board, and instructed them concerning the chasing signals, with a sharp admonishment carefully to heed the pursuit of the out-coming enemy. At about 3 o'clock there came a King's convoy of 10 sail; the 10 ran into the Scheur whilst Captain Barle[1] made for Ostend with his ship and 2 merchantmen, but grounded on the west end of the Brake; and as this was happening, two ships looking for the English convoy joined us from the west; they were 2 French double-shallop privateers, tho' we did not know whence they were,[2] which privateers laid on board one of the merchantmen (a small ship) in the gap in the Brake and carried him off with them.

Captain Burley therefore came aboard us and asked us to stop the same, but we had no orders to justify our interfering, whereon he went away discontented; we fired 5 guns as a salute and offered to help him with men and cables or whatever else he

---

1 From the lists given in Peter White, *op. cit.*, it appears that this officer was Captain John Burley in command of the *Second Whelp*. In 1647 Captain John Burley, who was a gentleman of good family in the Isle of Wight, beat the drum in Newport to rouse the populace to rescue King Charles, then a prisoner in Carisbrooke Castle. The response was ludicrous in the extreme, only one man with an old musket, and a few women, responding to the call. Although no harm was done, Burley was nevertheless tried by a packed jury, found guilty of treason, and duly beheaded.

2 This is all very involved, but the original is still more so.

stood in need of, for which he thanked us. At sundown the wind E. afterwards E. and south-east.

About one of the clock our boats that were lying on watch signalled that an enemy's ship was coming out, and the oared yacht of Captain Meij chased after her firing off his guns as signal.

With high water Captain Burley and his merchantman got off the shoal and continued their voyage.

The 29 August in the morning the wind was southerly with fair weather. Saw lying in the Scheur a small frigate with a little boat, which had come out of the harbour at night.

At daybreak a ship of the watch off Mardyke beat up to westwards, whilst both the chasers—Dorrevelt and Meij— rejoined us. With the flood tide the frigate ran into the harbour again together with the English merchantmen arrived with the last convoy; the packet-boat and another ship came from westwards into the Scheur, whilst the enemy warped 2 stout frigates up to the harbour entrance.

(54)
Verso
Ships come from the harbour into the Scheur by night.

There came a shallop from Calais aboard, with a letter from the Heer Gouverneur with an extract from one of Noijers,[1] His Majesty's Secretary, stating that the Spaniards would do their utmost to bring their troops in La Coruña over to Dunkirk, wherefore he (the Governor) should inform the Admiral of Holland thereof; there was yet another excerpt out of a letter from Dover dated the 27 instant, stating that a friend who had come from La Coruña had understood from Vice-Admiral Rombout,[2] that there was such sickness raging in the fleet, worse than the plague, that there was no likelihood of the Armada leaving before All Saints' Day, albeit the ships lay ready.

De Glarges wrote that our men had marched away from Gelder and our whole army now lay at Rijnbercq; that the Marquis de Lede[3] with one army and the Cardinal-Infant[4] with

Tidings from Gelder.

1 De Noyers, secretary of Louis XIII. A number of his letters are quoted in De la Roncière, *op. cit.*

2 A great Dunkirker privateer, for whose life and portrait see H. Malo, *Les Corsaires Dunkerquois*, 1, p. 400, Paris 1912.

3 General of the Spanish forces on the Maas.

4 Ferdinand of Austria, the victor of Nördlingen and Governor of the Spanish Netherlands.

plundering by the
French Armada.

another were near our army; further that the Admiral Monsieur de Bordeaux[1] had again landed in Biscay, plundered Laredo, captured the Castle of San Antonio with 100 guns, and seized much booty; on the way he had sunk one Spanish galleon and taken another, each with 40 bronze cannon;[2] we answered his letter.

4 enemy frigates
come out of the
harbour and are
pursued by our
ships.

The 30 *ditto* in the morning at one o'clock our boats made signal, 4 frigates came out of the harbour, and were pursued by Captain Keert de Koe, the oared yacht and Dorrevelt eastwards, the wind at S.W. by west; we fell in with Mathijs Gillisz. who likewise ought to have followed; we immediately sent him in pursuit to westwards, and in the event of his not finding them to warn the fishery in all haste, and thence after 7 or 8 days to find his Commander, whether Keert de Koe or Catz. At southern sun Captain Joris with the oared yacht rejoined us; an hour before daybreak he had anchored, Nieuport bearing from him S.E. by east, 4 miles off, having then lost the enemy in a thick squall of rain; tho' our three ships pursued the enemy N.N. eastwards yet he had seen but one frigate. When the sun was in the S.W. we signalled all Captains to repair on board, gave them further signals for chasing the enemy, and ordered Captain Jan Gerbrantsz. to anchor right over against the harbour, so as to afford a refuge for our boats lying on the watch; and when the boats should give the alarm with their muskets, then Captain Gerbrantsz. should fire as many shots with his great cannon, and hang up lanterns and leave them hanging until half ebb, if enemy ships should come out, so that the whole fleet can see how many ships have come out.

(55)

Commander Catz made a great pother about following the enemy eastwards, because his pilot was dead and his mate did not wish to take the responsibility, but would on the contrary steer out to the offing if the enemy came out; we considered that this would be the greatest disservice for the Land, if when the enemy came out we turned our backs on them instead of following them; many words passed over this matter and finally

---

1 Henri de Sourdis, Archbishop of Bordeaux.
2 De la Roncière, *op. cit.* pp. 53–4. This feat occurred at Santoña on Aug. 16th.

the pilot of Vice-Admiral de With was ordered to go over into Cats' ship.

At sunset the wind was E. by S. and E.S.E. with hard rain and wind; at 10 o'clock the wind shifted S., then S.S.W. with thick heavy rain; about high water the wind at S.W. with rough squally weather of rain, wind and lightning.

The 31 *August* in the morning at break of day the wind was W. by S. blowing a storm. The Vice-Admiral de With dragged his cable and drove betwixt Cats and us, his bowsprit topsail yard[1] fouled Cats' main shrouds and he brought up the ship with the sheet-anchor. When it was day we missed 2 small frigates, each with a top-gallant mast, from the harbour, and saw that the boat had likewise run out of the Scheur, whilst our boats which had lain on watch before the Scheur were driven hither and thither by the storm, Captain Camp's boat in one direction, we and our boat in another, whilst Captain Jan Harmansz.'s boat had got loose and drifted away without anyone in her. At sundown it was handsome weather, so that at the turn of the ebb tide the boats again rowed to before the harbour on the watch, viz. ours, the Vice-Admiral and Jan van Duijrens' boats.

2 frigates come out of the harbour & the boat from the Scheur.

The first September in the morning before daylight we set up our topmasts and squared the yards. The wind at S. it blew a hard gale, the enemy lying as before. At 8 o'clock we signalled all Captains to repair on board, and asked whether anyone had seen the enemy come out at night, they all answered no. The Court-martial treated of the collision between the ships of Captains Sluijs and Halfhoorn on the 8 of last month one hour before daybreak, when Sluijs lost his beakhead and Halfhoorn had a great hole made in the side; withal after examination of both parties by the Court it was pronounced to be an accident and disaster of the sea notwithstanding both sides having done their best to prevent the same, and therefore were not liable to punishment. At southern sun the wind chopped S.W. with hard rain and weather; we struck our topmasts and lowered our yards. At sundown the wind W.S.W. with hard raw weather.

(55)
Verso

Jan Teeue and Halfhoorn on board.

1 MS. *bovenblindereede* (spritsail-topsail yard).

The 2 September in the morning the wind was W.S.W. with a steady gale. At daybreak we set up our topmasts and squared the yards. When the sun was in the S.W. a Scotchman came out from the harbour who declared that a small frigate had come out at night and that altogether 12 or 13 frigates were out, including 2 galliots, whilst there still lay 6 or 7 inside, some which were to be fitted out; there was news ashore that the fleet in La Coruña was lying ready to set sail above 14 days since. Captain Colster with his 5 sail then joined us, having separated from Commander Bancque on the 24 August off the mouth of the Tees;[1] he (Bancque) was sailing with about 100 herring-fishers to the Texel, and Colster with 3 herring-ships to the Maas, with the intention of coming here under the flag after having brought the herring-ships home in safety. Towards evening a French pinnace joined us, bringing a letter of recommendation from de Glarges which stated that in the said vessel was the King's courier, with letters of importance, besides the son of the Chancellor of Denmark, the Heer Rantzow de Jonge with a party of noblemen[2] and other gentlemen of quality who asked, if it was possible, for convoy to the Wielingen; we therefore immediately sent Captain Tjaert to bring these people to the Wielingen, after which he is to rejoin the flag here forthwith.

The 3 ditto in the morning the wind was S.S.W. and S.W. with handsome weather. Skipper Willem Adriaensz., our victualling ship from Amsterdam, got under sail, and beat up to westwards out of the Brake; towards evening the wind W.S.W. with rain; in the evening an English King's yacht joined us in the Brake, bringing a letter from the Great Admiral[3] Pennington with a copy of a letter of the Lord High Admiral[4]

Colster's squadron Vijch, Pr. Pieterse, Post, Tjaert.
Bancker's squadron Brederode, Abram Crijnssen, den Oven, Hollaert, Farant.

A King's yacht arrives with letters from Pennington.

1 MS. *Tese.*
2 MS. *Engelsman*—obviously a copyist's error for *Edelman.* (N.)
3 MS. *Grooten Admiral.* Whether Pennington really was the "Great Admiral" of England or not I do not know, but the post certainly existed. *Vide* article on "Naval Executive Ranks" in the *M.M.* 11, pp. 106–112. The office was instituted in 1406 and was ninth in order of precedence of the great State offices.
4 Also *Grooten Admiral* in MS. but Northumberland was really the Lord High Admiral, having been appointed to the post on April 13th/23rd, 1638, in substitution for the infant James, Duke of York. His term ended in 1642. Over the

of England dated the 11 August, old style, wherein Pennington (56)
was ordered to show us the letter of the Lord High Admiral
stating that His Majesty of England forbade that any of us
Hollanders should visit any of his subjects' ships, on pain that
if the same occurs after this warning His Majesty will regard
it as an affront against his honour, and would revenge himself
on that person [who committed it]; whereon we answered
Pennington that we had only sought for Spanish soldiery, and
that we were sending the aforesaid letter and copy by express
to our Supreme Authorities who would decide regarding the
same.[1] In the evening we sent an order to Commander Ham
off Mardyke, that he should send Lambert Halfhoorn to Calais
for the boats bound for Vlissingen.

The 4 ditto in the morning the wind at S.W. with handsome
weather, Captain Dorrevelt joined us at 9 o'clock; after he had
gone in pursuit of the enemy on the night of the 29th last, in
the morning of the 30 he had sighted only one Dunkirker, close
to him, whilst Keert de Koe had lost his main topmast,
wherefore he (Dorrevelt) put about in order to rejoin us. Held
a Council of War. Discharged Van Diemen's ship of all his
victuals, so as to go to the Goeree Gat with express letters
and Calais boats. Before noon the English yacht grounded on
the Brake, whence he got off at one o'clock. At about 4 o'clock
there came Frans Jansz. from Vlissingen and Tjaert, both of
whom anchored near Camp[2] before the Sleu. At sundown a
boyer and a small boat came out from the east end of the
Scheur. We fetched the skippers aboard, and they declared that
no men could be obtained to take the King's ships to sea, whilst
there were 7 or 8 privateers at sea, whereof 2 were likewise
merchantmen, one being Fredrick Stadt's and the other from
Denmark. During the evening the inhabitants of Calais fired
salvos for the taking of the little place of Salsie.[3]

Dorrevelt rejoins us, after having pursued the outcoming enemy.

Victory rejoicings over the taking of Salsie.

office of Lord High Admiral which was instituted in 1547 see W. G. Perrin's
article in the *M.M.* xii, 1926, pp. 132–159.

1 The letters of Tromp and Pennington are printed in full in *Cal. S. P. Dom.*
1639, pp. 444, 457.

2 *I.e.* near Captain Camp. I cannot identify the Sleu unless it be the Snouw bank
which forms a westerly continuation of the Braek, or the Splinter of English accounts.

3 Unidentified. Some petty hamlet in Flanders no doubt.

Van Diemen's ship goes home.

The 5 September in the morning the wind was W.S.W. Captain Halfhoorn came from Calais with 3 boats, wherewith the ship of Van Diemen [carrying] the Lieutenant Bagijn with our letters set sail at southern sun, running straight over the banks to the offing; we all careened our ships; we sent Captain Commander Tjaert with a written order to Mardyke for Commander Ham, that he should get under sail tomorrow and follow us. We resolved that the Vice-Admiral de With should stay in the Brake with 10 ships, whilst we would cruise westwards between Beachy and the Narrows with 13; furthermore, when Commander Bancker should arrive to take over the chief command in the Brake, then Vice-Admiral de With should follow us with some ships. In the evening the wind southerly with a stiff gale.

Remain in the Brake
Vice-Adm. de With, Cats, T Hoen, Frans Janssen, Sluijs, Waterdrincker, Adrian Domensz., Zeen, Dorrevelt.

(56)
Verso

Go to cruise to the Westwards
Admiral, Colster, P. Pieters, Ham, Halfhoorn, Tjaert, Post, Jan Gerbrants, Ringels, Bachuijsen, F. Pietersz., Vijch, Camp.

The 6 ditto in the morning the wind was S. with a stiff gale. We weighed our anchors and steered westwards, leaving the Vice-Admiral lying. An English merchantman also put out of the Scheur ahead of us. Skipper Willem Adriaensz. had again come off Mardyke and followed us westwards; during the day the wind veered S.W. by S. with a topsail gale. At southern sun 3 Lübeckers sailing before the wind passed us, which were spoken by our ships. We beat up to windward until the turn of the ebb tide and then came to an anchor in 16 fathom, Calais bearing S. by W. from us. We set taut our main shrouds. At the turn of the flood tide we again got under sail and plied to westwards.

The 7 ditto in the morning the wind at S. We were close under Calais Cliff and steered for Calais. I went ashore in person, congratulated the Lord Governor, the Comte de Charost, and at south-western sun we returned aboard. Some salutes were fired from the town, and the Governor came on board our ship with his wife and all his retinue, and after having stayed for 2 hours he returned to the land. We saluted him with several guns, and got under sail an hour after midday; we steered westwards and were joined by the ship of Vlieger, which had left Teer Veer on Sunday, having on board some letters for Glarges and passengers for Dieppe; we therefore

Jan Pouwels joins us with the ship of Vlieger.

gave him an order to come and find us about Beachy after having landed the passengers.

The 8 September the wind south with a fresh gale; an hour before daybreak we tacked eastwards and came thwart of Boulogne,[1] and at 8 o'clock tacked westwards. Skipper Willem Adriaensz. meanwhile continued to stand to westwards; the sun S.S.W. we again lay over out to sea and the sun S.S.W.[2] to the north again. We discovered 7 tall ships and made sail after them, and coming up with them they were English King's ships steering for the Downs. We tacked away from them, being still a long way out of range. At sunset [they were] W.N.W. from us 6 miles, the wind mostly at west; 7 glasses in the first watch the wind backed W.S.W. Tacked westwards.

The 9 ditto in the morning the wind at S.W. by W. In the forenoon we again tacked to southwards, and were close under Beachy. We spoke a small English ship of London whither he was bound, but we could not understand whence he came. At ten o'clock we again lay over to the west and towards evening the wind backed S.E. with handsome weather. At sunset Beachy bore 3 miles north from us. We took in our topsails and stood to westwards. We saw another sail W.S.W. from us and presumed that it was skipper Willem Adriaensz.;[3] when the first watch was out the wind was again S.S.W. We tacked to the south-east.

The 10 ditto in the morning the wind was S. with a gentle gale. We saw Beachy S. by E.[4] from us 6 miles and at 8 o'clock tacked westwards. At southern sun we cast about to the northward and sailed straight before the wind to England; we discovered a sail and followed him to Fairlight; it was a laden flyboat, apparently a free man. At 4 o'clock we clapped upon a wind westwards, and sailed west by north. Towards evening we discovered yet another 2 sail off Beachy, and held towards them, and on its becoming calm at sunset we brailed up all our sails and so drifted to southwards, Beachy N.W. from us 3 miles

7 English King's ships pass us.

(57)

1 MS. *Bolonie.*
2 Should be either S.W. or W.S.W. (N.)
3 See under Sept. 6th.   4 Probably N. by W.

off. It lightened a great deal, and an hour after sunset the wind was E.N.E., whilst during most of the night it was stark calm.

The 11 *ditto* in the morning at daybreak the wind at west with handsome weather. We saw 2 sail under Fairlight that were doing their best to beat up to westwards, besides another 2 sail westwards of us which were first sailing in the offing, and when we made sail they bore up round and stood over to the land; Fairlight bore N. 3 miles; it being rainy; when it became calm we sent [some of] our Captains to the ships; one of them was an Englishman from London, come from Smyrna, the other being Dirck Pietersz. Dol of Enchuijsen, come from Livorno; they knew no news and were each of them homeward bound. We careened some of our ships; when the sun was in the S.W. there came a small breeze at S.W. by W. We lay over to the south. At sundown a ship came out of the wind towards us, we presumed it to be the ship of De Vlieger; we tacked to the north-west, Fairlight bore N.N.W. from us 7 miles off; we took in the fore-topsail. At noon we tacked to the south and at daybreak north again.

The 12 *September* in the morning little wind yet what there was W.N.W. by N. with variable squalls of rain. We discovered and there were round about us 4 boyers and some English ships, the boyers were Hamburgers with coals bound for Rouen, including amongst them a skipper Gerrit Jansz. of Amsterdam in the ship *Fortuijn* come out of Bayonne in France[1] on the 19th August bound for Hâvre where he had unladen some goods, and thence to London; he said that the enemy's Armada still lay ill-appointed in La Coruña, 30 ships strong, bound for Dunkirk.

News of the enemy.

The said skipper had also been off Belle Isle on the 21 ditto when he had met the French Armada, 35 warships strong with 4 or 5 fireships and 3 victualling ships, carrying about 1,000 foot-soldiers and again bound for La Coruña. He also declared that he had seen and spoken our flyboat in Wight, Jan Jacobsz. who was then still on his way to Portland. The sun E.S.E.

1 MS. *Bayoene de Frans.*

we bore up round and stood over to Hythe to water the fleet, and passed 2 English King's ships which lay off and eastwards of the point of Dungeness. About southern sun we came to an anchor thwart of Hythe Castle, sent our boats with casks to the shore, for water, but when they had landed them the wind shifted S.S.E. and blew a hard gale so that 3 or 4 boats became water-logged and the rest had perforce to return without water leaving their casks ashore; at sundown the wind was again west. We sent an order to the ship of Vlieger to get under sail and cruise westwards of us, so that if any enemy was discovered we could be at once warned thereof by him, who forthwith sailed out to sea.

The 13 *in the morning* at 3 o'clock light airs at W. Our boats all went for water; when day had dawned many Englishmen came out from the Downs and stopped the flood at the turn of the ebb tide. At southern sun the wind shifted S.W. again. Our look-out ship of Captain Vlieger rejoined us, not having seen anything except some sails that were English. Towards evening Cornelis Bos came on board; he said a fortnight last Saturday 2 English ships had come into Dover road from Spain, who had met 24 Lübeckers & Hamburgers, one of which had 30 guns and the others less, together with a Spanish galleon [of] Don Antonio [de Oquendo] which was convoying them to La Coruña for reinforcement of the fleet of 36 Spanish ships, already lying there, to bring over the infantry.

Cornelis Bos comes on board from under Hythe, bringing news of the enemy.

Saturday last there had also come into Dover road an English[man] with a Hamburger ship coming out of Spain; he said he had likewise met the Easterling fleet, and a few hours after passing them he had fallen in with the French Armada, whilst he had heard heavy gunfire at night so that he presumed they had encountered the Easterlings. He declared that he subsequently understood that the aforesaid Don Antonio had been sunk by the French.[1] Cornelis Bos added that the Commissary of the Directors of Enchuijsen had hired [a ship?] to

(58)

---

1 Nonsense. Don Antonio de Oquendo had safely effected his junction with Lope de Hoces in La Coruña.

take in the salved goods of the *Eendracht* for 23 pounds sterling.[1] [We weighed] with the fore-ebb towards evening and at 10 o'clock came to an anchor in 18 fathom; we spoke a Hamburger boyer who said that he had rode at anchor yesterday under the North Foreland near 5 Zeeland cruisers—apparently Commander Bancque with his cum socio [= consorts].

The 14 *September* in the morning at daybreak it was calm and slack water; we weighed our anchors and got under sail. Before sunrise a feeble breeze came out from the south; we did our best to ply to westwards; the sun south-west, the wind came S.W. and soon after we stood off from Beachy; at sundown we took in our topsails, Beachy bearing N.N.W. from us 3 miles off, we sailed S.S.E. out to sea. We had sent a written order to Captain Vijch to scout between the French coast and us for the Spanish fleet and other enemies.

The 15 *ditto* in the morning the wind was S.W.; we set our topsails; saw 3 or 4 English round about us; Captain Vijch left us for his rendezvous; Beachy bore 2 miles from us. At 7 o'clock we discovered 10 ships S.W. from us which were steering northwards; we finally saw that they were English merchantmen which we had met yesterday.[2] About S.W. sun saw a fleet of about 59 sail coming out from the west; we presumed that it was the Spanish Armada, put abroad the white flag and summoned all Captains to repair on board; we immediately resolved to dispatch Captain Tjaert to scour the sea with all haste to beyond the point of Dungeness, shooting 4 times in a glass[3] until in the Brake[4] inclusive, so as to warn our ships that they should proceed with all speed to Calais and thence to the westwards and into the Narrows to succour us, to the end that we might hold up the fleet which we hoped to near this evening, and thus to attack it with some hope of advantage.

1 Another obscure passage. Cf. note under Aug. 22nd.
2 Nothing is said of these ships under Sept. 14th. I think they were really the squadron of Vice-Admiral Mainwaring, who had been detached by Pennington to cruise between Beachy and Dungeness, though De Mello says that on the 15th the Spaniards met an Englishman who had encountered Tromp on the day before.
3 Four times every ½ hour.   4 Dunkirk road.

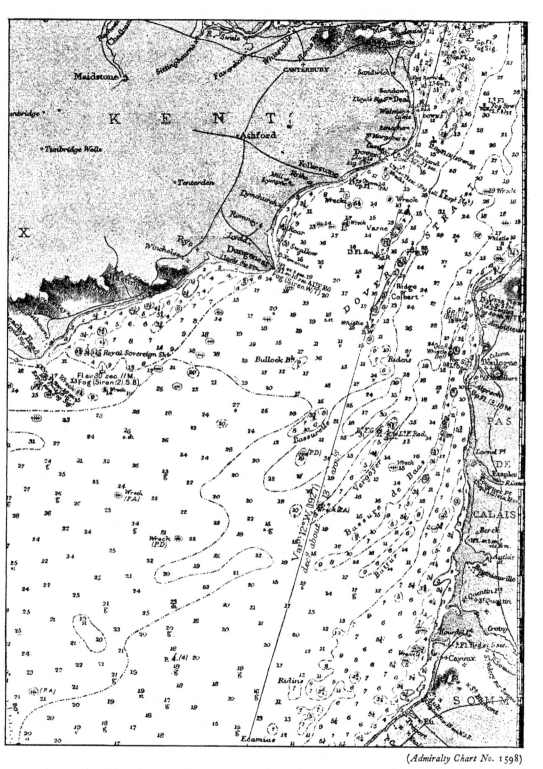

(*Admiralty Chart No.* 1598)

CHART TO ILLUSTRATE ACTIONS OF 16TH AND 18TH SEPT. 1639

At sunset they lay hove-to with the head to the south, N.W. from us 3 miles off. We lay over with the stem towards them and hauled up our fore-topsail and laid it aback, and brailed up our foresail so as to wait for them, the wind at W. b. S. We lit 2 poop lanterns at our stern and 2 lights in the main top, and fired 4 guns off every glass to discover the sea.

The 16 *ditto* in the morning the wind at west.[1] At sunrise the Spanish Armada was 67 sail strong, N.W. from us 2 miles off, and made chase after us. We would gladly have had the wind of them, but could not get it, and seeing 5 sail to leeward we bore away before the wind with brailed up courses and topsails low set S. eastwards. At south-eastern sun we came up with the aforesaid 5 sail which were those of our Vice-Admiral de With[2] to whom we immediately made signal to repair on board and [then] resolved to attack the enemy forthwith, wherefore we sailed close-hauled with our starboard tacks aboard,[3] and began to fight, in the beginning of which action the *Grooten Christoffel* wherein was the Commander Frederick Pietersz. t Hoveling of Enchuijsen, being a hired ship, was blown up through its own powder, and thus we fought on with our 16 sail until the sun was S.W.,[4] when the Spanish Admiral was out-fought and many others with him, wherefore he cast about to the north and lay by the lee with the Armada, and struck his [topsail] yards. Captain Vijch came north-about them and joined us whilst Lops came round them to south-wards. We cast about with the head to the north and lay by the lee, and let ourselves drive. We saw another 5 sail under the English coast, and presumed that they were English King's ships.[5] At nightfall the wind was south-west when the enemy

We were strong: Lt. Ad. Tromp, Ham, Halfhoorn, Ringels, de Boer, Vlieger, Jan Poulus, Post, Jan Gerbrants, Bachuysen, Pr. Pietersz., Camp, Fred. Pietersz. blown up.

(58)
Verso

Adm. de With, Adriaen Domensz., Farant, Water-drincker and the ship of Brederode join us.

Grooten Christoffel blown up.

Vijch and Lobs join us in the evening.

---

1 At N.W. according to Dom Francisco Manuel de Mello (*Epanaphora* IV, p. 502); N.N.W. according to Peter White.

2 Who had left Dunkirk on Sept. 13th and had met Captain Tjaert de Groot off Dungeness on the night Sept. 15th/16th.

3 The wind was west, thus with his starboard tacks aboard, Tromp's course was S.S.W.

4 *I.e.* about 2 in the afternoon. Peter White's times agree with Tromp's journal, and De Mello's approximately so.

5 In actual fact Vice-Admiral Mainwaring in the *Henrietta Maria* with his squadron of five ships; cf. note under Sept. 15th.

lay W.S.W. from us 2 miles off and drove as formerly.[1] We brailed up our foresail and hauled the fore-topsail to the mast. Fairlight bore W.N.W. from us 5 miles off, at midnight we missed the enemy's lights wherefore we lay over to the E.N.E. under small sail, and it became calm.

The 17 *September* in the morning the wind at S.S.W. Cap Grisnez bore E.N.E. from us 4 miles off with hazy weather. We had not sight of the enemy and lay over to the south a little and then tacked to the N.W. At 9 o'clock we saw the enemy at N.W. by west from us.[2] We stood towards them the whole day, but owing to the calm we could not come up with them either by sailing or by towing. In the evening at sundown the enemy came to an anchor off Folkestone at the turn of the flood tide, as we did a mile out to sea from them, the Spanish Admiral being N.N.W. from us. At 11 o'clock at the turn of the ebb tide we weighed our anchors and stood towards the enemy. The whole of the night we had fired 4 shots per glass, whereto we had heard answer from the E.S.E.[3]

The 18 *in the morning* at one of the clock little wind yet what there was S. We got the weather-gage from the enemy and began to fight.[4] During the fight we discovered some ships to windward which we perceived towards daybreak to be the Commander Bancque with the ships under his command coming out from the Brake, who came on board us for a short time to ask for orders, and then we all together fell upon the enemy in the Narrows, and so fought until ten o'clock, when 2 enemy ships being hopelessly disabled, tacked westwards out of the fight; these 2 ships were chased by the ship[s] of Ringels, Bancke, Vlieger, Forant, Vijch, Abram Crijnsz. and Camp and

(59)
Commander Bancker, Cats, 't Hoen, Zeeu, Frans Jansz., Abram Crijnsz., Sluijs, den Oven, Veen, Joris Dorrevelt and Tjaert join us.

1 Thus the Spaniards were still to windward; this agrees with Peter White, *op. cit.*, "...the wind came to the S.W. fair weather". De Mello says it was a "terral" or offshore breeze.

2 Oquendo had "lain all night by the lee" and until noon on the 17th, having then drifted between Beachy Head and Fairlight. Here Mainwaring came up with him, and forced him and his Vice-Admiral to strike after firing "a fair shot at the Admiral" (Peter White, *op. cit.*).

3 *I.e.* by Banckert who joined the next day.

4 De Mello says that the action began at 11 p.m. (on the 17th) and adds that it was a calm but dark night.

yielded after a short dispute. The whole Armada tacked and we with it. Ere we could prevent it one of the captured ships, being a great galleon,[1] fell amongst the enemy's main body again through heedless plundering; the other was an Easterling-built [ship] with 10 bronze and 6 iron guns;[2] it was captured by Captains Crijnsz. and Vijch. The enemy beat a retreat towards the Downs, whilst we were at the end of our powder albeit we[3] had taken 4 barrels out of Captain Veen, and since all our ships had likewise no more powder left we were forced to give over the fight, and to make for Calais, so that the enemy steered for the Downs and we for Calais.[4] At 8 o'clock we had sent Captain Joris with the oared yacht to Calais for more powder and shot. At 4 o'clock we came to an anchor before Calais and towards evening 3 bilanders put off to us with 28,000 lbs. of powder, 300 shot of 33 lbs. calibre, 700 of 18 lbs., 600 of 8 lbs., 400 of 6 lbs. and 20 lbs. of Lunt which we got on board and distributed.[5] The wind at south-west.

The 19 *September* in the morning at daybreak the wind was S.W. with a stiff gale. We summoned all Captains to repair on board, and found that we still needed a quantity of powder and shot in the fleet; we therefore ordered Commander Catz to remain lying before Calais to procure the same from the Governor. The Vice-Admiral is to go to Goeree with the prize, taking also the prisoners, wounded and letters for our Rulers. Abram Crijnsz. is also to go with the prisoners' wounded and some small boats to the Wielingen. At 8 o'clock we weighed our anchors and stood over to England. On coming into the Narrows, we saw the enemy lying at anchor off Dover point; they immediately made sail and steered into the Downs near the English King's ships close under the Castles, whilst we came to an anchor near them at 2 o'clock, what time we heard

Commander Keert de Koe, Mathijs Gillisz and Meij join us.

Vice-Adm. de Wit and Abram Crijnssen go home with the prize.

(59)
Verso

1 The flagship of the squadron of Bartelosa commanded by the Almirante Matteo Esfrondati, who had been shot dead during the fight.
2 Dom Francisco Manuel says it was a Danish urca (*anglice* "hulk") named *Esgueven*.
3 In the sense of "I".
4 Where Tromp cut off the enemy's approach to Dunkirk, since the fairway for ships of deep draught lies through Calais road. (N.)
5 All this was duly returned. See Sept. 20th and Oct. 5th and 26th.

that the enemy's force had lost a Galleon sunk[1] with 700 men, of whom only 7 had come ashore at Dover with a little boat. At evening there joined us from the North Sea Commander Keert de Koe, Matthijs Gillisz. and Cornelis Meij.

The 20 *September* in the morning the wind south with a fresh gale. Signalled all Captains to repair aboard and distributed the powder and shot; when the ebb-stream began, the English ships plied from southwards; the Admiral's Captain[2] came aboard us and said that Admiral Pennington had ordered all the Spaniards to run somewhat more to the north,[3] and that we being under sail should not think that the Spaniards got under sail of their own accord, whilst we were to remain south of them with our fleet. At about 10 o'clock Rear-Admiral Cats joined us from Calais bringing with him 12,000 lbs. of coarse grained gunpowder, 3 shot of 6 lbs. calibre, 100 of 8, 400 of 4, 80 of 33 and 500 of 18 lbs., 20 boxes of lunt, 1½ quires Cartridge paper,[4] all of which we distributed. During the day some Dutchmen living at London and Dover came on board; we dispatched a missive to the Heer Ambassador Joachimi and also letters to their H.M. and Great Mightinesses[5] and to His Highness, wherewith Captain Vijch took his departure in the evening. At nightfall Captain Slingsby[6] came aboard us requesting that we should not fire a gun at the posting of the watch;[7] he also said in the name of the Spanish Admiral that he would gladly exchange prisoners; we answered him that all ours had been sent home, tho' we would have a search made amongst our ships to see if there were still some left, and then treat further of the business.

The 21 *ditto* in the morning it was calm. The English King's boat [with] Captain Fielding[8] came aboard; he said that we should still stay berthed south of the English ships, and that

1 There is no confirmation of this in any trustworthy contemporary source.
2 Peter White. See his *Sea-Fight, etc.* p. 11.
3 So as to be berthed in the northern part of the road.
4 *Kardouspapier.*
5 H.M. were the States-General, and G.M. the States of Holland only.
6 Captain of the *Providence* in Pennington's squadron. MS. has *Slinsby*.
7 *I.e.* the night-gun at about 8 p.m.
8 Captain of the *Bonaventure*.

Admiral Pennington assured us that the enemy would not escape out of the north end by night; we therefore anchored just outside the English Admiral with a number of our ships. We summoned the skipper of the victualling flyboat of Hoorn on board and asked for his ship as a fireship, which he was reluctant to consent to, but we took it as by force and gave him a certificate to that effect. We issued orders that if the enemy attempted to send away their light and Flemish ships, these should be pursued by Commander Bancque with his attached Captains as per margin. We sent Captain Colster ashore to seek materials wherewith to prepare the fireship, but he could not get hold of any. In the afternoon 4 English Captains came aboard us to request us that we should wear no colours on our bowsprit top, nor any astern.[1] They declared that the enemy would have to leave within 5 or 6 days, since the Agreement between Spain and England stated that only 7 or 8 Spanish warships together might ride in English road-steads. In the forenoon there passed through the Narrows a fleet of 38 or 40 sail steering eastwards,—apparently a Hollands fleet.

The 22 *September* in the morning the wind at W.S.W. We missed some of the enemy's frigates. We sent our shallop sailing through the enemy's fleet, whereby we found and learnt that 11 or 12 frigates and light flyboats had escaped north-wards[2] during the night with, it was said, 4,000 soldiers, flat contrary to the promise made us yesterday by Admiral Pennington, at which we complained very bitterly; yet he excused himself denying all knowledge of it; we therefore at once ordered Commander Bancque with his squadron to anchor just

Marginal notes:

Take the victualling flyboat of Hoorn (skipper Maerten Claessen) for a fireship.

Commander Bancker, Capn Cats, Ham, Keert de Koe, Frans Janssen, de Zeeu, Halffhoorn, Farant, Sluijs, M. Gillisse, Vijch, T. Hoen, Joris Pietersz., den Oven.

(60)
English Captains
Henry Stradling, Richard Fielding [in the] *Bonaventure*, Edward Popham [in the] *Unicorn*, and Slingsby.

---

1 On the outbreak of hostilities with England in 1652, Tromp drew up a report on the former usage regarding the striking of the flag to the English wherein the following sentence occurs: "Binnen haer Havenen ende Casteelen komende, salueerden de Casteelen met Eer-schoten (die oock wederom antwoorden), en namen de *Vlagge* in, en lieten in plaets een *Wimpel* wayen, soo lange die van desen Staet binnen haer Havenen lagen, insonderheydt wanner eenige Konings schepen daer waren die de Konings *Vlagge* lieten waeyen" (Aitzema, *Saken van Staet en Oorlogh*, III, p. 731). The numerous difficulties with Dutch ships caused by the exaggerated tokens of respect demanded for the English flag are fully discussed in Fulton, *op. cit.*

2 *I.e.* via the Gull Stream.

northwards of the Spaniards, which was accordingly done in order to prevent further escapes.[1] The Spanish Admiral sent us all the prisoners that he had picked up, both from the exploded ship of Fredric Pietersz.[2] as those who had jumped out of Vice-Admiral de With's ship, whilst we sent him back in return those Spaniards that we had, viz. 6 men and 4 boys; we kept 2 of his men who did not wish to go as they were Provençals. The Admiral Pennington asked us to give him a written certificate wherein we should promise not to attack the Spaniards here, which we excused ourselves from doing.

The 23 ditto in the morning the wind W. by S. with a hard gale, the enemy and ourselves lying as before. During the day we took some victuals out of Lob's in payment of what we had lent Captain Pietersz. In the forenoon another 8 English ships full of Spanish infantry came to an anchor near us,[3] wherefore we sent Captain Cats to Admiral Pennington complaining that the English merchantmen carrying Spanish soldiery were still coming here, contrary to His Majesty's intentions, wishing that we had them in the offing; when we could hope to give both Spaniards and Englishmen a short shrift; he—Pennington —offered excuses over this and also did not approve of what the English merchantmen had done; he therefore placed the ships under embargo charging them under the King's Seal not to leave until further order from the King; we advised the

1 Dom Francisco Manuel de Mello, who was on board one of these ships which escaped, states that 13 ships—the majority of them Dunkirkers—*together with* 56 bilanders were detailed to carry across to Dunkirk the money and soldiers demanded by the Cardinal-Infant. He also adds that all the ships with 49 of the bilanders (*Balandras*) got safely into Dunkirk at 9 a.m. on the next day, but that seven or eight of the bilanders carrying some 300 soldiers with their officers and flags were taken by the Hollanders. Dom Manuel wrongly dates this exploit on the night of the 27th/28th. It is extraordinary that Tromp makes no mention of either the 56 bilanders, or of the 320 men who were taken, and probably Dom Manuel confuses two separate incidents.

2 The *Groot Christoffel* blown up on Sept. 16th (*q.v.*), and some men who had jumped out of Witte de With's ship in a panic at a fire which had broken out during the action. (See *Leven en Bedrijf, op. cit.* p. 114.)

3 These were eight ships under Edward Chapell of London, which had left La Coruña with the Spanish Armada, and put into Plymouth on Sept. 1st/11th with 2,000 soldiers on board. Cf. De Mello, *op. cit.* pp. 496–8, and Gardiner, *op. cit.* I, p. 263.

Ambassador per express of this occurrence and the trick by which the enemy had escaped, requesting him to bring the same to the knowledge of His Majesty himself. Another 2 small boats came from the direction of the Goodwin Sands,[2] coming first from La Rochelle and not being able with this wind to discharge off the Goodwins, they came here to the roadstead; they were both of Vlissingen laden with salt. During the day the Spanish Admiral struck his topmasts and yards.

Tam Trasaert[1] posts to London.

The 24 *ditto* in the morning the wind at W.S.W. with handsome weather; the Heer Commander Bancque came aboard us; we issued orders concerning the pursuing and fighting of the enemy's fleet should they attempt to put out to sea; we also instructed Commander Bancque to hand the copy [thereof] in our name to all the Captains under him, and to order them to act in accordance therewith; we subsequently fished our main yard and stopped shot-hole leaks. In the afternoon it blew a hard gale.

(60)
Verso

The 25 *September* in the morning the wind was S.E. At 9 o'clock there came a Calais shallop with a letter from the Governor which we answered. During the day the Spanish Admiral got a new fore-topmast and his foresail yard was greatly fished. The Secretary of the Heer Ambassador Joachimi came on board bringing a letter wherein he [the A.] asked that some noblemen might come on board us to fight against the Spaniards out of love for us; also stated that if we attacked the enemy here it would be very badly taken in this country, withal he had already written to our Rulers on that score. Towards evening there came into the Downs an English convoyer Captain Burley with Jan Schep from Dunkirk; they declared that 13 ships with 500 wounded were arrived at Dunkirk, but he would not confess that they were those which had escaped by night from this Armada;[3] there was as yet no preparation

Letter from the Comte de Charost received & answered.

1 Probably the "servant of the Heer Joachimi's son-in-law". See Sept. 28th and elsewhere.

2 MS. *Gom.*

3 "This day came the second *Whelp* from *Dunkirk,* and Captain *Burley* certified our Admirall, that there was 13 sayle of the *Spanish* fleet arrived there with 3000 men" (Peter White, *op. cit.*).

made there to come here with some ships. Today 4 frigates had sailed out from Dunkirk to the west, whilst on Thursday last a flyboat of 16 guns, being a Muscovy trader, had been brought as a prize into Dunkirk. There were still 6 or 7 frigates lying within but few men could be secured. At sundown the wind south-east.

The 26 *ditto* the wind was at south with rain, when it was daylight the wind veered west. The Captains from Zeeland joined us, viz. Cornelis Evertsz., Mangelaer and Regemortens, bringing with them 44 men from the regiment of the Grave van Zolms under Captain Jan van den Bos, with 60 men of the regiment of the Heer van Beverwaert commanded by Lieutenant van Lier, which soldiers we at once distributed; we also dispatched Captain Mangelaer to convoy the Zeeland vessels to Calais in safety, and having done so to rejoin us here forthwith. I sailed in person through the Spanish Armada and reconnoitred it.

The 27 *ditto* in the morning the wind was S.S.W. with thick rain and wind; all the ships' topmasts were struck and we let fall the bower to stop the leeward tide. At the flood tide it blew a hard gale; a Spaniard dragged his anchors but held himself again with his sheet-anchor. Towards evening Captain Slingsby representing Admiral Pennington came on board with 3 propositions; the first that the King had not broken his word in [allowing] the bringing over of Spanish infantry,[1] because he had said that he would forbid his subjects to do so on condition that other Kings and States likewise forbade the same, and whereas even our own State had not forbidden it, he was not therefore bound to do so; secondly he asked me for a certificate of discharge to the effect that he (Pennington) had not kept his word in assuring us that no Spanish ships should escape northwards; thirdly that two Hamburgers had been taken by [our] ships out of the Spanish fleet,[2] whereof he asked restitution.

Towards evening we weighed our bower; a Zijtsche[3] pink

(61)

---

1 See Sept. 23rd.   2 MS. *boot* instead of *vloot*.
3 The Dutch coast from Hook of Holland to Den Helder is (or was) called the Zijde. (N.)

came aboard, bringing the duplicate of the letter and resolution
of Their H.M. taken on the 21 of this present,[1] wherefore we
[.....] Captain Regemorter [the next few lines are incom-
prehensible] concerning the reinforcements to be dispatched.
There further came aboard us the son-in-law of the Heer
Joachimii, bringing a letter which stated that the King had
propounded in the Privy Council the matter of the two fleets
lying in the Downs, wherein the King's authority had been
heavily disputed, and that it was very injurious for the same
that His Majesty's friends should be blockaded in His Majesty's
roadstead; it is also regarded as certain that His Majesty will
order both the fleets to leave; furthermore that the King has
given orders for a great number of his ships to be fitted out;
that all merchantmen in the River were detained for their
crews including those that the Spaniard had hired on the London
Exchange to come into the Downs & there to take in soldiers
to carry over to Dunkirk, for which they were to get 30
shillings per head; that the King had assembled 30 ships
together, and that he would act against the first party to attack
his enemy in the roadstead; withal he could not as yet hear
that His Majesty had brought himself formally to release the
English ships carrying soldiers. There also joined us the 2
Zierickzee pinks convoyed by Captain Cornelis Mangelaar in
the ship *Ter Toolen* carrying 26 guns & 77 sailors, with Captain
Gillis[' ship] mounting 18 guns & 70 sailors.

The 28 September in the morning the wind at west with fine
weather. At sunrise we sent a letter to Calais, together with
a copy of the Heer Joachimi's letter, to the Comte de Charost,
as also Captain Regemorters to act as convoy for the Zijtsche
pink[2] and the victualling boyers of Captain Joris, and the little
English boyers which had on board some goods salved from
the *Eendracht*, to Zeeland with letters for Their H.M. and
their G.M., as also for His Highness and the College of Zeeland.
During the day there came aboard us 4 English Captains
with the skipper of Vice-Admiral Pennington, Mr White,[3]

(61)
Verso

1 *Vide* Appendix III. 2 See note under Sept. 27th.
3 Peter White, Master of the *Unicorn*. This interview is recorded *in extenso*
on pp. 16–17 of his *Sea-fight, tc.*

with whom we discoursed at length concerning the point which Captain Slingsby asked me about yesterday evening, namely that I should give a certificate under my own hand to the effect that Admiral Pennington had not passed his word that the Spaniards would not sail off to northwards; and after long discourse Captain Fielding and Mr White acknowledged that they had ordered us in the name of Captain [*sic!*] Pennington to remain berthed south of them,[1] whilst Captain Catz further declared that Pennington had offered to forfeit his head on a charger that they could not and should not escape to northwards, and yet they had subsequently done so.[2] Today we also resolved the Vice-Admiral de With with 7 ships should cruise off and on to southwards for English merchantmen carrying Spanish soldiers, whilst Commander Bancque with 14 sail is to go likewise north of the Armada to snap up those which try to get away northwards, to the end that we may forestall this bringing over of the infantry.

In the afternoon an English King's Captain named Edward Popham[3] came on board, warning us in the name of Admiral Pennington not to attack the Spanish fleet between the two Forelands, and he asked whether we would do this or no, repeating the question several times. We made answer that we had no order therefor and were not yet resolved to do it.[4] He

1 Peter White acknowledges no such thing in his own account.

2 Peter White in his version says: "Capt. Cats being there present, denied in secret unto us that he never mentioned, should not, but that his Admirall had added that unto the message that he brought him...But Cats durst not openly deny it, for then he should have given his Admirall the lye; so the fault was wholly laid upon Capt. Cats, with which answer we returned".

3 This is a mistake. It was Peter White who wrote: "Afterward I was sent again single aboard of Admirall *Tromp* as it were to give him a visit by myself, and to have an hour or two conference together, to which he had divers times invited me familiarly & called me brother; hoping thereby to get something out of him being single more than we could when there was more company with him", etc. *Vide Sea-fight, etc.* p. 17.

4 Actually Tromp had the order in his pocket (see under Sept. 27th), but he could scarcely be expected to tell the English as much, in view of the outspoken terms in which it was couched, and in view of the fact that he was ordered to keep it secret even from his own captains. Peter White has a most amusing account of the efforts of Tromp and himself to "pump" each other. Cf. his *Sea-fight, etc.* pp. 17–18.

then asked whether we would get any order? We declared
that we did not know, whereupon he said that if we attacked
the Spaniards between the two Forelands, we would render
them [*i.e.* English] our enemies, and that in that case they
would prepare to help the Spaniards; whilst if the Spaniards
should attack us, then they would help us and fall on the
Spaniards. We also wrote an order for Captain Mangelaer to
convoy 2 Zeeland merchantmen to Boulogne in safety, and then
rejoin the flag here. Towards evening we sent ashore the
servant of the son-in-law of the Heer Joachimi[1] with a letter,
being in answer to his 2 letters of the 25 and 26 of this present
from London.

The 29 *September* in the morning the wind was S.W., during (62)
the night it had blown hard; we saw a Spanish galleon stranded
ashore near the third Castle[2] having been driven there at night;
in the forenoon it got off again and came to an anchor a little
way to the north of the innermost Castle.[3] Towards evening
we signalled our Captains to repair on board and gave each[4]
of them order to cruise under the Vice-Admiral on the English
who tried to steal away soldiers from the Spanish Armada to
Dunkirk. The skipper of Admiral Pennington also came on
board and showed us a letter of the Lord High Admiral
Northumberland, written in the name of His Majesty, stating
that the Holland Ambassador had complained to His Majesty
that some small English vessels had been hired at London, to
take soldiers from out of the Spanish Armada to Dunkirk,—
the names whereof as per margin,[5]—and that His Majesty's
will was that he (Pennington) should make search to see if any
such ships had come into the Downs, and finding such to
detain them, and put a stop to the business; furthermore that
all the merchantmen lying here in the Downs were detained
to hold themselves in readiness at any moment at the King's

Vice-Ad. Squadron
Pr. Pietersz., Vice-
Admiral, Post,
Camp, Tjaert, Corn.
Mangelaer, Gillis,
Jansen, Ringels, Jan
Poulus & Dorrevelt.

Letter from the Lord
High Admiral.

Richard Gilbert,
Hugh Lawes, Harry
Read, Richard
Tattom, Wm.
Williams.

---

1 See note under Sept. 23rd.
2 Walmer Castle (?). Peter White has a similar description, *ibid.* p. 18.
3 Sandown Castle (?).   4 Probably "some" is meant.
5 These names are from Peter White's account. The Dutch originals are fairly
close. White says that the detention of these vessels caused Tromp "to rejoice
exceedingly". Cf. his *Sea-fight, etc.* pp. 18–19.

service, so that if need arose, they could help fight those who first fired on the enemy; and thus he hoped to prevent his friends from fighting in his King's Chamber. At sundown the wind at west south-west.

The 30 September 1639 in the morning the wind at S.W. Set up our topmasts and squared the yards. We wrote to Commander Bancque what Captain Popham on the day before yesterday, and Mr White yesterday evening, had told us in the name of Admiral Pennington. We got under sail and hacked a piece out of our cable [and came to an anchor again]; we were then joined by Captain Bastian Tijssen, who brought a letter from His Highness written from the army in the Cruijspolder[1] on the 24 of this present, besides 2 letters for the Heer Joachimi, to which we added another letter wherein we enclosed a copy of the letter showed us by Mr White on the day before yesterday. Towards evening an English Captain Hall[2] came on board us, accompanied by the owner of the ship of Captain Brown,[3] who was Admiral of the English merchantmen lately come from Plymouth with Spanish soldiers; he declared that he had sold to the Spaniards of the stranded galleon a cable of 15 inches thick, & 120 fathoms long with an anchor weighing 2,100 lbs.; he had received 570 pieces of eight in payment thereof. He added that he was obliged to serve with his ship through the King's press, whilst the Spanish infantry on board were to be transferred into the Spanish ships.[4]

(62)
Verso

From Zeeland
Capn Swart, Vice-Adm. Jan Everts., Abram Witboom, Pr. Arentsen, Gillis Vlaminck, Jan de Vrachter, Jac. Verhel.

The first October 1639 in the morning at sunrise the wind was S.W. During the night there had been much lightning and variable wind. During the day were joined by the Heer Vice-Admiral Evertsz. with his squadron, together with the Maas people as per margin. Captain Mus came bringing a quantity of shot of all kinds, with 45 barrels of powder, and Captain Brust brought 200 barrels, all of which we immediately

1 Near Hulst in Zeeland-Flanders.   2 Of the *Dreadnought*.
3 *The Exchange.* Cf. Peter White, *op. cit.* p. 13.
4 "But this order came something too late for the most of the Souldiers were sent away before by *Dover-men, Deall*, and *Ramsgate-men* with other small craft, that tooke them aboard in the dark nights and carried them away". Peter White, *op. cit.* p. 19.

distributed. Captain Van Diemen also joined with 11 new sailors for us and 18 for Vice-Admiral de With, 68 of his own men whom he took in the ship *Prins Hendrik* from Gelderland; there also arrived Lieutenant Verhaef whom we appointed as Lieutenant to Captain Stier. We also heard that the Cardinal-Infant was at Dunkirk,[1] where 6 ships were being fitted out, but there were only slender crews for them and they could not come out of the harbour this spring tide;[2] also 100 Flemings from Dunkirk had come out of Flanders into the Downs, amongst whom were 30 gunners who had been distributed amongst their fleet. We had received from His Highness 2 letters in answer to mine, stating that he would assist us with all his power, and that we should keep our courage high; also received a letter from their H.M. dated 22 September. We ordered this evening that all Zeelanders should place themselves under the command of the Heer Vice-Admiral Evertsz. to northwards of the Spaniards. At 2 o'clock in the evening Captain Farant came aboard us, declaring that he had spoken ashore with 2 noblemen, one of them the Grave van Stamvoort & the other the Master of Horse of the Queen of England, who said that they had heard in Sir John Pennington's ship, that 6 or 7 Dunkirk frigates were to come into the Downs this evening in order to take soldiers out of the Armada and bring them to Dunkirk.

From the Maas Silvergieter, Sier de Liefde, Brustens, Pr. Brouck, Mus, Vijch.

The 2 October in the morning the wind was W.S.W. All the Zeelanders ran northwards of the enemy to join Vice-Admiral Evertsz. Captain Maetroos joined us in Jan Romboutsz.'s ship, bringing a missive wherewith was enclosed a copy of one of His Highness' dated 23 September from the army near Roversberch[3] together with several resolutions tending to the effect that all possible assistance would be sent us; he also brought 150 musketeers from the garrison of den Bos, 10 men from each company, and others totalling 450 altogether in all

Capn Maetroos with the ship of Jan Rombouts. Skipper Reijer Pietersz., Symon Cornelis, Symon Joppen, Gerrit Senten, Jan Verhagen, Job het Kint, Aert Roelen, the polish joncker, the straw joncker.[4]

1 This was quite true. He had done this to facilitate negotiations with England, and the ferrying over of Spanish soldiers.
2 Full moon Oct. 10th–11th. (N.)
3 Just north of Hulst in N. Flanders.
4 Nicknames of captains. See *infra*.

the ships. When the sun was S.W. we were joined by the skippers as per margin from the fishery who came to an anchor near us. We distributed as many musketeers as we could; the Scheveling Hoy[1] returned with letters and resolutions of their H.M.; we immediately sent it back per express to Holland and Zeeland with our letters for their H.M., His Highness and the Admiralty of Zeeland, under the convoy of Bastiaen Tijsz.; about 15 of our men went away, some on leave & [some unfit?]. In the evening there arrived the Master's mate of Captain Abram Crijnsz., named Servaes van den Berch, who had come in an English ketch from Vlissingen with a letter of His Highness dated the 29 ditto in the Cruijspolder.[2] Three English Captains also came on board in the name of Signor Pennington declaring that the Spanish fleet must away, but made the excuse that their main and topmasts lay at Dover, and that they could not fetch them through fear of our ships; they therefore asked either for an English convoy or for a promise from us that we would not hinder them. We answered that if they had no other excuse for not coming out than that, we would give our word not to hinder them even if they had to fetch a hundred masts, and that we ourselves would rather bring those on board them so that they could come out.[3] Our Vice-Admirals de With and Evertsz. were appointed as Commissioners to try to get 3 or 4 prisoners still amongst the Spaniards, withal they got a very civil answer. In the evening fairly calm weather.

On the Buss convoyers Dirck van Dongen, Teuine den Hengst.

(63)

The garrison from den Bos[4] distributed as follows:

Catz	25	Camp	10
Mathijs Gieles	15	Post	15
Ham	15	Corn. Engelen	35
Colster	15	Farant	20
Keert de Koe	10		

150 [*sic*]

1 Or Zijtsche pink of Sept. 27th, *q.v.*
2 See note under Sept. 30th.
3 Which actually happened! See Oct. 7th, and Peter White's account, p. 11, which corroborates Tromp word for word.
4 Hertzogenbosch (Bois le Duc).

From the garrison of the Briel of Governor de Grater's Company were distributed 100 men—

Thoen	15		Teunis Huijgen	20
Bachuijsen	15		Lieut. Vlugh	15
Van Dongen	20		Van Diemen	15

100

[From] *Breda and Terheij*

to	Capn Hitvelt Capn Veen	10
to	Capn Kijn Com. Meij	10
to	Capn Valckenhaen Capn Bleijcker	10
from to	Capn Haften Capn Juijnbol	10

From Crevecoeur the Ensign La Rue   20 men
    in Pieter van den Broeck   20 men
Ensign Govert van Stakenbroeck from Breda
    20 men, Capn Sluijs this 20 men.
Crijn Jacobsz. delv̄red from the garrison of
    Steenbergen   30 men

The Lt. Admiral Tromp	10
Adriaen Damas	20
	30

From the garrison of Worcum, Ensign Winteroij with
    20 men to Captain de Lieffde 20 men.
Elbert Henricx. Corporal from Westerbeecq 20 men to the
    Vice-Admiral these 20 men.[1]

Skipper Reijer Pietersz. has taken aboard 36 hogsheads with
    55 tuns beer.
Jan Gerbrantsz. 12 hogsheads.
Tjaert 12 hogsheads.
Veen 12 hogsheads.

(63)
Verso

---

1 In the "Epistle dedicatory" to Peter White's *Sea-fight*, we read that "*Tromp* had 1000 Land Souldiers in his Ships, which was too many by 999!"

Geert Senten some bundles of faggots with 4 small last of beer.

Jan Verhave 7 grappling-irons, one without a chain, and some faggots, tar-barrels, and some empty & full train-oil barrels.

Willem Cornelisz. "Straw Gentleman" 2 masts of 16 or 17 palms and a quantity of lumber.

Sijmon Joppe 8 casks of sulphur, 30 reams of cartridge paper, 26 axletrees.

Aert Roelen 2400 shot of divers kinds, 33 pipes, 44 hogsheads.

Job t Kint 60 hogsheads, 4 pipes of beer, faggots, a little cheese, butter and herring.

Sluijs 20 pipes; the Adm. 30 hogsheads, [Brustens?] 4 pipes, Bachuijsen 20 hogsheads, Corn. Engels 10 hogsheads.

The "Polish Gentlemen"[1] divers shot amounting to 3500 rounds.

Yet another amount, viz. 80 of 36 lbs., 335 of 24 lbs., 1100 of 18 lbs., 1375 of 6 lbs., 65 of 4 lbs., 25 of 3 lbs., 33 tuns of powder.

Have still had aboard 40 hogsheads, 36 pipes of beer.

Farant 40 hogsheads, Mathijs Gillisz. 15 pipes, de Liefde 15 pipes.

The 3 October in the morning an hour before daybreak we dispatched our shallop with a letter, being the answer to the letter dated the 29 September from the Cruijspolder,[2] after Captain Bastiaen Tijsz. who had been ordered to Vlissingen, tho' Captain Tijsz. had left at night.

Assembled in the Council of War, Lt.-Adm.Vice-Adm. de With, Everts, Cats, Bancke, Ham, Halfhoorn.

Yesterday we divided our ships into squadrons as follows:[3]

Cornelis Engelen, Waterdrincker, Van Dongen, Frans Jansz., Farant, Captain Regemorter, Commander Joh. Hend. de Nijs, de Zeeu, Juijnbol, Melcknap.

1 A nickname, of course.
2 See under Sept. 30th.
3 This list is valueless as the copyist (perhaps wilfully?) has repeated several of the names three or four times, sometimes twice in each squadron! (N.)

Follows the Lt. (Adm.) Squadron Cats, Ham, Colster, Half-hoorn, Farant, Sluijs, Veen, Joris Pietersz., Vijch, Bachuijsen, Waterdrincker, Diemen, Mus, Pieter van den Broeck, Brustens, Corn. Engelen, de Lieffde, Van Dongen, Den Hengst, Juijnbol, Appelman, Melcknap, de Lapper, Turkoijs, Schellinckhout.

Vice-Admiral Evers' Squadron Bancque, Ringels, Jan Pouwels, Corn. Everts, Regemorter, Frans Mangelaer, Corn. Mangelaer, Bastiaen Matthijssen, Swart, Abram Crijnsse, Den Oven.

Hired ships Abram Witboom, Pieter Arentsz., Gillis Vlamingh, Jan den Trechter, Jacob Verhal, Pieter t Lam, Jacob de Bruijne.

Fireships Jacques Tybout, Den Oven, Keert de Koe.

Vice-Admiral de With, Camp, Post, Tjaert, Dorrevelt, Keert de Koe, Captain Lieven, Vlugh, Mathijs Gillis, Meij, t Hoen, Adriaens Lops, Jan Garbrants, Sier de Lieffde, Claes Juijnbol, Jacob Nieuvelt, Jaersvelt, Bleijcker, de Zee[u], Crijn, Claessen van Hoorn, fireships [of] Vice-Adm. de With, de Zeeu, de Lieffde.

In the forenoon the servant of the son-in-law of the Heer Joachimi came aboard us, bringing with him a letter for me, containing a request for a copy of the extract given by me to Pennington, with another letter for their H.M. and one for His Highness; we dispatched Regemorter with these, instructing him to send a sailor in a pink to the Wielingen, or else set him ashore to forward the aforesaid letters, who at once left. We detailed Captain Juijnbol to act as convoy to a Maas Galliot as far as Etretat, and then to return again forthwith. During the

There join us from the Maas:—
Marinus Juijnbol.
The College of the North Quarter.
Cap. Warnar, Kappelman, Bleijcker, Melcknap.
Amsterdam Directory
Jacob Nieuvelt, Jaersvelt.
From the College of Amsterdam
Jan de Lapper.[1]

---

1 A man whose name still lives in the folk-lore of Holland: He was a cobbler of Haarlem, where he had been born in 1620, who in the intervals of a seafaring life followed his old occupation ashore. On one of his voyages the captain of the ship being killed in action, De Lapper brought the vessel safely into the Texel. He was vice-admiral of a squadron in the first English war, being present at the battles of Nieuport and Ter Heide in the ship *Fazant*. In 1656 he went to Danzig in the *Maarseveen* in the fleet of Jacob van Wassenaar, under whom he also served in the Swedish war of 1658. In one of the actions of 1666 he lost an arm, but had himself bound to the mast and continued to encourage his men until his head was blown off by a cannon-ball (or so it is said).

day we distributed ammunition, victuals and soldiers, and also ordered an inventory to be made out of all the fireships, and gave instructions that each one was to be made ready. There was also brought on board us a soldier from de With's ship who had jumped out of the round-house and been fished up by the Spaniards. We ordered Vice-Admiral de With to take 4 six-pounders out from the ship of Claes Pietersz. of Rotterdam, in order to use them temporarily on board the ship *Prins Hendrick*; similarly Colster 4 six-pounders from Claes Pietersz., and Silvergieter 4 four-pounders from Skipper Jan Verhagen. During the day some English merchantmen got under sail.

The Adm. Tromp's Mate, Pieter, in the fireship of Claes Pietersz.

The Vice-Adm. de With's Lieutenant, Quack, in the fireship of Zier Pietersz.

The Lieutenant of Mathijs Gillisz., Hendrick Steur, [in the fireship of] Gerrit Senten.

Captain Ham's Lieutenant, Gerrit Mint, [in the fireship of] Sijmon Joppen.

Captain de Zeeu's Lieutenant, Pieter Gerritsz. and Job 't Kint.

(64)
Verso

Captain Colster's Mate, Pieter Duijf—Jan Verhagen.

Captain Zier de Lieffde, Jan Arents Verhaef, the "Polish Nobleman".

Captain Farant, Lieutenant Dirck Crijne Veen, Symon Cornelisse.

The skippers Aert Roele and Willem Cornelisz. "Straw Nobleman" were left over to accommodate the merchants' goods and the crews of the fireships.

Captain Nieuvelt of the Amsterdam Directory brought with him 33 recently enlisted men and some provisions, the muster-roll whereof together with the lists of provisions I have handed to Rear-Admiral Cats with orders to distribute them where most needed.

Enchuijsen Admiralty
Cap. de Zeeu.
Hoorn Directory
Cap. Crijn Claes.

The 4 October in the morning the wind was east. During the day we were joined by the ships named in the margin; we ordered the inventory of the fireships to be pushed on, so that these could be fitted out with all speed, which was accordingly done; the materials were found to be insufficient, and we sent Cornelis Bos, Captain Snip and Cornelis Meij with ships to Dover to buy firewood. We signalled all Captains to repair on board and charged each one to make everything ready, and to those that wanted something, we sent munitions, victuals, soldiers and whatsoever was lacking. In the evening the wind at east with calm.

The 5 ditto in the morning the wind at E.S.E. with a stiff gale; we dispatched our shallop to the Narrows [to order] the fireships to be prepared, and asked them when they would be ready. We got answer that they were doing their best and would let us know when they were all ready. In the morning we collected the inventories of the fireship skippers and gave Captain Maetroos his order, thanking him.[1] At ten o'clock the servant of the Heer Joachimi's son-in-law came on board us, bringing letters for their H.M., His Highness and the States of Zeeland; he [*i.e.* Joachimi] wrote me that he had been told on behalf of the King that as a favour he would not assist the Spanish fleet, nor the convoyers should they slip out, provided that he could be assured on behalf of the States that the Spaniards would not be attacked in his roadstead; he [Joachimi] had written to their H.M. and to His Highness informing them of this same. We forthwith dispatched Captain Elias Van der Base [in his] frigate of the Amsterdam Directory with the aforesaid missive, together with mine for their H.M., His Highness, and the College of Zeeland. We were joined during the day by those named in the margin. At sunset the servant of Rear-Admiral Cats came aboard, bringing 2 letters with him; one from the Governor of Dover asking us when we threw our dead overboard to sink them by attaching a heavy weight, because the people dwelling along the foreshore had made great complaint that many corpses were washed up on the beach and stank,—albeit praise God they were not from our fleet, but out of the Spanish. The other was from Captain

Zeeland hired ships
Cap. Pieter Claes, t'Lam, Jacob de Bruijne.
The College of Amsterdam
Cap. Jacob Turquoys.
Zeeland fireships
Jacob Tybout, Den Oven, Keert de Koe.

The North Quarter's Corn. Schellinckhout.
The College of Amsterdam
Elias van de Base.
Directory of Enchuijsen
Jacob. Corn. de Boer.

(65)

---

1 For what? This whole sentence is unintelligible in the original—through some copyist's errors probably.

D.,[1] relating that a little ship without a fore-topmast was lying close inshore, which had carried away some Spaniards; and we received further tidings that two ketches laden with Spaniards had run in under Margate pier, which tidings we sent to the Vice-Admiral Jan Evertsz. for him to send a frigate thither to hinder the same, and if they caught any of them they were to be brought into Vlissingen. In the evening Skippers 't Lam of Middelburch and Jacob de Bruijn of Vlissingen came on board with 40 thousand pounds of gunpowder, which we ordered to be sent with a letter on board of 2 ships to the Comte de Charost in restitution of what he had lent us on the 19 September.[2] In the evening the wind at E.S.E. with handsome weather.

On account of the East-India Company Commander Houtebeen, Reijndert Wijbrants, Jan Jacobs Strijck, Com. Jansz. Saijer.

West-India Company Dirck Claessen.

From the College of Amsterdam Commander Denijs Schrevels, Balcq, Nieuhoff.

The 6 October in the morning it was handsome weather. We saw 8 or 10 sail in the Narrows, and were extremely busy with the fitting out of the fireships. In the forenoon Master White came aboard us on behalf of the Vice-Admiral Pennington, requesting me very earnestly to come and dine with him, tho' we excused ourself and ordered Vice-Admiral de With and Commander Cats to go instead.[3] We were joined by the ships shown in the margin, and Commander Houtebeen had on board 174 barrels of gunpowder, whilst Reijndert Wijbrants brought 150 barrels, each of 100 pounds. The Commander Vice-Admiral Jan Evertsz. had sent a frigate to Margate, in

1 Probably Dorrevelt: see under Oct. 8th.
2 Sept 18th to be exact.
3 Cf. Peter White, *op. cit.* p. 23: "Sir *Iohn* sent me aboard of Admirall *Trump* to invite him to dinner, but he desired to be excused for two reasons, the which he did relate unto me that I might give Sir *Iohn* our Admirall to understand that it was not for want of love and respect unto him, for he said in the first place, I have so much businesse that I cannot be absent from my ship one half-hour, much lesse three houres which is but a usuall time for a dinner; secondly he said that he had a great many clownish Boars amongst his Captains, that neither understood civility nor manners, and that they would be ready to make the States acquainted with my being absent from my businesse, and would not stick to say as they had formerly done by my Predecessor, the *Grave Van Dorp*, which was cast in his teeth divers times by the States, that he did neglect his businesse and lost many oportunities of doing them good services, by feasting with our Admirall Sir *John Pennington*, to whom he desired to remember his humble service, and said that hereafter he was in hope to come hither when he should not have so much businesse, and then he would wait upon him".

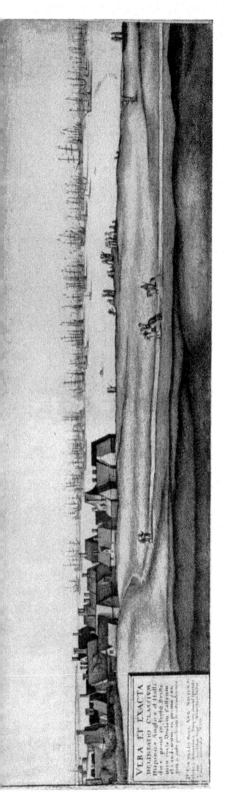

From the print by Hollaer in the Macpherson Collection

ENGLISH, DUTCH AND SPANISH FLEETS IN THE DOWNS, OCTOBER 1639

accordance with my order of yesterday, to prevent the bringing over of the Spaniards in the ketches mentioned yesterday; in the evening Sir Henry Mainwaring with Mr White came aboard, complaining that one of our frigates had been before Margate, wearing English Royal standard and jack, and had taken the 2 English ketches with Spaniards out of the roadstead, which Admiral Pennington took very ill, since we had misused His Majesty's flag—albeit we declared we knew nothing thereof. The Count of Warwick[1] came on board with his suite; he stated to us that he would represent all our actions in the most favourable light, so far as he could. In the evening a light breeze easterly with handsome weather.

The 7 ditto in the morning a faint breeze with very handsome weather. At daybreak we sent our shallop for the Heer Vice-Admiral Evertsz. with the members of the Council of War from the Zeeland squadron. At 8 o'clock there came aboard us Vice-Admiral Mainwaring, & Captains Slingsby, Popham and Richard Fielding; they asked three things,—firstly that we should restore to them the Spanish soldiers taken by Mangelaer in Margate road yesterday in 2 barques carrying 230 men; we answered that his orders were to take any Spaniards that he might catch to Vlissingen, whither we felt sure he must have sailed since we could not see him; the second point, that he [Mangelaer] had taken the aforesaid Spaniards under the King's colours, whereby His Majesty was affronted; I answered that I had given no order to that effect, and could not be held responsible for what others did, but I would nevertheless forbid the same;[2] thirdly, that the Spanish Admiral had requested that our fireships should ride somewhat further off from him, which we [said we] would do on the request of the English Admiral Pennington. We gave them the names of some prisoners, to try to procure their freedom. There also came on board us the Vice-Admiral Evertsz., Bancque, Frans Jansz., and the Vice-Admiral de With, Catz and Colster; communicated to them the resolution of Their H.M. anent the last point. Marinus

(65)
Verso

1 MS. *Baricq*. In actual fact it was Lord Conway; cf. Peter White, *op. cit.* p. 24.
2 Cf. Peter White, *op. cit.* pp. 24–5.

Juijnbol came from the Hâvre convoy, whither we had dispatched him; he had spoken the west-bound Texel and Maas fleet.

Since the Spanish Admiral had complained several times that he could not set sail for want of his spars, which lay at Dover and could not be brought aboard him owing to our watch, we therefore had sent Captain Dorrevelt to Dover yesterday, who now, at 10 o'clock, came here with a small barque carrying the masts in tow, which we sent to the Admiral of Spain who presented Dorrevelt with a demijon¹ of sack. After we had assembled the flag officers of the fleet, we told them that we were of opinion that the time had come to reveal to them the last item of Their H.M.'s resolution which had been entrusted to us in secret, and we therefore ordered all the papers concerning that point to be read out frankly to them; and having deliberated upon the same we came to no other decision than that, since our Zeeland fireships were not yet ready, we would equip them in all haste; and the wind not being favourable, we would keep our secret for the present from the General Council of War until a fitter opportunity, to lessen the risk of its being discovered. In the afternoon we signalled all Captains to repair on board and charged each one to prepare his things well, and to be ready enough to fight at any hour, whilst those who still had something to fetch or bring should do so forthwith;² shortly after sunset the breeze was N.W. with mist and calm weather.

The 8 in the morning the breeze at N.W. We assembled the Council of War in the ship of Vice-Admiral de With, to be free of the English who were continually importuning us in our ship; here we propounded and clearly demonstrated Their H.M.'s resolution of the 21 September, and it was decided by 13 votes that we had no advantage over the enemy who were

Margin notes:
- Dorrevelt with his frigate tows their masts to the Spaniards.
- The Lt.-Adm. Tromp, Vice-Adm. de With, Vice-Adm. Evertse, Rear-Admiral Cats, Frans Jansse, Colster, Bancque.
- Council of War. Lt.-Ad. Tromp, Vice-Adm. de With, Vice-Adm. Everts, Bancque, Cats, Colster, Ham, Frans Jansse, M. Juijnboll, Van Dongen, Corn. Engelen, Corn.

1 MS. *boot*, derived from the Spanish "Botyo". Dom Francisco Manuel in his account of this incident (*Epanaphora*, pp. 557–8) says that Oquendo first offered Dorrevelt a large sum of money for this service, and when this was declined he presented him with the wine.

2 This entry is made in such obscure and ambiguous language, that it would appear this was deliberately done on Tromp's order for some reason or other.

54, and the English 24 sail strong, whilst we were now only 65 sail. In the evening we were joined by the ships of Bastiaen Tijsz. and Regemorter; [the latter] brought a letter from His Highness dated the 5 instant at Bergen-op-Zoom; there had also been aboard us 4 English Captains, Edward Popham, Slingsby, Richard Fielding and Henry Strandling,[1] with a merchant of Dover, who complained that Dorrevelt had carried off a bilander from the English convoy under the Castle; we therefore gave them a written order commanding the vessel to be restored, even though there were Spaniards in it;[2] we likewise gathered that the frigate was lying stranded on the shore, whither we dispatched Cornelis Bos, who returned at sundown with the news that the frigate lay high and dry whilst the Captain was a prisoner in the Castle. At sunset it was calm, and towards the evening the servant of the son-in-law of the Heer Joachimii came on board, bringing a letter for me and letters for Their H.M., His Highness, and the Lord States of Zeeland with a request to deliver the same.

The 9 October in the morning the wind at N. Sent the Heer Ambassador's servant with a missive to London, and also dispatched Captains Halfhoorn and Juijnbol to Scheveningen with letters for His Highness and Their H.M. concerning our situation, together with a copy of the resolution taken in the Vice-Admiral's ship and also the Heer Joachimi's letters. The Zijtsche pink[3] joined us bringing a letter from Their H.M. wherein they instructed me to inform them from time to time of how we stand, and exhorted us to carry out their resolution to the full when the opportunity should present itself; this pink and the flyboats of Aert Roelen and the "Straw nobleman",

Marginal notes:

Melcknap, Corn. de Zeeu, Halfhoorn, Jan Teeue, Hendrick Denijs, Houtebeen, Farant, Waterdrincker, Diemen.

(66)

Juijnbol, Halfhoorn, Aert Roelen, Strawnobleman, Zijtsche pink go home.

Post, Camp, Cats, Veen, Meij, Lobs, Mus, Nieuvelt, Gaersvelt, Bleijcker. There join us:— Capn Berchout, Wijbrant Dircxsz. & Jonas Amont's ship.

---

1 And the ubiquitous Peter White, who says they followed Tromp aboard De With's ship!

2 Cf. Peter White: "unto which he made answer that the Captaine and the men that were in that Frigot, were drunke with the Butt of Sack that the Spaniards gave him the day before, for he had no Commission for what he had done, and vowed that he would punish him for it". Curiously enough, Dorrevelt actually *was* drunk! His written apology to the Lord Warden of the Cinque Ports, the Earl of Suffolk, for his "drunken contempt" is printed in *Cal. S.P. Dom.* 1639, p. 536, along with other documents on the affair.

3 See under Sept. 27th.

together with all the skippers and sailors of the aforsaid 8 fire-ships, sailed homewards with the said Captains. We ordered Cats to cruise with 10 ships between Dover and Ostend on the 4 King's ships and 10 frigates which it was said were to come from Dunkirk, as also to visit all English ships bound for Flanders. The Count of Arundel came aboard, who was received with a salute of cannon, but we could not draw anything out of him to our advantage.[1] We learnt however that a Mestre del Campo[2] with some other Spanish officers would try to cross over from Dover to Dunkirk; we therefore ordered Captain Van de Base to cruise about for them, and we sailed once through the Spanish fleet in Captain Joris' yacht, accompanied by the Vice-Admiral de With and Captain Colster. A musket shot was fired from out of the Admiral of Naples[3] through our mizzen, wherefore we sent Captain Colster aboard and told them that they had broken the King's Peace in the roadstead, and that they could tell their General that we would shortly come to lay them on board with our ships.

The 10 in the morning the wind at east. Yesterday afternoon there came aboard us Sir Henry Mainwaring with 3 other Captains of the English King, who declared to us in the name of Admiral Pennington that he had that day received letters stating that the Lord High Admiral[4] had put off his intended journey hither, and there was every likelihood that the distrained ships pressed here for the King's Service would be released ere long. Master White of Sir John Pennington came aboard and brought us a copy of the order which had been issued to all the Royal ships, concerning the matter of safeguarding their roadstead and the striking of the flag. We learnt from him that the English Captains had made a bad report on us yesterday, saying that we had said that he [*i.e.* Pennington] could do his best, whereas on the contrary we had said that if

(66)
Verso

1 As Arundel was a Catholic this was not very surprising. He had been commander-in-chief of the English army on the Scottish border, and was then (1639) over 80 years old.

2 *I.e.* Colonel. This was our old friend Dom Simão de Mascarenhas. *Vide Cal. S.P. Dom.* 1639, p. 522.

3 The ship *Orfeo* of Don Pedro Velez de Medrano.

4 Northumberland.

it so happened that we received orders to attack the Spaniards here, we asked him to do as best he could by us.[1] We asked him what was the reason why the English Royal ships were getting under sail; he said that the Spaniards had reported, that we had told them that they had broken the peace in road through their musket shooting yesterday, and therefore we meant to come and board them; yet they excused themselves by saying that it had happened at nightfall and they had fired because they feared that it was a fireship which was about to clap them on board; but this was a lie since the sun had not yet set, and Mr White admitted that it was still daylight and we had then fired 3 saluting shots for Pennington, and he had answered with one.[2]

On the same day we received a letter from Their H.M. per Abram Crijnsz. in the Scheurwater yacht, together with an extract from the resolutions of Their H.M. dated 21 September, which charged us to put that into execution, as also did His Highness in his letter wherein he most earnestly charged us to carry out the same. At nightfall the Heer de Glarges left us with a number of French officers who had visited us; there had also been aboard the Governor of Dover Castle[3] with some gentlewomen and his own lady.

The 11 *ditto* in the morning the wind at N.E. We sent a yacht for the Commander Cats who joined us at noon, when we made signal for the Council of War to repair aboard. We also learnt that the French had taken the Spanish Sytie[4] last

1 All this is related by Peter White at great length in his account, pp. 22–4, who gives Tromp's answer as follows: "God forbid that I should say so; for that were a kind of challenging the King of *England* in his owne Road; I pray you, said he, mistake not my meaning, for my *English* is not very good, and I speak in our *Dutch* phraise, to doe the best for us, my meaning was that you should shoote over us, and not to hit us" (*Sea-fight*, p. 24). After further assurances by De Glarges, who was present, Pennington accepted this explanation.

2 This agrees with Peter White's account, p. 28.

3 Sir John Manwood.

4 Cf. Peter White: "*Don Carolus* sent one of his Captains aboard unto Sir *Iohn* to complain that his Sattee (light Iberian craft) was taken out of the Road last night. Sir *Iohn* answered him that the fault was their owne, for to Ride with such a small vessell so far from their Fleet, for an Adviser as he conceived should ride closse by the Admirall" (*op. cit.* p. 30). The Saetia in question was called *Santa Tereza. Vide* Appendix IV.

night. We unanimously resolved that we would attack the enemy with the first opportune wind and weather, and defend ourselves against whosoever should try to hinder the same. We ordered the Vice-Admiral de With with 30 warships and 4 fireships to observe the motion of the English and to resist them in the event of their attempting to attack us. During the day 2 different Zijtsche pinks came alongside, each with letters from Their H.M. wherein they commended to us in the most drastic wise the attacking of the enemy, and stated that we could rest assured that they would come to no other decision.

(67)

The Count of Warwick with three great Lords came aboard us this day;[1] some galleons came out from under the shore and anchored near their Admiral. In the morning 17 Flemish fisher-boats arrived with some men for the Spaniards.

The 12 *October* the wind at N.E. then E.N.E. Made signal for all Captains to repair on board, and told them frankly what we had resolved on yesterday, with regard to the Resolution taken by Their H.M. on the 21 September, and exhorted them to demean themselves courageously, and gave written orders to all those who were allotted to the Vice-Admiral de With's squadron. We also appointed tomorrow morning early as a day of prayer in the Armada. At noon the Heer Ambassador's servant came on board, bringing letters to be delivered in Holland. We weighed our anchor and plied up to northwards and came to an anchor over against the Spanish Admiral, Don Antonio. Towards the evening there came further letters from the Heer Joachimi which we sent on by Claes Juijnbol[2] with the Zijtsche pinks, which were already under sail with Captain Veen, who was carrying our letters wherein we sent to Their H.M. and His Highness our resolution taken yesterday. At sunset the Flemish fishers made sail northwards, but being pursued by our frigates some of them turned back. At sunset the wind at E.S.E. with a hard gale.

De Lieffde, Juijnbol, Nieuvelt, Jaersvelt, Bleijcker, Zeeuw, Crijn. Claesse, Berckhout, Loncque, Regemorter, Mangelaer, Swaert, Abram Crijnsse, Pr. Arentsse, de Vlamingh, Jan den Trechter.

Fireships to wait on their ships, as follows:—
Vice-Adm.   1
de Zeeu   1
M. Gillissen 1
de Lieffde   1
              —
              4

1 Cf. Peter White: "after dinner the Lords went all abord of the Dutch Admirall, who entertained them with 11 pieces of *Ordnance*, & gave them 21 pieces of *Ordnance* at their parting from him" (*op. cit.* p. 30).
2 See under third note in List of Captains at end of *Journal*.

The 13 *ditto* in the morning the wind at E.S.E. Captain Frans Mangelaer joined us from Vlissingen; he stated that before daybreak his convoy, consisting of 3 Zeelanders, had been taken by 6 stout Flemish frigates. We signalled all Captains who were in our division[1] to repair on board, to [? decide whether to?] attack the enemy, and divided them in squadrons as follows:—

The Lieutenant Admiral Tromp with his aim on Don Antonio
    1 fireship, Lt. Adm. Tromp, Colster, 1 fireship, Ham, 1 fireship, Sluijs, Vijch, Diemen, Corn. Engelen, den Hengst, Van Dongen, Van Galen,[2] Jacob den Boer.

The Vice-Admiral Evertsz., his aim on the Portuguese Admiral
    Vice-Admiral Evertsse, Ringelssen, Corn. Everts, Bastiaen Tijssen, Jacob Verhal, Pr. Claes t Lam, Mus, Abram Witboorn, Gillis Janssen, den Oven with 1 fireship, Bachuijsen, Waterdrincker, Frans Mangelaer.

Rear-Admiral Cats, his aim on the Flemish Admiral
    Cats, Farant, Turcquois with another 1 fireship, De Lapper, Schellinghout, Elias Balck, Melcknap, Pr. Brouck.

Commander Denijs on the south side of the fleet
    Commander de Nijs [*sic!*], Schrevels, Balcq, Nieuhof, Antonis, Davit Bont, Cappelman, de Bruijne.

Lourens Houtebeen opposite the northernmost ships of the Armada
    Houtebeen, de Robbe, Jacob Struijck, Corn. de Zaijer, Dirck Claesse, And. Cornelisse, Brustens.

Furthermore each Commander was ordered to anchor over against his allotted enemy, as most of them did. We propounded to the Council of War whether it would be advisable to begin the action with this easterly wind; it was unanimously resolved No,—by reason of the lee shore giving the enemy too much advantage;[3] we then asked with what wind would it be ad-

(67)
Verso

---

1 *I.e.* excluding those in De With's detached squadron.

2 See under his name in list at end of *Journal*.

3 *I.e.* they could run their ships aground easily, and thus deprive the Hollanders of the satisfaction of making prizes.

visable, whereupon it was unanimously resolved that we should commence in the name of God with a N.W. by W. to W.S.W. wind.[1] We sent the Captain[2] and Van Galen as envoys to Sir Pennington to ask whether he had received any order for the Spaniards to leave.

He made answer that he had told the Spaniards this morning that they should have to leave, whereon Don Antonio had replied that he would leave within half an hour when once he was ready.

Van der Zee and Michiel Fransse go with the Rouen Convoy.

It was further ordered this evening that Captains Michiel Fransz. and Van der See should go with their convoy to Rouen, and thence take the homeward-bound ships safely to the Maas, and then do whatsoever the Council would command them; many Spaniards also got under sail.

The 14 *October* in the morning the wind at E.S.E. with a steady gale. Some more of our ships got under sail. In the morning the *Wakend Hart* went to Calais with letters. We weighed our anchor and hacked a piece out of our cable; it became calm with misly and hazy weather. Most of the Council of War were aboard and we discussed the attacking of the enemy. During the day an English Royal *Whelp*[3] steered northwards and came to an anchor between the Quarles[4] and Goodwin. In the afternoon the Pfalzgraf Frederick[5] came on board Admiral Pennington's ship. He likewise sent to greet me through some noblemen, accompanied by the Count of

1 MS. has *N.E. by W. tot W.S.W.* which seems to have been written thus intentionally, to mislead. Cf. Oct. 15th.

2 *I.e.* Tromp's flag-captain, Barents.

3 MS. *Whulp*. There were ten of this class of vessel—*Lion's Whelps* as they were called—in the navy built by Charles I. They were all square-rigged with three masts and fitted for using sweeps. The original armament of each was four culverins, four demi-culverins, and two brass sakers; but to these two demi-cannon were added. The *Whelps* were built by contract at £3. 5s. a ton. Cf. Clowes, *Royal Navy*, II, p. 10 and note.

4 Peter White has "Quearns" for this bank.

5 This must be a mistake. Frederik V the Elector Palatine and "Winter-King" of Bohemia was already dead and his eldest son Frederik Hendrik had been previously accidentally drowned in Holland in 1629. The Pfalzgraf—or Elector Palatine—in 1639 was Karl Ludwig, elder brother of Princes Rupert and Maurice, and it is he who is intended here.

Warwick, whilst we congratulated him by shooting off some guns, as also did some others of our ships; the Spaniards did likewise, and they also shot dead a man in Captain Balck's ship with a musket. In the evening 2 English Royal ships went away with the Pfalzgraf; they beat up to southwards, being bound for Dieppe.¹

The 15 ditto the wind at E. by S. At sunrise we put abroad the red flag and held a Council of War. We decided that it would certainly be most advantageous for us to have the wind between N.W. by W. and W.S.W.² in attacking the enemy, but considering the season of the year, the uncertainty of the weather, and the reinforcing of both the English and the enemy, I propounded to the Council whether or no it was advisable to attack the enemy with such winds, when we could sail 4 or 5 points over the tide, whether it was ebb or flood, and the weather was such that we could bear out our lower tier of ordnance; a resolution was taken and signed regarding this matter, wherein we opined that it was seemly that we should begin.

(68)

In the morning the Vice-Admiral Sir Henry Mainwaring, Captain Hall and Captain Stradling came on board us; they asked us on behalf of Don Antonio whether we would oblige him with 5,000 lbs.³ of gunpowder and let pass 1,000 of his sick men to Flanders, in which case he would then sail out of the road tomorrow morning to fight with us. We agreed with the Council of War that we would do that, in order to get the enemy to come out of the road, provided that he paid therefor one hundred and ten pounds sterling, as he had been charged this amount at London;⁴ with regard to his sick, we could only

1 On his way through France to try to raise an army in Germany for the recovery of his Electorate, Karl Ludwig was thrown into prison at Vincennes by Richelieu's orders to Charles I's intense annoyance (*vlg*. Gardiner, *op. cit.* I, pp. 268, 274).

2 MS. has *b. N.E. to N.S.W.* (!!)—probably inserted thus deliberately. Cf. Oct. 13th. (N.)

3 Peter White (*op. cit.* p. 33) has 500 lbs.

4 In addition to paying for the powder, the Spaniards were forced to disgorge £5000 to the King and £1000 to the Earl of Newport (Master of the Ordnance) in bribes! For further details over this unsavoury transaction see Gardiner, *op. cit.* pp. 264–5. Curiously enough Peter White has it that Tromp offered to supply

say to him that a free country lay by him. When the sun was in the S.E. Captain Van Nes joined us.

We appointed three of our Captains, Colster, Van Galen and Pieter Claesz. 't Lam, to go with the Englishman on board of Sir Pennington, to tell the Spaniards through them of what we had determined about the powder.

The Admiral Pennington had received tidings from his Admiral that both the French and Holland Ambassadors had assured His Majesty that no act of hostility would be committed in the roadstead here, whereby 6 detained merchantmen and 1 Royal pinnace had been dismissed.

Towards evening our Commissioners returned from Admiral Pennington bringing no other tidings save that the Spanish Admiral thanked us for our offer of the gunpowder, but could not keep his word unless his sick were let pass, and with more flimsy excuses which we felt assured the English had made up.[1]

In the evening we were joined by the *Waeckende Hart* with the King's Lieutenant from Calais, accompanied by about 40 Frenchmen who wanted to view the fleet, yet they must needs wish to stay in our ship to fight against the Spaniards; we eventually with great trouble set them in Captain Veen's ship to take them to Calais; which Veen had convoyed the Zijtsche pinks as far as Schouwen having left here on the [blank]. In the evening the wind at east.

the powder *free*, but that Pennington said "that he would not upon those terms send unto the *Spaniard*, but if so be that they would set a reasonable price upon their Powder and sell it unto them, then Sir *Iohn* would give them notice of it".

1 MS. *blaeuwe redenen*. Tromp does the English less than justice. From a perusal of Peter White, *op. cit.* pp. 33–5, it is obvious that Pennington did nothing of the kind, ". . .also he [Pennington] told him [de Oquendo] that the *Hollanders* had been with him, and proffered to give them 500 barrells of powder". *Ibid.* p. 35 and again on p. 36: "discoursing with Capt. *Slingsby*, he [de Oquendo] said, the *Hollanders* it seemes have too much powder, for they proffer to spare him 500 barrels, the which if they will performe, and give him but leave to send away a thousand sick soldiers for *Flanders*, as he was a Gentleman he would goe out of the Road with them, & give them fighting work enough. Sir *Iohn* sent Capt. *Slingsby* and me abord of the *Hollander*, to certifie him, what the *Spanyard* demanded, who answered, that on the morrow he would send some of his Captains to treat with them about that busines".

The 16 *ditto* in the morning at 3 o'clock the wind at E. by S. We summoned the Vice-Admiral Evertsz., de Wit, Bancke, Commander Denijs and Cats with Houtebeen, Jan Van Galen and Forant. Some of those lying close inshore were towed out, since it was a flat lee-shore; we asked them their opinion whether we should begin, whereon it was unanimously resolved that this was inadvisable, since we could not bear out our lower tier and the wind was right against the land. We got under sail to clear our anchor, but we sailed our ports half in the water.

On the same day another 3 ships joined us, 2 from the Texel and 1 from the Vlie. At night 17 Flemish shallops arrived, bringing soldiers' straw-mattresses and women.[1] Before sunset Captain Keert de Koe's boat came alongside with the news that their captain was dead. We were joined by Captains Halfhoorn and Juijnbol, who had sailed from Scheveningen yesterday evening; they brought 2 letters from Their H.M. and 2 from His Highness, wherein they again urged us to attack the Spanish fleet, and most highly encouraged us to do so, but they had not been able to approve of sending one of their number hither;[2] in the evening it blew so hard with a hard loom gale that we had to veer more cable. The wind at E. by S.

The 17 *ditto* in the morning the wind at E. by S. and E.S.E. A number of the chief officers came on board again, viz. Vice-Admiral Evertsz., Bancke, Catz, Colster, Van Galen and others. The Vice-Admiral de With was sickly. We resolved, as yesterday, that it was inadvisable to attack the enemy. During the day Captain Veen rejoined us, having landed at Calais the French officers who had been aboard us on the 15. Mr White came on board bringing news that His Majesty was annoyed at our taking 2 ketches laden with Spaniards under the cannon of Margate, whilst wearing royal colours, for which cause we should punish our Captain; we thereupon said that no order had been given for this, but that I could not punish him, since

Margin notes:

From the garrison of Den Bos. Skipper Arent Aeckersloot, in the *Wapen van Amsterdam.* guns soldiers 18 : 61 : 20. Also brought 10 soldiers for Houtebeen. Skipper Scheur of Amsterdam in the *Geecroonde Walvis* 24 : 67 : 20. Commander Denijs 20 soldiers.

Marinus Juijnbol and Halfhoorn join us.

---

1 *I.e.* whores for the Spanish soldiers.
2 It was not until the days of Jan de Witt that one of the deputies of the States-General actually proceeded to sea with the fleet. Jan and his brother Cornelis often did so.

if he had not worn those colours, perchance the Spaniards would have taken him.[1]

The same day we dispatched Colster to set ashore Tam Trasaert to take horse for Rochester in order to spy out the King's ships there,—how many and how ready they might be, and where they lay. Colster, coming on board again in the evening, brought tidings that Don Antonio had dismissed 7 Easterling ships from his fleet,[2] whilst 3 English ketches and 7 or 8 Flemish fishers full of soldiers lay inshore ready to cross over to Dunkirk. During the day we had issued orders for Commander Regemorter, Mangelaer and Elias Base, to cruise between the Goodwin and the Flemish banks, on the look-out for English ships and Flemish fishers. At sunset another 2 stout Holland ships came round the Goodwins to join us; the wind at east with fine weather.

Hector Pietersz. and Jacob Lamberts join us.

(69)

The 18 *October* in the morning at daybreak the wind at east, with handsome weather; 2 captains came aboard us from the 2 ships arrived yesterday evening, namely Captains Hector Pietersz. and Jacob Lambertsz. Some members of the Council of War likewise came on board, tho' it was decided that it was not prudent to engage; at ten o'clock the wind was shuffling about between E.S.E. and E. Tam Trasaert returned from Rochester and declared that 6 royal ships were lying ready at Chatham to come here as speedily as possible, whilst there were 4 others at London which had been placed under embargo for the King's service.

The 19 *October* in the morning in the third glass of the day watch there came light airs at N.N.W., at daylight W.N.W. We were completely ready to fall upon the enemy if the wind had continued thus, but at 10 o'clock the wind chopt to E. by N. with a small gale, wherefore the onslaught was postponed.[3] In

1 In Peter White's account this is justly termed "a Baffling answer not worth the writing".

2 This is confirmed by Manuel de Mello, *Epanaphora* iv, p. 557, who says that most of the guns and men were taken out of these ships to reinforce the others. These Lübeckers still remained with the fleet on the 21st.

3 The English knew what was up. Writes Peter White: "...we hove out both our top-sailes, and were ready with all our fleet to attend on the *Hollanders*, and to assist the defendants, but the *Spaniards* rode still fast moored, albeit Capt.

the afternoon the Spaniards weighed their anchors and some of them drifted to rejoin their consorts.

The 20 *ditto* in the morning the wind at E. by S. and E.S.E. with a small gale; we were joined by Commander Regemorter and Frans Mangelaer and Captain Elias van der Base. We had hauled from off the Goodwins an enemy frigate which had sailed out of the Downs yesterday with 80 Spaniards and 8 or 10 Flemings. We placed one man in each ship. During the day we held a Council of War and propounded whether or not it was advisable to anchor near the enemy, so as riding at an anchor to attack them, tho' we were dissuaded from so doing by a majority of the Council, wherefore we continued to adhere to our former Resolution. Yesterday 4 English ships sailed out from the Downs and returned in again today. We sent a request to the Spanish Admiral asking him whether he would exchange Hollanders for Spaniards, whereof he asked a list of names, which we sent him and await an answer.

The 21 *ditto* in the morning at 2 hours before daybreak[1] it was misty and calm with the wind northerly. At slack water of ebb[2] we made signal to get under sail; before daybreak we said prayers, and at sunrise it became a little clearer, the wind being at N.W. We weighed our anchors and dropped to northwards of the enemy, and at about half-past eight we opened fire on the enemy who cut their cables and made sail; shortly after the action began it became very misty, so that we remained driving with our sails laid aback on the mast for a good half-hour, until it began to clear somewhat, so that we saw the enemy; *we fought him again and drove the enemy, to the total of* 23, *ashore*, close under the castles, including the Vice-

Chase the enemy out of the Downs.

Slingsby advised him to get his fleet loose, and rather to put it to a sea-fight, than to be burnt at an Anchor", etc. (*op. cit.* p. 40). He also notes that "the *Hollands* Admirall was fitted for fight, having taken downe all things, even his Bed-sted, and Table out of his Cabin"

1 At 4.30 o'clock, as the sun rises at 6.35 a.m.

2 Roughly about 8 o'clock or a little later. On full and new moons it is high-water at Dover at xi h. 12 m. (Deal xi h. 15 m.). Oct. 25th, 1639, was a new moon's date, therefore on the 21st it was high water at about vii h. 36 m., at which time the tide began to ebb, and with that tidal stream (which flows in a northerly direction) Tromp dropped with the ebb northwards of the enemy. (N.)

Admiral of Spain,[1] who was shot under the water, and lay waterlogged,—and we trust many others besides; we also fired a Dunkirker and a Spaniard. The Castles fired on us but did us little harm, whilst the English King's ships also did little or none. The remainder we drove fighting out of the Downs, some of them kept close inshore, whilst the Spanish Admiral went with a compact body of 19 or 20 sail steering his course towards Dungeness; we fought this body, as did the Vice-Admiral and other officers, and at about 3 o'clock Captain Mus became fast entangled with the Vice-Admiral of Portugal. 5 fireships came to burn the Admiral of Portugal, whereof three miscarried and were burnt out, but the other two fired the Portuguese Admiral, and meanwhile the Spanish Admiral made sail and took to flight with his attendant ships, being 17 sail strong, which we immediately pursued. At nightfall our headmost ships were up with his sternmost and plied them very hotly, but we could not see whether he had struck or no. We followed the enemy, but lost sight of him in the evening. The wind at N.N.W. afterwards [blank] we sailed S. west.[2]

During the fight two of the enemy's galleons, which ran foul of each other, fell away to leeward, and we felt sure they had also struck because there was a large squadron of ships near them. Three were also taken to windward under the land, so far as we could see; at night when the middlewatch was over the wind shifted N.W. We tacked northwards; in our ship were slain Pieter Jansz. Qual, Pouwels Pietersz., Jacob Jorisz., whilst Jan de Ruijter and Jan van Luijcq had their legs shot away.

Killed, Pr. Jansse
Qual. Pouwels
Pietersz., Jacob
Jorissen.
Their legs shot off;—
Jan de Ruijter, Jan
van Luijcq.

The 22 *October* the wind was west with variable hard weather and squalls of rain, Beachy bearing N.N.W. from us 3 miles off. We lay over to the south-east, and saw our ships

---

1 *San Agustin* commanded by Don Andrés de Castro. She had originally been the flagship of the Naples squadron and was one of the finest ships in the fleet. The names of the 23 ships driven ashore are given, in English, *S.P. Dom. Charles I*, vol. 431, no. 76, Record Office MSS. Cf. Appendix IV.

2 Tromp told Peter White on the 24th, that on the 21st "Before midnight the wind Westered so, that so farre as they were a head of the Hollanders, so much they were to windwards of them; yet the *Hollanders* plyed to and fro all the night, expecting that on the morrow, by shift of wind, they might recover them".

From the painting by Hendrik Van Anthonissen (1606–c. 1652) in the Nederlandsch Historisch Scheepvaart Museum at Amsterdam

BATTLE OF THE DOWNS (OCT. 21ST, 1639)

In the centre the Vice-Admiral of Zeeland, Jan Evertsen, is engaged with the flagship of the Portuguese squadron, the great *Santa Tereza*. On the right is Tromp's flagship the *Amelia*, and on the extreme left the English coast and forts.

scattered about; we counted 55 sail altogether, but could not perceive that there was an enemy included amongst them. When the sun was S.E. we discovered a galleon to which we gave chase, whilst it began to rain and blow hard, so that we had perforce to take in our topsails, and the aforesaid galleon stood stem for stem with us, and blew both his topsails with the mainsail out of the bolt ropes. We stood with him and shot twice at him, then mastered him and set our pilot, Jan Poupse, therein, together with the mate, Pieter Pietersz. and the boat-swain, who remained on board; we sent him to Vlissingen under the convoy of Captain Brust, in whose ship we placed Monsieur Billicq with letters for His Highness and the States-General; there were 12 bronze and 12 iron guns in the prize. Towards the evening a storm blew asunder our mizzen, mainsail and spritsail. We presumed that the enemy were to windward, and we likewise learnt from a Flemish prisoner, that during the night some of the enemy with a number of our ships had run before the wind. After sunset we bent the courses and steered northwards. At 5 glasses in the first watch we tacked south-wards until after midnight, when we cast about to the north. At about 11 o'clock we had to lower our foresail on the bow by reason of the storm.[1]

(70)

The 23 October in the morning the wind at west with hard gusty weather. During the day we hove out our foresail and ran northwards. Our fleet was very scattered; we discovered another galleon amongst our main body, that was captured by our ships. We made landfall about Dungeness at mid-day, where we found some of our ships lying at anchor here and there, whilst one vessel ran ashore; we discovered no more enemies, but a great fleet of over 50 sail came out of the west. We bore away before the wind to the Downs. Coming before Dover we saw another Spanish galleon lying right under the Castle, whither we sent Captains Farant, Post and Joris Pietersz. to take him, whilst we put into the Downs and found the Spanish fleet destroyed, most of them having run aground. We fired divers salutes for the Castle of Dover and for the

During the fight we were joined by,— Gerrit Symons, buss-convoyer, Teunis Conde, Corn. Lastdrager, and Jacob Schot. We sent home-wards;—

1 See note under May 4th.

of *the E. I. Comp.*
Comm. Houtebeen,
Reijnert de Rose,
Jacob Struijck,
Corn. Saijer.

West Ind. Comp.
Salamander.

To the great fishery
Comm. Voorburgh,
Van Dongen, Teeus
Pieterssen, den
Hengst, Corn. de
Zeeu.

Captain Vijch goes to
the Scheur to spy out
the ships lying there.

(70)
Verso

royal ships in the Downs, but got no answer.[1] At nightfall the aforesaid fleet passed us, sailing along outside the Goodwins to the north. 3 fresh Captains came aboard as well as the Haven buss-convoyer.[2]

The 24 ditto in the morning the wind was N.W. with a loom gale. The Admiral Pennington came on board, asking what we still wanted to do here, now that we had recently affronted the King in his Chamber, and what we meant by it. We answered that we hoped that the King would not take it as an affront from us, and that in accordance with the orders of our High Authorities we had acted as faithful servants, and that finally we had come to see whether all the Spaniards who had been chased ashore were disposed of, and if not we would gladly destroy them. He replied and swore by all the Saints that there was not a single one left entire, and those that were still drifting about had been surrendered and sold to the English, who were plundering the Spaniards as much as they could. He said that altogether there were 22 Spanish ships left here either burnt, sunk or spoiled. Master White, Captain Fielding, and another redcoat[3] have also been here. We made signal for all Captains to repair on board and ordered 2 ships to cruise under the command of Captain Colster for safeguarding the sea, as per margin. Captain Dorrevelt came to say that another Spanish prize lay under the point of Dungeness, wherefore we gave him order to take it home. We also felt sure that Captains Farant and Joris Pietersz. must have captured the Spaniard left lying off Dover yesterday, since they did not reappear.[4] During the day 5 English King's ships came from north of the Downs, and fired numerous discharges.

1 Little wonder! Tromp must have dictated this entry with his tongue in his cheek! Cf. Peter White, *op. cit.* p. 49: "But we did not answer him one Piece of Ordnance".   2 *I.e.* Gerrit Symonsz. See marginal entry.

3 MS. *roorock*. Compare Peter White, *op. cit.* pp. 49 ff.

4 Writes Peter White, *inter alia*: "Amongst other discourse with him [Tromp], I did inquire for my friend Captain *Forran* a French Captaine formerly mentioned, and how he had behaved himself in the fight; he answered me, that he was a stout man of Warre, and said that if so be that all his Captains had been such as he was, they might have done more than they did. But hee imployed him about a businesse of Consequence, otherwise he had been in the Road. Which as I was afterwards informed, [was] to take the *Spanish* Galeon that rode in *Dover*

The 25 October in the morning the wind at north. An hour after sunrise we weighed our anchors and ran under Hythe Castle to fetch water for the whole fleet, whilst we ordered Houtebeen to ride in the Downs with the West-India ships and buss-convoyers which we had sent off yesterday. We issued out written orders to the Captains serving under Commander Colster, and ordered Pieter Broucq to go to Nantes and to pick up Aert Roelen and another Hollander on the way. There passed us a west-bound fleet of about 20 English sail, who fired [? salutes?]; in the evening the wind at N.N.E.

Corn. Lastdrager, Jacob Schot, Gerrit Claessen, Ringelssen, Turquoijs, Schellinghout, Melcknap, Hector Pieters, Schrevels, Balcq, de Bont, Hendr. Jansse, Corn. Meij, Arent Ackerslot, de Zeeu, Jan Gerbrandsz., Jacob Lambertsz., Loncq, Vlaming.

Pr. Broucq goes to Nantes.

The 26 ditto in the morning the wind at north; during the morning watch at about 8 o'clock, we weighed our anchors and drove eastwards on the flood-tide with our 27 sail. We handed over to Commander Regemorter all the borrowed munitions which the Comte de Charost had lent us,—about 4000 rounds,—and ordered him to restore this amount at Calais,[1] and then to convoy with his squadron the vessels lying there homeward-bound. At southern sun we shaped our course for Calais, and came to anchor in 15 fathom with that place bearing S.E. from us. A Calais frigate with a letter from the Comte de Charost came alongside, to which we replied. The Frenchmen told us that three enemy ships were stranded between Boulogne and Calais, whilst 10 ships had run into the Scheur, including Don Antonio with another great galleon, both of which had stranded in entering the Scheur—or so he said[2].

3 enemy ships stranded.

The 27 ditto in the morning the wind at west. We weighed our anchors before daybreak and set our course for Gravelines. We were joined by Captain Vijch who told us that he had been off the Scheur yesterday, and seen lying therein the Spanish Admiral[1] and another galleon[2] with 11 other Flemish and Dutch-built ships; 5 of these he had seen run into the harbour

road. The which service he performed; for the next day there came Complaints unto our Admirall, that she was taken out of the Road in the night and carried away, which was impossible for us to prevent" (*op. cit.* p. 50).

1 See Sept. 18th and 20th, and Oct. 5th.

2 This news was exaggerated, see next entry. One of the ships stranded on the French coast was the great galleon *S. Christo de Burgos*, flagship of the squadron of San Josef.

(71)

with high water, so that there were now left 6 Flemish ships lying in the Scheur and 2 Spaniards in the harbour. We therefore summoned the Council of War and asked each one's advice as to what we should do, and it was unanimously resolved that since the enemy lay in the Scheur, we could do nothing with him, and should continue on our course to the fatherland. We left Commander Regemorter and his attached ships before Calais, and set our course N.E. by N. About 2 of the clock the Vice-Admiral Evertsz., Bancker and skipper de Bruijn left us, we complimented each other with several salutes; an hour before sunset the Amsterdamers left us, shaping their course for the Texel; we were joined by Captain Cappelman, whom we dispatched to the fishery; there also came out of the Texel for news Claes Symons Cramer, whom we sent after Captain Colster. When the first watch was over, we hauled our foresail to the mast and drove with the head to the south, the wind at W.S. west with fine weather.

The 28 *October* in the morning at 3 hours before daybreak we had 12 fathom depth of water. We cast about to northwards. At daybreak it began to be misly.[4]

Left us;—
Vice Adm. Evertsze, Bancque, de Bruijn.
To the Texel
De Nijs, t Hoen, Waterdrincker, Jan de Lapper, Elias Basse, Nieuhoff, Snip. A. Damasse, Lobs, Bleijcker, Berchout.
Cappelman to the Fishery, Claes Symons goes after Commander Colster.
Lt-Adm. Tromp. Vice-Adm. de With in Colster's[3] ship. Diemen, Vijch, Ham Keert de Koe, Halfhoorn, Cats, M. Gillisse, Post, Borrevelt, Veen.

1 The *San Tiago*.
2 The flagship of the Bartelosa squadron, which had been temporarily captured by Tromp in the action of Sept. 18th, *q.v.* She was subsequently wrecked in the harbour, the crew being saved.
3 In Colster's ship as he was ill. Cf. under Oct. 17th, and *Leven en Bedrijf*, p. 118.
4 The next day Tromp made his report to the States-General. *Vide* Aitzema, II, p. 615.

LIST and NAMES

of the

CAPTAINS and COMMANDERS and SKIPPERS

of the WARSHIPS

present in the Downs

the 21 October 1639

for the purpose of helping to destroy the Spanish Fleet there

under the flag of

ADMIRAL TROMP

which have divided together the plunder therefrom.

GELDERLAND.

Captain Pieter Pietersz. de Wint, in whose ship[1] was the Vice-Admiral De With.[2]

WARSHIPS OF ROTTERDAM serving under the said Flag.

The Lieutenant-Admiral Tromp.

Captain Willem Van Coulster.

Captain Sijvert Vijch, Captain Van Diemen.

---

1 *Prins Frederick Hendrick.* See Oct. 1st.

2 Witte Cornelisz. de With (1599–1658). First served in the East Indies 1616, where he took part in the operations round Jacatra (Batavia) in 1619. Under the West India Company in 1623, after which he was again in the East Indies in the voyage round the world of the Nassau fleet. Served under Piet Heyn at Matanzas, and under Tromp at the Downs. In June 1640 he captured Matthys Rombouts, the celebrated Dunkirk corsair. In 1644 he convoyed 900 merchantmen through the Sound without paying the tolls. He was sent to Brazil in 1647 to restore the situation there, but failed, and returned to Holland without orders, for which he was imprisoned by the Prince of Orange (1649). In 1652 he was reinstated in his former rank and fought in the first English war at the battles of Nieuport, Texel, and Ter Heide, etc. He was killed in action against the Swedes (Nov. 8th, 1658). A man of headstrong personal courage, he was hated by the majority of his seamen owing to his severity and hot temper. His manuscript seventeenth-century *Life* was recently published by S. P. L'Honoré Naber under the title of *Leven en Bedrijf*, etc. in the *Transactions* of the Historical Society of Utrecht, 1926.

WARSHIPS FROM THE SAME COLLEGE serving as Convoyers.

Captain Cornelis Engelen Silvergieter.
Captain Marinus Juijnbol.
Captain Musch.
Captain Pieter Jansz. van den Brouck.
Captain Jan Jacobsz. van Es.
Captain Ban Brustens.
Captain Sier de Lieffde.
Captain Claes Juijnbol.[1]
Commander Skipper Teeus Conde, with a hired ship.

BUSS-CONVOYERS FROM THE MAAS.

Captain Dirck Claesz. van Dongen of Rotterdam.
Captain Gerrit Symonsz. Voorburch of Delft.
Captain Teunis den Hengst of Schiedam.

WARSHIPS, distributed under the aforesaid Flag.

Jonkheer Joris van Catz,[2] Rear-Admiral.
Captain Jan Theunisz. Sluijs.
Captain Post in Voorn's ship. [Post's own ship was the *Deventer* (28).]
Captain Mathijs Gillisz.
Captain Gerrit Meijnertsz., "the Owl", in Brederode's ship. [*Utrecht* (28).]
Captain Barent Pietersz. Dorrevelt.

WARSHIPS of the same College destined to act as Convoyers.

Captain Sijbrant Waterdrincker.
Captain Jacob Turcquois.
Captain Jan de Lapper.[3]
Captain Elias van de Baese.
Captain Jan van Galen.[4]

(72)

1 Presumably Nicolaes Juijnbol who had served under Piet Heyn at the capture of the Spanish Silver Fleet in Matanzas Bay, Cuba, in 1628. He saw much service against the Dunkirkers, including the capture of the port in 1646. Other members of the same family were Marinus Juijnbol (*vide supra*), whose name frequently occurs in this journal, and Dirck Juijnbol, who was blown up with his ship in the battle with the English off Dungeness, Dec. 10th, 1652.

2 Joris Cats, a man of the Van Dorp type. He had been employed in diplomatic dealings with Algiers in 1617–23, and despite his flag-rank in the Downs seems to have seen little or no fighting at sea before or since. In 1651 he was dispatched to the Mediterranean, where he commanded until relieved by Jan Van Galen. Cf. further, J. C. M. Warnsinck, *Een Nederlandsch Eskader in de Middellandsche Zee*, 1651–1653 in the *Marineblad* of 1923, pp. 441 ff., and Elias, *Schetsen*, III, pp. 116–38 for details.

3 See under Oct. 3rd.

4 Jan Van Galen, a German by birth, first saw service against the Dunkirkers in 1631. For the next twenty years he saw much fighting against Dunkirk corsairs,

Captain Hendrik Cornelis Denijs.
Captain Hendrick Schrevelsz.
Captain Aucke Balcq.
Captain Willem van Nijeuhoff.
Captain Evert Anthonisz.
Captain Davit Jansz. Bondt.
Captain Jan Gerbrantsz.

NORTHERN DIRECTORS' SHIPS OF AMSTERDAM.

Captain Gerrit Fredericxsz. of Zuurwoude.
Captain Cornelis Claesz. Lastdrager.
Captain Jacob Tijsz. of Nijeuvelt.
Captain Claes Bastiaensz. of Jaersvelt.

HIRED MERCHANTMEN, both East and West India Company's ships
    at Amsterdam.
(These seventeen are Commander skippers.)

Laurens Pietersz. Bachuijse.
Hector Pietersz.
Lambert Henricxsz. Smith.
Admiral Houtebeen.¹
Reijnert Wijbrantsz. de Vos.
Jacob Struijck.
Gerrit Claesz. de Ham.
Cornelis de Zaijer.
Claes Claesz. Schienmaecker.
Dirck Claesz.
Arent Pietersz. Aeckerslooth.
Henrick Jansz. Schuijr.
Joannis Ijsbrantsz.
Adrian Domassz.
Jan Jacobsz. Lobs.
Jacob Lambrechtsz.
Jacob Schatt.

(72)
Verso

WARSHIPS from Zeeland serving under the aforesaid Flag.

The Vice-Admiral Jan Evertsz.² in the ship of Captain Frans Jansz.

Barbary pirates and the like, until in 1652 on the outbreak of war with England
he was appointed to command the Dutch forces in the Mediterranean. He
succeeded in driving the English out of this sea, but was mortally wounded in
the victory he gained off Livorno (March 14th, 1653). For further details see
J. C. M. Warnsinck, *Een Nederlandsch Eskader in de Middellandsche Zee,*
1652–1654.

    1 See note under Oct. 6th.
    2 Johan Evertsen (1600–66) served in countless actions and campaigns, the
chief of which were La Rochelle (1625), West Indies (1626), The Slaak (1631),

Commander Joost Bancker.[1]
Captain Cornelis Ringelsz.
Captain Adriaen Swart.
Captain Cornelis Regemorter.
Captain Abram Crijnsz.[2]

WARSHIPS from the same College destined to act as Convoyers.

Captain Vlieger's ship wherein was—
Commander Jan Willemsz.
Captain Cornelis Evertsz.[3]
Captain Bastiaen Thijsz.
Captain Gloeijenden Oven[4] [= Glowing Oven].
Captain Frans Mangelaer.
Captain Cornelis Mangelaer ⎫ both fisher-convoyers of Zierickzee.
Captain Cornelis Jansz. Teer ⎭

HIRED MERCHANT SHIPS from Zeeland.
(These ten are Commander skippers.)

(73)   Jacob Verhelle.
Pieter Claesz. "the Lamb".
Abram Witboom.
Jaques Thybout.
Pieter Arentsz.
Gillisz. de Vlamingh.
Jan den Trachter.
Jacob de Bruijn.
Loncque.[5]
Andries Cornelisz.

Dunkirk (1636), The Downs (1639), Sas van Gent (1647), the whole of the war of 1652–4, and part of the Swedish war. Appointed Lt-Admiral in 1664 he was temporarily, and unjustly, dismissed after Lowestoft, but reinstated to die in St James' fight, July 25th (Aug. 4th, N.S.), 1666.

1 His proper name was Joost van Trappen. He served at Matanzas (1628), Pernambuco (1630), against Dunkirk (1636) and at the Downs. Appointed Vice-Admiral in 1646, he died in the following year. His two sons also achieved fame in the wars against England.

2 See under May 6th.

3 Brother of Jan Evertsen, and known as Cornelis Evertsen de Oude to distinguish him from his sons and nephews of the same name. After much service against the Dunkirkers he saw service against the English (1652–4), Swedes, and Barbary pirates. Appointed Vice-Admiral in 1664 and Lt-Admiral in 1665, he fought at Lowestoft and was killed in the Four Days' Fight of June 1666.

4 See under May 9th.

5 I suppose this is Hendrik Cornelisz. Loncq, who served at Algiers in 1624, under Piet Heyn in 1628, and commanded the fleet which took Olinda and Pernambuco in 1630, though it seems curious that he should now be occupying such a subordinate post. Perhaps it was a son or nephew, or Cornelis Lonck.

WARSHIPS from out of the North-Quarter serving under the same Flag.
Captain Claes Jansz. Ham.
Captain Keert de Koe.
Captain Lieve de Zeeu.
Captain Lambert Ysbrantsz. Halfhoorn.
Captain Bleijcker.

WARSHIPS from the same College destined to serve as Convoyers.
Captain Jan Pietersz. Berchout.
Captain Cornelis Jansz. Schellinchout.
Captain Melcknap.
Captain Jan Warnars Cappelman.
Captain Cornelis Meij.
Captain Cornelis de Zeeu.

NORTHERN DIRECTORS' SHIPS from the North-Quarter.
Captain Crijn Claesz. of Hoorn.
Captain Jacob Cornelisz. de Boer of Enchuijsen.

WARSHIPS FROM FRIESLAND serving under the aforesaid Flag.
Captain Joris Pietersz. Broeck.
Captain Hendrik Jansz. Camp.
Captain Tjaert de Groot.

ON BEHALF of the PROVINCE of OVERIJSSEL.
Captain Jaques Forant. [In the *Overijssel* (26).]

HALF FOR GELDERLAND, HALF FOR DRENTH.
Captain Gerrit Veen.

N.B. Names in brackets from *Cal. S.P. Dom.* 1639, p. 411.

There follows in the Manuscript an extract from the Resolutions of Their High Mightinesses The States-General, dated 4th December 1638, concerning Tromp's messing-allowance, and another note on the Dunkirkers, which are omitted as being of no very great interest to the campaign of 1639.

APPENDIX I

Dom Francisco Manuel's account of the fights in the Channel,
September 16th and 18th

(Dom Francisco Manuel, *Epanaphora Bellica* IV, *Conflito do Canal*, pp. 502–23,
2nd edition, Lisboa 1676.)

At daybreak on Wednesday the 16th of September, the Spanish vessels
were seen scattered about far apart from each other, as if on that night
the fortune of their enemies had controlled them; for each one plied about
whither he chose, whilst all were seeking for the fittest place for the
battle, and thus they confusedly ploughed through the waves, some cutting
across the courses of others, with incredible disorder. For this cause, and
by reason of the zeal with which I attempt to write, availing myself
of historical lessons, I would advise those who may have to give battle
with a great force, *That previous to doing so, they should divide their
ships into squadrons, which are to fight separately.* Because Experience
has shown, that both to that Captain who knows best how to dispose of
it, as to him who knows how to keep it, this formation matters not less
than victory itself.

It would be about seven o'clock in the morning when the whole of the
Hollander's Armada was discovered, that with the very north-west
wind before which the Spaniards were steering, bore up towards them.
Withal so few were those ships, that it was thought perchance we might
be mistaken and that it was some English squadron. Only eleven Dutch
ships could be counted together, besides another six further off which
were standing on a different tack.

General Oquendo, anxious for the fray, once more showed (and
this time with the most disastrous results in his life) how much he preferred the heart of a soldier to the spirit of a Captain. He set every stitch
of canvas,[1] and without paying the slightest heed to the remainder of the
Armada, he sailed on the same tack as did the enemy flagship, followed
only by the lightest Dunkirk ships which were posted in the vanguard,
and in support of the Flagship; among these, the *Capitana* of that squadron
made sail ahead of the others, whilst those which were smaller remained
always close to the Flagship, including the galleon commanded by the
Sergeant-Major D. Juan Ascencio.[2]

Many were saying, that until then there had never dawned a day in
which the fear of an approaching battle could have been better excused,
for it came to pass that through the want of any orders whatsoever to

1 "Largou todas as vélas ao vento."
2 The galleon was the *San Juan Bautista*.

take up any suitable formation,[1] many Captains who were near the enemy steered away from them, on pretext of seeking their post according to the place which had been assigned to them in the plan.[2] Some who found themselves to windward of the enemy, lost the weather-gage easily, since the chiefs of the squadron in which they were included were to leeward of the remainder of the fleet at dawn. These disorders, almost instantaneous in affairs of navigation, are—once committed—most difficult to remedy. Whence as regards Generals at Sea, it is better for them to watch rather their friends than their enemies in the time of battle; contenting themselves with being the cause of the successes of their men,—as also they are of their errors when they do not apply thereto the remedy that they ought.

General Tromp, whose proper name was *Martim Herps*, with the title of Lieutenant-General of the sea (since its rule strictly speaking pertains to the Prince of Orange), was not completely informed of the strength of the Spanish Arms; for it is certain that the States-General,—either because their spies had not informed them of the coming of the Italian contingent, or because they thought to dissimulate the advantage which the Spaniards thereby had over them,—had always told their Commanders that they had only to deal with the arm of Don Lope de Hoces, encouraging them to battle. And since the forces of Holland were stronger than his, in order that such an honourable fight should not escape them, the Dutch General divided his ships into three squadrons; one of which he sent into the North Sea under the command of Captain Ban Kart [= Banckert], to see if perchance it was true (as was said) that we were coming north about round England, as indeed the Spaniards had originally intended to do; another entrusted to Viten Viticen [= Witte de With], which was to cruise round all the ports of that island; whilst that which he had with him was to cruise off the coast of Flanders, albeit it did not exceed eleven ships, although they were the best of the States'.

Tromp, then, recognizing his mistake and also that of his superiors, on sighting the huge power of the Spanish fleet, and seeing that only valour could save the situation, put abroad the flag of council in view of the enemy, and having thus summoned those of his Captains who were with him, he spoke to them (as he told me afterwards) in this very sense:[3]

1 The original is far from clear, but the general sense is that Oquendo issued no orders of any kind, whence his captains acted on their own judgments.

2 The *meia-lua* or crescent formation prescribed in Appendix IV.

3 Despite a great deal of high-falutin' and Iberian flourishes in the speech that follows, there are some sentences in it which might very well have come from the lips of Tromp himself. It must be remembered that Tromp would have no reason for lying to Dom Manuel when they met at Falmouth and talked over the battle of the Downs. At any rate, the words attributed to Tromp here, are more honourable to him than those alleged in Witte de With's *Leven en Bedrijf, q.v.*

"*Our birth obliges us to die for our country, our duty for the Common weal, and our honour for our own sake. It is for this hour that for many years the States of Holland have sustained us; nobody can say that he has been deceived, when that happens to him for which he should always have been waiting. Yonder is the Standard of Spain, which we have never yet seen in these seas save to lower it before our banner. Do not suffer yourselves to be intimidated by its arrogance, nor because it is accompanied by many who acknowledge its sway; because from the formation which they have taken up on seeing their danger, you can perceive how much they will try to avoid running into it. If only the sight of you has sufficed to disorder them, what will not your force achieve? He who fears appearances is bound to yield to mere empty demonstrations. 'Tis true that I see yonder some powerful Spanish ships, but those vessels, which resemble fortresses, are like bodies without a soul, since they are not animated by the courage of the brave men who are lacking therein to defend them. Those Burgundian staves which wave upon the poops of those Brabant ships,[1] have more virtue in the hands of their pirates than in those of their Captains,—as everyone knows; for interest aided by practical experience greatly exceeds any result of obedience to one deserving thereof, always remiss on similar occasions.[2] Because those men whom Greed renders daring, seldom or never risk their lives when not animated thereby; for ruled by vice, they do not find in Glory the pleasure which Plunder gives them. The other ships which you see sailing about in disorder merely increase the numbers of the Enemy and not his force; and since they only serve to increase their confusion, the more of them that you find the surer will you be of victory. Withal I say that if with the eleven ships which we have here, we wish to give battle to the seventy which we see before us, it will appear rash; but if we of these eleven, can make one single ship, then those who form such an unwieldy monster, if they attack us, they will be the rash ones; for who in his senses would try to attack an unbreakable rock defended by the five hundred cannon which we have amongst us? Whence I do not know whether its fury or handiness will be the greater. I will soon see, when we have thus built this new machine, what we will do to those ungainly louts who form the greater part of their soldiery. To attack us thus would be extremely difficult even to brave souls; united then, my friends, in body and soul, let our resolution likewise be one, and our arms like those of one body; and as we make common Death and Life, so if one of us be killed, let us avenge him as if we all had been injured, whilst if only one survives he will triumph for all together. It is necessary; for all those who hear me now are practised seamen; work in such a manner that these our ships unite so closely, that by no chance will they allow any contrary force to penetrate between them. Let each one die at his post, because should he perish elsewhere*

1 *I.e.* the red diagonal cross on the Dunkirk ships.

2 I am aware that this is unintelligible, but so is the original so far as I am concerned: "o interesse ajudado da prática, excede muyto qualquer efeito da obediencia, a quem desserve a vontade, sempre remissa em semelhantes accidentes".

neither Death nor Life will be of service to him. But if, despite all our valour and skill, misfortune should overtake us, it will be an hour which has been thus decreed in Heaven; for what does it matter what this may chance to be? Fortunate are they who at the price of their blood purchase the safety of their Country, wives and Religion!"

The Captains who were present at Tromp's Council were:—Colster, Nam, Cornicem, Foraõ, Port, Kamp, Brederode, Baosk, Honcling and Ringelsz;[1] they all without any other reason than that of obedience forthwith repaired aboard their ships; and assembling them diligently, they compassed them together in such a manner that the bowsprit of one was always touching the taffrail of the other next ahead,[2] whilst there was not room for the smallest falúa[3] to pass betwixt them. The formation of the Spaniards on the other hand was disordered in the extreme, partly owing to the novelty thereof and partly to want of skill. The Dunkirk squadron, in better order than the rest, followed the Flagship. The remaining vessels were each trying their best to get up with the enemy from where they were so as to engage them.

The General Oquendo was obsessed with the vainest pride, and desired to have all the glory of the victory for himself, whence it came to pass that he took it from him and his, giving it to the enemy, as not seldom happens to those men who blindly seek to carry out their designs by the same means which frustrate them. His whole idea was to board the enemy Flagship without discharging a single cannon or musket shot; with this end in view, followed confusedly by some ships, he bore down alongside the Hollanders so that when the two flagships were level he could clap that of the enemy on board. However since maritime affairs are so violent and uncertain that they usually confound all human skill and foresight, when the Spanish Flagship tried to run aboard the Dutch it was already too late, and she was left so far astern of the Hollander that she could not grapple him as had been tried and intended. He at once hauled to the wind to improve his position, but at the same time all the enemy ships passed him. Withal Oquendo did not wish to fail in this effort which he regarded as constituting the victory of the battle;...He therefore next tried to board the Almiranta[4] which dextrously evaded his grappling irons, leaving the Spaniards bereft of their fantastic and presumptuous conceits. But Tromp, not content with what had happened, tacked with all his Captains, who falling upon Oquendo gave him such furious broadsides with their eleven ships, as to cause him such damage that when the smoke of the first discharges had cleared away, the Spanish Flagship was only recognizable to the remainder of the Fleet by the place in which it was. The flags with which it was adorned were fluttering about loose in the air.

1 For correct names see under Sept. 15th–17th in the *Journal* of Tromp.
2 "que os goroupezes de huãs, beijavaõ sempre os forões das outras".
3 *falúa* would correspond to an English hoy, smack, catch or what-not.
4 De With's flagship.

The shrouds hung like pennants, trembling sadly in the breeze, and cut by the chain shot of the enemy. Then Oquendo, like a brave bull which is ferociously attacked by a pack of hounds and blindly charges those which assault him, so he with his ship full of dead, wounded, and mutilated (who it is affirmed amounted to over 150 in this first action) gallantly tacked upon those which were nearest him, whom he plied upon most hotly with continual broadsides and discharges of musketry, from which the near-by enemy received no little hurt. At this time there were already numbers of her own fleet near the Flagship, and these engaging closely with the Hollanders sufficed to detain them until such time as the rest of the Fleet came up, from which the enemy could not escape despite all his arts. The fight now greatly increased in violence on both sides whilst several persons thought that Fortune was declaring for Spain, because I suppose that although the Almirante Viten Viticen with five great ships (and subsequently another two of the same squadron) had joined the General Tromp, this reinforcement could only have served in that hour to make his loss the greater and to enhance and increase the victory of Spain; for victory, without a doubt, was already beginning to declare itself thus, with the firing of a Dutch ship, that by reason of its size was known as the *Graõ Christovaõ*, which was burnt by some chance fire due to misfortune or neglect. But since the Spanish Commanders were so avid of Glory, they would not admit this; but I believe that six persons of high position claimed the honour of causing this tragedy, each one of them attributing this occurrence to his own force; there perished in the explosion nearly 120 Hollanders, for the remainder of the crew saved themselves indifferently amongst friends and foes.[1]

Tromp now found himself in a parlous plight, more by reason of the place in which he was, than through the great Armada which beset him. That portion of the land of France which forms the arc of the Gulf of Boulogne (within which, amidst vast sandy shoals, the River Somme, already mentioned, flows into the sea) formed a Lee shore to the Hollanders, since the wind was from the west-north-west; it was impossible to round it,—as they were obliged to do in order to save themselves,—without falling into the hands of the Armada, which, formed in a squadron after the fashion called *Grande ferente*[2] by soldiers, had penned them into a narrow space between the river[3] and the shore. On the other hand, towards the south-east, south, and south-west ran the banks and shoals which extend all along that coast and those ports; in view of this fact, in the opinion of experienced persons, the Spaniards had only to continue on the same tack on which they already were, in order to

1 Actually only one man was picked up by the Hollanders. See *Journal* under Sept. 22nd.

2 Unfortunately I cannot explain this word, but I should imagine it means a crescent formation.

3 *I.e.* the Somme.

assure themselves securing the spoils of the enemy; for since their ships of great burthen were being forced towards the shore, the Hollanders, in order to avoid stranding on the banks (which would be crueller enemies to them than the Spaniards), thereby imperilling all their lives, they would, of the two pressing dangers to which they were exposed, rather choose that of surrender than of shipwreck. And how much the more since, when yielded to at discretion, men would always give them a better chance than rocks.[1]

In this manner the Armada of Spain bore down upon them, almost exactly as happens in the Chase when the Hunters form a superb wing[2] which alternately contracts and extends, when Heaven, which had destined another end to the business, by the secret judgements of God allowed General Oquendo to throw away the Glory of that day. Many persons said:—*That it was because he would not consent to divide it with his rivals; since his proud and twisted spirit would not suffer them to be conquerors when he could no longer fight.* An unworthy thought, in truth, to enter into a great heart; and one reprehensible in that of an equal and worse still in that of a superior, who in all the actions of his subordinates should have the heritage of Glory or Dispraise.

Don Antonio de Oquendo resolved to steer in the opposite direction to that in which he was then sailing. He said "*For two Reasons*", both of them obvious. *The first,—because being afraid of the course that the enemy were taking, it was prudent to run the risks of the vanquished in order to forestall the conquerors; the second,—that by tacking, he could not lose the victory, but rather would ensure rendering it more useful, reserving for a better fate those gallant ships that were being borne to be the spoil of the waves on the neighbouring shoals.*[3] Whether he erred in his reasoning the sequel will show; for the wind changing at evening, as is usually the case, Tromp sailed merrily along the French coast without running the slightest risk therein, in such a manner that on the next day he was already outside of the Gulf, and of the inevitable loss he would otherwise have suffered, and had the weather-gage of the Spanish Armada.

It caused all of us a sorrowful sadness to see the Good Fortune which was sweetly leading us on to a notable triumph escape us in that way. It would be about twelve hours of daylight and after six hours of battle when the Flagship cast about to the northward, but for two hours longer

1 It is not quite clear from the text whether the Spaniards had penned Tromp's fleet in between (say) Étaples and the mouth of the Somme, or between the latter and ± Tréport. Probably the latter, but in either case Dom Manuel overestimates the importance of the banks and shoals off this part of the coast. See Admiralty Chart, No. 1431, for details.

2 "huã fermosa ala".

3 The original text is cryptic in the extreme, but in any case Oquendo could have had no adequate reason for breaking off the fight, except the fact that he had had the worst of it, and this in all probability was why he did so.

some of the other Captains declined to follow her, until the General repeated the usual signals for retirement with numerous cannon shots, thus forcing all to withdraw, leaving Tromp (as it were) free of the prison wherein we already held him a captive.

Both Armadas remained under sail during the afternoon, whereby the Dutch was sensibly bettered in position, strength, and wind, getting clear of the narrow sea in which the battle had begun. Shortly afterwards it was joined by the second squadron of fifteen stout ships under the command of their Almirante Viten, whose person was of no less help than they.[1] Already the air was breathing gently o'er their poops, and already the Hollanders were breathing again at seeing themselves delivered from the deadly peril in which they had been shortly before. For similar reasons, the Ancients were accustomed to depict some maxims of great utility in the guise of fables and mystic symbols to corporal and spiritual eyes; thus that Virgin called *Opportunity* they painted with the back of her head void of the beautiful locks that enriched her brow & adorned her forehead, wisely showing how he will always be left flouted who on chancing to meet with that wayward damsel, neglects to seize her by the first tresses that she offers him, in the hope of detaining her by the last.

The night of the sixteenth of September and the whole of the day following were spent by both sides in curing the wounded, preparing their arms and repairing their ships. Tromp, however, with greater deeds in view, prepared for the ensuing battle.[2] Wherefore, in order not to be driven by the tide (which runs there with great violence) beyond the favourable position in which he found himself, he came to an anchor and his fleet with him. When the Spaniards saw this they did likewise, or at least some of them; as also did the Flagship shortly afterwards on seeing the peril to which it would be exposed if it continued on its course. However, the *Tereza*, which amongst her perfections had not been endowed with that of handiness (not by reason of her build, but of the rigging), without casting anchor like the others, spent the whole of that day & night in forging ahead of the rest of the Spaniards under small sail; by this means she found herself in the van on the eighteenth, whilst some of the heaviest and strongest galleons were close to her, all of whom served to strengthen [us?] in the fight, as we shall see.

Scarcely was a quarter of the third watch over when General Tromp began to move. This watch is commonly called by those who watch by

1 As Dom Manuel himself has already stated, De With joined Tromp on the 16th (and actually before the action began). The man intended here is Banckert, who had come from Dunkirk with his squadron. See Sept. 17th and 18th in the *Journal*.

2 It is clear from De Mello's own version that the Spaniards were now definitely on the defensive, and Tromp had passed from the attacked to the attacker. Thus Sept. 16th was the decisive action of this campaign, as it marked the passing of the initiative from the Spaniards to the Hollanders.

night by some vulgar name such as *Modorra* in our tongue, because the
heaviness of sleep weighs more at that time than any other; but if we
revolve our learning in our minds we will find that *morros* in Greek is
what the Latins call *morio* and we *amadorrado*,[1] which clearly defines and
signifies the effects which slumber produces in animals at that hour.
Tromp, founding his plans upon these, bore down to fight. We never
discovered the reason why at such an extraordinary time (it would be
about eleven o'clock at night), he began an action upon the result of which
so much depended, only to avail himself of the exhaustion of our men.
However, when I subsequently spoke with Tromp himself on this matter
(having met him at Falmouth, a celebrated English port, when I came
from Holland in charge of the Armada which had been entrusted to me
there by order of the King), he gave me to understand:—*That an Astrologer
whom he had on board, had strongly urged him to commence the battle in
that hour and at no other; since the stars promised him good success.* For
without the favour of the stars, he could found the hope of his betterment
upon the good measures he had taken.[2]

The ships of the Spanish van were, as we have said, the least handy
but not the least stout of the Armada, & these were already giving and
receiving tremendous broadsides; but the enemy, knowing full well that
they had as much advantage over the Spaniards therein, as these latter
had over them in musketry-fire, gave a general order to his ships that they
were all to keep out of musket-shot.

The night, though calm, was dark; but the flame of the discharges of
cannon and musketry was so continuous, as it blazed up in first one and
then another part, that it lit up the sea; and as it never died down, it
maintained a certain brightness before the eyes which atoned for the

1 "Drowsy".

2 It is to be feared that Tromp (or his interpreter) was pulling the worthy
Dom Manuel's dignified leg, when (and if) he told him this fudge about the
Astrologer. The meeting at Falmouth in September 1641 is however referred to
in Tromp's manuscript *Journal* for that year, now in the Rijksarchief. After
convoying the young Prince William of Orange over from London after his wedding
with Charles I's daughter, Tromp was sent on a cruise against the Dunkirkers,
in the course of which, on Sept. 17th, he put in at the Cornish port of Falmouth
to careen. Here he found Dom Francisco Manuel, who had left Holland in
charge of a fleet of eleven ships bought in the Netherlands for the Portuguese
navy. Tromp and De Mello struck their flags to each other, and had several
interviews in the next few days of which Tromp gives accounts in his *Journal*.
At the last of them, the Portuguese (impecunious as usual!) asked for a loan of
800 guilders as he could get no credit in the port, and had no money. He offered
a present of a gold chain and a hat-band decked with pearls in part security.
Tromp accepted the gift and lent Dom Manuel 800 guilders out of his own
pocket, in return for which the latter gave him letters of credit on Salvador
Rodrigues, a Portuguese financier at Amsterdam. Dom Manuel left Falmouth for
Lisbon on the 23rd, and Tromp departed two days later.

absence of daylight. The discharges of Ordnance pealed out ceaselessly, so that it appeared to be a continuous thunder, as if the world was dissolving in a universal disorder.

Carlos de Brevil, Priest of the Society of Jesus, a wise man, and one of singular virtue, who was my companion in this voyage, affirmed:— *That in the fourteen hours for which this appalling conflict lasted, he could never reach the third word of the Pater Noster which he was continuously saying, without hearing the echo of some cannon.* We do not know that the sea has ever witnessed a conflict of arms more horrible, whether ancient or modern; for from eleven at night until five in the morning these waters appeared like those which Poets depict as the Infernal Lake; because if it, as Lucretius and Strabo say, was called thus by reason of its lack of birds, since flying in the air they fell dead, stifled by the sulphurous fumes of that Lake (which signifies as it were *Averno* in Greek),—so now with more reason could this sea be named thus; for the surrounding air was corrupted by envenomed ships which poured forth fire and powder, so that it blazed with so furious a thundering, that on writing of it at a remoter time (albeit we witnessed it with our own eyes, as have many others who are now reading this) we would not dare to affirm the effects thereof; because we saw and learnt that in the Downs, an English place five leagues distant from the scene of combat, the earth shook in such a manner that the people rushed out into the fields during almost the whole of the time that the fight lasted. At Calais in France, which was distant more than seven leagues from that place, nearly all the glasses of the windows were broken; whilst at Cambray, two and twenty leagues distant therefrom, the cannon-shots were distinctly counted in that great city.

Withal, however, the damage caused was not equal to the terror aroused, for since the Armadas were jumbled confusedly together in the shades of night, there was no opportunity for skilful use of the broadsides or dexterity in aiming. Both sides received but little hurt,—albeit despite the fact that both the contending parties realised it, this did not suffice to stop the Hollanders, who steadily increased the intensity of their fire. For this reason some of the Spanish Commanders thought and said:— *That Tromp with great cunning was deliberately expending his munitions in that way, so as afterwards, when he must of necessity experience the superiority of the Spaniards' strength and power, at the same time that he was enforced to retire he could say that it was due rather to lack of munitions than to the enemy's strength.* Perchance this idea was in reality conceived from the malice of his Rivals.

At length the day dawned and the struggle began with renewed fury but not in better order. For since the Armada of Spain had not received any order other than their first, the Captains thereof were only guided by their own Judgement, or Discipline, both of which were unequal in some and uncertain in others. . . .

The enemy Fleet was discovered, formed in two wings, one of which was led by Tromp, the other by Viten, which in the manner of dexterous cavaliers on a civic festival, wended in and out, vomiting heavy broadsides on the Spaniards who were already beginning to receive them in a similar formation. For joined together in one elongated body,—like that formation which soldiers call *Dobrete*[1] and *Parallelogram*, almost the *Gramino*[1] of the Geometricians,—their right side served as vanguard, since they were being attacked on that part; the whole was composed of four or five rows of ships in such a fashion that only the first gave and received reasonable broadsides, whilst the remainder, finding themselves out of danger, made no effort to thrust themselves therein, as they considered that they could each of them do their duty in those places which were assigned to them. However, adding one error to another, it was a most melancholy spectacle to see the barbarity with which they fired their broadsides on the enemy, for the least hurt they did was to expend these on the waves, whilst many of them lodged in their own comrades who were closer to them than the enemy, which only served to dishearten those same comrades.[2]

Oquendo had occupied his post in the battle, for the *Tereza* in the vanguard fought in such wise that almost everyone else's courage was obscured. Neither to friend nor foe would she yield pride of place, and it was averred that this ship fired during those hours more than one thousand five hundred and twenty cannon shot from the *Starboard* (as mariners term the right side) battery alone, as was reckoned by counting up the cartridges expended:—*Cartridges* are kinds of receptacles made of canvas, parchment, or paper (whence the term *Cartridges* is derived from *Carta*), which contain a certain measure of gunpowder, with which any cannon is charged in order to fire it off well, and they are made in mathematical proportion to the diameter of the piece of Ordnance. There were also many other shots which were fired without cartridges, and these latter served notably to increase the total number of rounds expended. The sight that resulted from the heat of this action was a terrible but most beautiful one, for it was founded not only upon the valour and numbers of the combatants but on that very fortress of a ship, which like as if she had been forged of flawless steel,—as Antiquity depicted the

1 I do not know the correct translation for these words.

2 The foregoing paragraph is especially interesting as it contains the origin of the statement that Tromp invented the manœuvre now known as "the breaking of the line". It will be seen from the text that Dom Manuel does not state anything of the kind, as he specifically says that the Spaniards were ranged in four or five *parallel lines*, forming a sort of vast parallelogram altogether, whilst Tromp's force was in two squadrons. But Quintella in his *Annaes* thought that Dom Manuel meant that the Spaniards were in one single line, and that Tromp broke through it, and this statement of his was copied by Duro in his *Armada Española* and thence by other writers.

arms of Achilles,—appeared to be wholly impenetrable throughout all her great bulk. So robust are the woods of that renowned Province of Lusitania which lies between *Douro* and *Minho*, and is thus called; whence are found and taken better plants than those celebrated ones from the mountain of Nicomedia in Asia,—so precious that the Grand Turk sent them, borne on land by camels, to be transported to the Red Sea, in order to construct therewith the Armadas which were to combat ours upon the Indian Ocean, as we read in Portuguese Histories. I certify that on the next day I saw the General Don Lope writing letters to the King, which he gave me to read as a person interested in the praises of my country, wherein amongst other discreet remarks he had written: *Those mountains of Portugal were worthy of being kept like the Hill of Potosi*[1] (which is the richest place on earth), *since such woods were grown thereon.*[2]

The enemy, piqued at seeing a single ship wreaking such havoc in theirs and offering so much resistance to all, several times essayed to beset her with squadrons composed of their best ships and Captains; eight or ten together tacked upon the valorous *Tereza*, which, awaiting their onset without any movement until they were within close range, then plied upon them with her musketry and heavy Ordnance, from whose force they recoiled forthwith, and tacked about with more hurt than reputation. This incident was repeated several times during the battle, in such wise that the Hollanders always fought better against the flank and rearguard than in the station of the forepart,[3] as we Portuguese called it, or *Vanguard* as it is termed nowadays.

General Oquendo, as usual, sailed out from the main body of his Fleet and being ahead thereof, he spread more sail with great daring, continually giving and receiving broadsides. He behaved himself with skill and courage, but his choleric spirit plunged him so blindly into the thickest of the fray, that during the whole time of the action he never gave, nor ordered to be given, a single order to remedy the confusion which he observed amongst his subordinates. The Almirante Don Andrés de Castro acted in a similar manner, but without having done so far anything worthy of either praise or blame. Not thus other Commanders, for some, by their behaviour (whether due to fear or ignorance), contributed to the ill-success of that day. There was one who, because he knew that the chief object of the expedition was to succour Flanders, tried to give over the battle and seek refuge in Ostend or Dunkerque, with his own ship

1 The famous Bolivian silver mines.
2 Actually most of the European-built Portuguese vessels were built of pine which was not very satisfactory material, and was frequently contrasted disadvantageously by their shipwrights with the hard teak of which their superb Indian-built galleons and *náos* were constructed. Probably the *Santa Tereza* was built of oak, as the wood came from North Portugal.
3 "Dianteira".

and others who were of his mischievous opinion and cowardly fear, under pretence of bringing in the relief. Were it not that Duty compels me to write nothing in this History but the Truth, I would not sully my Narrative with the remembrance of so base a proposition. With my own eyes I saw and observed this Commander twice try to carry out his nefarious design.

Not thus the Almirantes, Francisco Sanches Guadalupe and Matteo Esfrondati, both of whom lost their lives in the pursuit of Honour. The first, whilst commanding his squadron of San Josef[1] (of which we have already given a long account), was slain by a cannon-ball which cleft him in twain, but could not destroy the glory of his name. The second had a worse fate; for he, being the only one amongst the Spaniards who tacked upon the enemy and steered for the enemy flagship, at the same time that he charged amidst his foes, had his head carried away by a bar-shot, leaving all his soldiers not only without a head[2] but deprived of their heart; whence it happened, that as there was some dispute amongst the Infantry Captains who commanded the raw recruits by whom this Flagship was manned, as to who was to command her, the crew were thrown into such a state of confusion that the ship drifted aimlessly on her course into the midst of the main body of the Hollanders; these, perchance fired by a new fury because of the havoc she had caused amongst them, attacked her with five stout ships, which, after a short tho' sharp fight, boarded and captured that brave vessel, whilst a Danish urca named *Esgueven*, which was hired by the Spaniards, had just previously met with a like fate.[3]

The loss of that chief ship of Bartelosa was so generally felt, that each one took upon himself the avenging of such a humiliation. The Flagship had originally been standing on the same tack as the Almirante Matteo, but after having retired to the main body of the fleet, she now, like a furious lioness bereft of her whelp, again tacked upon the enemy, sounding her clarions as if to some forlorn hope; the remainder followed her, firmly resolved to board the enemy ships and fire themselves with them,—should they wish to await such an onset as they had formerly shown their willingness to do. However Tromp, who had already achieved the object of his victory, which even though he had not yet completed he had at least rendered certain (humanly speaking), did not wish to await the shock of the Armada of Spain; whose Star, it seems, at this hour assumed a more favourable aspect, infusing into the Spaniards an extraordinary valour by way of restitution for the ordinary courage of which it had begun to deprive them at the beginning of that expedition. Tromp told me afterwards,—*That he had broken off the fight through lack of powder, before the enemy could animate themselves with this knowledge.* Clumsy is the man who cannot find spacious reasons wherewith to justify his pro-

1 In his flagship *Santo Cristo de Burgos*.
2 I cannot say if the pun was intentional!
3 Compare *Journal* under date of Sept. 18th.

ceedings, but since we write of facts and not of opinions, we are only concerned to deal with events and not the reasons thereof.

The Flagship had only steered for a short while towards the enemy Fleet, when it likewise tacked, and shaped its course for the port of Calais in France; it would now be about four o'clock in the afternoon, and since the captured Flagship of Bartelosa hindered the Hollanders through the difficulty of managing her in her dismasted state by the towropes with which other ships were towing her, Tromp resolved to cast off that prize, contenting himself with displaying her flags in France and Holland as the proofs of victory. This they at once proceeded to do, before they were able to scuttle the ship; for the light Spanish galleons, making all the sail they could, bore down upon her so swiftly that the Hollanders preferred to suffer the ignominy of a retreat rather than the peril of this onset. Don Antonio de Oquendo being informed of this, and considering that the narrow and uncertain sea was compelling Tromp to seek the shelter of some port (he being as versed in that coast as a native thereof), thought that there was all the more reason for him to do likewise. Wherefore without delay, after receiving the recaptured ship in the midst of his Armada, he immediately cast about and steered for the Downs in England (hoping to arrive there before nightfall), since he was closer to this anchorage than the Hollanders were to that of Calais in France; in which two ports, the two Armadas of Spain and Holland cast anchor at almost the same time.

APPENDIX II

Letter of Tromp to the States-General, August 9th, 1639[1]

(Extracts concerning his views on cruising in the Channel)

(*Archives of the States-General,* Lias Admiraliteiten, No. 5509.)

...We have resolved on the 7th of this present concerning the blockade of Dunkirk, whither Commander Banckert sails this evening with his six sail in order to unite with Commander Brederode and so blockade the harbour as before. We have thus been very busy for some time, providing his ships with supplies, and moreover with cruising on the look-out for the expected fleet, in regard to which we find ourselves in complete agreement with the views of Your H.M. and His Highness; save only that we, in place of remaining between Dover and Calais, should cruise between Portland and the Casquets, since that is the fittest place wherein to await the Spanish fleet, whereon our whole design is set and for which we have waited hourly up till now, and still are awaiting; withal shall we,—following the order of Your H.M. and His Highness,—proceed to cruise between Beachy, Dover, Hâvre and Calais, and correspond from time to time with Commander Banckert lying off Dunkirk and do whatever we shall find....

[Postscript]

Secondly that one should, so far as is possible, stop the expected Spanish fleet and keep it from reaching Flanders so that it cannot arrive therein; this will not and cannot be done by ships lying off the coast at Gravelines or Calais, when the opportunity of wind, tide and weather favours the enemy; for if there occurs a westerly wind, hard weather and a flood-tide, what time the enemy comes off Calais in retreat, it is only 1½ or at the utmost 2 hours' work on such an occasion to sail from Calais into the Scheurtjen; neither is it possible to lay them on board and destroy them since they are likewise bold and skilful seamen. This much is clearly shown by the former example, when the late Heer Vice-Admiral Hollare once lay off the Goodwin with 9 ships but could not stop some Dunkirker, who seized his opportunity of tide, wind and weather; yet undoubtedly it cannot be imputed to our Captains that they were wanting in courage or good-will, because many of those then present have quitted themselves well in other actions both before and since; wherefore I remain of my former opinion that in the whole Channel there is no better opportunity

1 A copy of the original was kindly furnished me by Captain Naber, R.N.N. (rtd.). Cf. Dr Graefe's article, *op. cit.* p. 61.

of intercepting ships from Spain than between the Casquets and Portland, where the Channel is narrowest, and the enemy on a Summer's day cannot easily slip by without being seen, whilst on sighting him we have 24 hours sailing in which to fetch up and fight with him, and do whatsoever is best on such an occasion as aforesaid; whereas in the Narrows on the contrary, if the enemy takes due advantage of weather, wind and tide, we cannot do so in a short space, and furthermore run risk of losing anchor and cables and thus enforced to quit the sea untimely.

APPENDIX III

Tromp's Secret Orders

(*Secret Resolutions of the States-General*, September 21st, 1639, fol. 477 v.)

...And shall this Their High Mightiness's Resolution with two divers points, be sent in duplicate to the said Lt-Admiral Tromp for him to comport himself in accordance therewith...and that meanwhile he will hold the Spanish Fleet blockaded, and also attack it should a favourable opportunity present itself in the meantime, and that he being reinforced now at this present, as in the future, must and will not neglect to destroy the Spanish Fleet to the utmost of his power, without taking any heed or consideration whatsoever of the Harbours, Roadsteads or Bays of the Kingdoms in which the same might chance to be; and should he be the strongest, or consider that he has the advantage over the Spanish or other hostile ships, he will do this same; and in case any French, English, Scots, Swedes, Danes, Poles, or Easterlings should attempt to hinder the same, he will not on that account desist from his intended design, but attack the enemy and destroy them, in so far as may be possible, at the same time defending himself with force of arms against the aforesaid nations. Withal he, Lt-Admiral, will keep this paragraph of this Resolution secret, and refrain from communicating it to the Captains of the Fleet under his command until such time as he shall have to do the same in order to carry out the business.

(478)

APPENDIX IV

Order of Battle of the Spanish Armada, August 27th, 1639[1]

(Orden de Batalla en media Luna.)

	NAME	SQUADRON	GUNS	REMARKS
1	*Santiago*	Castile	60	Capitana Real or Royal Flagship. Escaped into Dunkirk, 22. x. 1639
2	*San Antonio* (pinnace)	Masibradi[2]	—	Driven ashore, 21. x. 1639
3	*San Agustin* (pinnace)	Martin Ladrón de Guevara	—	Driven ashore, 21. x. 1639
4	*Santa Tereza*	Portugal	60	Don Lope de Hoces, commander. Destroyed in action, 21. x. 1639
5	*San Feronimo*	Naples —	—	Vice-Admiral. Driven ashore, 21. x. 1639. Sunk 3 or 4 days later
6	*San Agustin*		—	
7	*El Gran Alejandro*	Martin Ladrón de Guevara	—	Taken by the Dutch
8	*Santa Ana*	Portugal —	—	—
9	*San Sebastian*		—	—
10	*Santa Catalina*	Guipuzcoa —	—	Driven ashore, 21. x. 1639
11	*San Lazaro*		—	—
12	*San Blas*	Masibradi	—	Driven ashore, 21. x. 1639

1 Ships' names from "Order of Battle" in Duro, *Armada Española* IV, pp. 225–6. Other information from list, *ibid.* P. 227; Dom Francisco Manuel de Mello, *Epanaphora* IV; and a list of ships run ashore, *S.P. Dom Charles I*, vol. 431, No. 76, etc.

2 This squadron was variously designated as that of Masibradi, Bartelosa, Ragusa and Seville!

Order of Battle of the Spanish Armada (contd.)

	NAME	SQUADRON	GUNS	REMARKS
13	San Jerónimo	Masibradi	—	Burnt in the Downs, 21. x. 1639
14	San Nicolas	—	—	—
15	Santiago	Castile	—	Burnt off Dover on the night of 23. x. 1639
16	San Juan Bautista	Guipuzcoa	—	Sunk, 21. x. 1639
17	Esquevel	A hired Dane	16	Taken by the Dutch, 18. ix. 1639
18	San José	Dunkirk	—	—
19	Los Angeles	Castile	—	Driven ashore, 21. x. 1639
20	Santiago	Portugal	—	Driven ashore, 21. x. 1639
21	Delfin Dorado	Naples	—	Driven ashore, 21. x. 1639
22	San Antonio	Naples	—	Driven ashore, 21. x. 1639
23	San Juan Evangelista	Dunkirk	—	—
24	El Pingue	Hired ship	—	Sunk in the Downs, 21. x. 1639
25	San Carlos	Masibradi	—	—
26	San Nicolas	Masibradi	—	—
27	San Miguel	—	—	—
28	Orfeo	Naples	44	Lost on the Goodwin sands, 21. x. 1639
29	San Vicente Ferrer	Dunkirk	—	—
30	San Martin	Dunkirk	—	Escaped into Dunkirk, 22. x. 1639
31	Nuestra Señora de Monteagudo	Dunkirk	—	Captured by the Dutch, 21. x. 1639
32	Santiago	Galicia	60 (?)	Taken by the Dutch, 18. ix. 1639, and retaken same day. Escaped to Dunkirk, 22. x. 1639. Wrecked 4 days later
33	?	Flagship of Masibradi	—	—

Order of Battle of the Spanish Armada (contd.)

	NAME	SQUADRON	GUNS	REMARKS
34	Santo Tomás	Martín Ladrón de Guevara	—	Driven ashore, 21. x. 1639
35	Nuestra Señora de Luz	—	—	—
36	Santa Clara		—	—
37	San Gedeón	Dunkirk	—	—
38	San Jacinto	—	—	—
39	San Carlos	Dunkirk	—	Sunk, 21. x. 1639
40	Santo Cristo de Burgos	San Josef	—	Lost off the French coast, 21. x. 1639
41	San Pablo	Masibradi	—	—
42	San Miguel	—	—	—
43	La Corona	Hired ship	—	—
44	La Presa or San Pablo La Presa	Castile	—	—
45	San Esteban	Martín Ladrón de Guevara	—	Taken by the Dutch, 21. x. 1639
46	San Pedro de la Fortuna	A hired ship	—	Driven ashore but got off, 21. x. 1639
47	Los Angeles	Hired ship	—	—
48	Aguila Imperial	—	—	—
49	La Mujer		—	—
50	Santo Domingo de Polonia	A hired Polish ship	—	Driven ashore, 21. x. 1639

Order of Battle of the Spanish Armada (contd.)

In addition to the ships given in the Order of Battle, the following have been traced from various sources. Why they are omitted from the above list it is difficult to explain.

	NAME	SQUADRON	GUNS	REMARKS
51	San José	Flagship of Vizcaya	—	Taken by the Dutch, 21. x. 1639
52	San Salvador	Flagship of Dunkirk	—	Escaped into Dunkirk, 22. x. 1639
53	São Balthazar	Vice-Admiral of Portugal	50 (?)	800 tons. Back at Lisbon in 1640[1]
54	San Francisco	Rear-Admiral of Dunkirk	—	Escaped into Dunkirk, 22. x. 1639
55	San Pedro el Grande	Flagship of Ladrón de Guevara	—	—
56	Santiago	Martín Ladrón de Guevara	—	—
57	Jesús María (pinnace)	—	—	
58	San Pedro Martir (Urca)	A hired ship	—	Driven ashore, 21. x. 1639
59	Fama (Urca)	A hired ship	—	Driven ashore, 21. x. 1639
60	Santa Cruz	Masibradi	—	—
61	San Daniel	Guipuzcoa	—	Driven ashore, 21. x. 1639
62	San Juan Evangelista	A hired ship of Hamburg	—	Driven ashore, 21. x. 1639
63	Santa Agnes (frigate)	Naples	—	Stranded but got off, 24. x. 1639
64	Grune[2] (?)	Castile	—	Driven ashore, 21. x. 1639
65	Santa Tereza (Saetía)	Castile	—	Taken by a French privateer, 1. x. 1639
66	Exchange	Hired English Transports with 5 consorts	—	Put into Plymouth, 3/13. ix. 1639, and reached the Downs, 12/22. x. 1639, where they were detained
67	Peregrine			
68	Assurance			

I have not been able to ascertain details of the remaining 7 sail of the Armada, which, when it left La Coruña (27. viii. 1639), must have totalled 75 sail including the 8 English transports, as when Tromp first (16. ix. 1639) met De Oquendo the latter was 67 sail strong without them.

1 Some authorities state that the São Balthazar did not accompany the Armada.
2 This name is obviously wrong, but it appears thus in the contemporary English List of stranded ships.

APPENDIX V

A note on the Amelia

Tromp's flagship the *Amelia* (also spelt *Aemelia, Amalia,* etc.) was built by the Admiralty of the Maas at Rotterdam, *circa* 1637.

She was named after the fair—though frail—Amalia von Solms,[1] the beautiful wife of the Stadthouder Frederik Hendrik, Prince of Orange. Most Dutch authorities call her a two-decker and give her 56 guns. This ship was sold by the Admiralty in 1647, in despite of Tromp's protests, and according to the *Hollandsche Mercurius* of 1651, was bought by the French and used by them as a privateer in the Mediterranean. In this capacity she made prizes of several vessels (including Dutch) until she was captured by the Spaniards and taken into Naples. *Sic transit!*

In the Great Church of Rotterdam are still to be seen two organ pillars which are reputed to be made from the *Amelia's* mainmast, presumably from that same mast which went by the board in a storm off Hellevoetsluijs on April 14th, 1641, when Tromp was conveying Prince William of Orange over to England for his marriage with Charles I's daughter, Mary Stuart.

[1] Financially speaking only. Her morals otherwise were beyond reproach. Many stories are told of her weakness for gifts and presents of jewelry or money. Some of these are doubtless exaggerated, but it is certain that towards the end of the Thirty Years' War she was in the pay of Spain, whilst in 1643 she was also in that of Portugal. (Cf. Blok, *Frederik Hendrik*, Amsterdam 1924.)

BIBLIOGRAPHY

(Arranged chronologically)

Pamfletten-Knuttel, nos. 4617 to 4632. Amsterdam, etc., 1639–40.

PETER WHITE. A memborable SEAFIGHT penned and preserved by PETER WHITE. one of the IIII Masters of Attendance in ENGLANDS Navie. (*Never before now.*) Published for the good of *Englands* Commonwealth, *By* ANDREWES BURRELL. *Gent.* OR, A *Narrative* of all the Principall *Passages* which were Transacted in the *Downes,* in the Year 1639. *Betweene* ANTONIO DE OQVENDO. Admirall of the *Spanish* Armado, *And* MARTIN VAN TROMP, *Admirall* for the States of *Holland.* Wherein (by a similary illustration) *Englands* (present) sluggish Navie is proved to be Unserviceable, and in a like Condition with the *Spanish* Fleet. *When* GOD *ordaines his Lights to shine, There's little need of* thine *or* mine. LONDON Printed by T. Forcet (Septem. 4. 1649) dwelling in Old *Fish Street.* London, 1649.
> An invaluable account of the blockade in the Downs, written by a man who had exceptional opportunities of observing all that took place.

ARNOLDUS MONTANUS. 't Leven en Bedryf van Iohan van Galen, etc. Amsterdam, 1654.

LIEUWE VAN AITZEMA. Saken van Staet en Oorlogh, in ende omtrent de Vereenigde Nederlanden, Beginnende met het Jaer 1633, ende eyndigende met het Jaer 1644. Tweede Deel. 's Gravenhage, Anno 1669.
> A first-class authority. Especially valuable for Waterdrincker's account, pp. 613–19.

V[AN] D[EN] B[OS]. Leven en Daden der Doorluchtighste Zeehelden, etc. Amsterdam, 1676.
> The account of the campaign of 1639 is almost word for word that in Aitzema.

DOM FRANCISCO MANUEL DE MELLO. Epanaphoras de Varia historia Portugueza, Epanaphora Belica IV. Conflito do Canal de Inglaterra entre as armas Espanholas, & Olandezas. Anno 1639. 2nd edition, Lisboa, 1676.
> The longest account extant—126 pages—it is also in some ways the most interesting and the most informative. But the author's fondness for classical allusions and cryptic sentences is often apt to obscure his meaning in a cloud of words; he also wastes time in delving into the meanings of all technical terms or foreign names which he uses—sometimes with comic results.

IGNACIO DA COSTA QUINTELLA. Annaes da Marinha Portugueza. Tomo II. Lisboa, 1840.
> Mainly based on De Mello's account. The author was a Vice-Admiral in the Portuguese navy.

J. C. DE JONGE. Geschiedenis van het Nederlandsche Zeewezen. II Druk. I Deel. Haarlem, 1858.
> An invaluable work. He used both Tromp's *Journal* and De With's *Leven* but nothing on the Spanish side. He is not an unduly critical writer.

Calendars of State Papers, Domestic Series of the Reign of Charles I. Vol. 1639 and vol. 1639–40. London, 1873–7.
> Invaluable for the English point of view. Numerous letters, orders, dispatches, etc. of Northumberland, Pennington, Thomas Smith, Windebank, Endymion Porter and others on the difficulties with the Hollanders and Spaniards, June–November 1639.

J. P. AREND. Algemeene Geschiedenis des Vaderlands, IIIᵉ Deel, vᵉ stuk. Amsterdam, 1874.
> Based almost entirely on the Resolutions of the States-General and States of Holland.

C. FERNÁNDEZ DURO. Armada Española desde la Union de los Reinos de Castilla y de Aragón. Tomo IV. Madrid, 1898.
> Especially noteworthy is the account of Feijo de Sotomayor on pp. 227–35.

M. G. DE BOER. De Armada van 1639. Groningen, 1911.
> The best account to date, based on excellent authorities. Its chief weaknesses are a lack of any modern map or chart, and a tendency to neglect the preliminary period of Tromp's cruise in favour of other and less important—but more striking—events.

T. W. FULTON. The Sovereignty of the Sea. London, 1911.
> An excellent book by one of the very few English writers who has drawn upon the voluminous Dutch sources for the period. Interesting for the fishery questions 1631–40 and the striking of the flag.

G. EDMUNDSON. Anglo-Dutch Rivalry during the first half of the Seventeenth Century (1600–53). Oxford, 1911.
> A good account of the diplomatic negotiations before, during, and after the affair of the Downs.

H. MALO. Les Corsaires Dunkerquois et Jean Bart, I. Paris, 1912.
> A valuable account of the Dunkirk squadron of the Spanish fleet.

D. F. SCHEURLEER. Onze Mannen ter Zee in Dicht en Beeld, Deel I. 's Gravenhage, 1914.
> Rhymes, prints, and popular poems on the Downs on pp. 127–42.

J. E. ELIAS. Schetsen uit de Geschiedenis van ons Zeewezen. Eerste Gedeelte, 1916.
> Supersedes De Jonge in the economic and administrative spheres.

G. E. MANWARING. Life and Works of Sir Henry Mainwaring. Vols. I and II. (N.R.S. publications.) London, 1920–2.
> The second volume contains the Seaman's Dictionary. The first is invaluable as regards the description of the Ship-Money fleets, but the part dealing with the Dutch and Spanish fleets is unreliable. Tromp is confused with De With, and other similar errors make nonsense of the description of the September battles.

C. DE LA RONCIÈRE. Histoire de la Marine française, V. Paris, 1920.
> A good sketch of De Sourdis' movements in 1639.

Sir R. TEMPLE. The Travels of Peter Munday, 1608–67. Vol. IV, Europe, 1639–47. Hakluyt Society, 2nd series, vol. LV. London, 1925.
> Munday visited the three fleets in the Downs, and saw the wrecks on October 24th.

J. F. L. DE BALBIAN VERSTER. Articles: Tromp bij Duins, and Tromp voor Duinkerken, both in the Jaarverslag of the Nederlandsch Historisch Scheepvaart Museum. Amsterdam, 1919, 1926.

S. P. L'HONORÉ NABER. 't Leven en Bedrijf van Vice-Admirael de With, Zaliger. MSS. of 1662 published for the 1st time in the Bijdragen en Mededeelingen van het Historisch Genootschap gevestigd te Utrecht. Utrecht, 1926.

F. GRAEFE. Militärische Seetransporte von Spanien nach Flandern (1631–9) in the Marine Rundschau. Berlin, 1927.

ADMIRALTY CHARTS of the English Channel. Nrs. 1406, 1431 and 1598.
Indispensable for a proper appreciation of Tromp's difficulties and dispositions.

N.B. This does not pretend to be a complete list, but it does cover all the ground. C. R. B.

INDEX

A. PERSONAL NAMES

(N.B. Throughout the translation of the *Journal* the spelling of the Dutch names has been retained as in the original, but only one form of each name is given in the Index. Thus *Banckert* appears in the text as *Bancque, Bancke, Banckers, Bancker,* and *Banckert*. C.R.B.)

B. PLACE NAMES

(For identification only. Cf. also maps and charts in the text.)

C. TABLE OF THE MOST IMPORTANT MATTERS
DEALT WITH IN THE TEXT

Printed by Printforce, United Kingdom